791.43

Film Curatorship
Archives, Museums, and the Digital Marketplace

Edited by Paolo Cherchi Usai, David Francis,
Alexander Horwath, Michael Loebenstein

Österreichisches Filmmuseum
SYNEMA – Gesellschaft für Film und Medien

A book by SYNEMA ☰ Publikationen
Film Curatorship. Archives, Museums, and the Digital Marketplace
Volume 9 of FilmmuseumSynemaPublikationen

We would like to thank David Robinson, Geoff Brown, Livio Jacob, Piera Patat,
Kellie Rife, Meg Labrum, Kristin Thompson, Edith Kramer

This book is jointly published with Le Giornate del Cinema Muto, Pordenone, Italy

© Wien 2008
  SYNEMA – Gesellschaft für Film und Medien
  Neubaugasse 36/1/1/1
  A-1070 Wien

Copy editor: Catherine A. Surowiec
Transcriptions: Teresa Devlin and Michael Loebenstein
Design and layout: Gabi Adebisi-Schuster
Project management: Michael Loebenstein
Printed by: REMAprint
Printed and published in Vienna, Austria
Printed on paper certified in accordance with the rules of the Forest Stewardship Council.

ISBN 978-3-901644-24-5

Österreichisches Filmmuseum (Austrian Film Museum) and SYNEMA – Gesellschaft für Film & Medien
are supported by BM:UKK – Abteilung VI-8 FILM and by Kulturabteilung der Stadt Wien.

Table of Contents

Chapter 1

The Work Print

This book was born around the table of a café in Vienna, Austria on New Year's Eve 2005. The fact that the conversation ended up revolving around the topic of film curatorship shouldn't come as a surprise. For us, it wasn't talking about business: when you enjoy what you're doing in your profession, the boundaries between work and leisure can easily become blurred. It is after hours, and in good company, that ideas often start flowing, unconstrained by the imperatives of deadlines, meetings, and written reports. So there we were, having a good time and in the mood for straight talk. We were concerned about our field, frustrated by what appeared to us like a profound crisis of the so-called "archival movement", and eager to do something to get out of the impasse.

For different reasons, each of us felt that a re-definition of "curatorship" was the best way to ensure that film archives have a chance to maintain a meaningful place in society. The "uniqueness" of their collections is no longer a defining feature of their identity, and the quality of their projection prints often appears to be lower than that of more cheaply produced digital copies. Nevertheless, we use *Film* in the title of this book (instead of "moving image") because we are preoccupied with the future of cinema as a cultural entity; *Curatorship*, because we believe that

interpretation is what differentiates a collecting body from a mere repository of audiovisual content; *Digital* and *Marketplace,* because we are convinced that the two words go hand in hand, leading to a dramatic redefinition of what is termed the "moving image experience".

The implications of our choice of words are obvious. By saying *film* we refer to a specific historical phenomenon, rooted in the 20th century, with all its distinctive characteristics. However, we also imply that many of the issues facing the analog heritage – especially the challenges of preservation and public presentation – also apply to the digital world, or are bound to do so in the near future. A corollary of the title is our intention to deliberately sabotage the traditional distinction between *film archives* and *film museums.* In our view, this separation should be scrutinized, and possibly even questioned, as we believe that any organization that needs to interpret its collections to the public should be driven by some form of curatorship. Finally, the digital marketplace is the arena where access to the film heritage is recognized as the main *raison d'être* of our activity, a blunt reality to which most archival institutions have reacted with passivity – often tinged with resignation ("film is dead anyway") – or by embracing the new regime without a proper identification of the principles and values underlying our profession.

If Vienna is the birthplace of this project, the Italian city of Pordenone is where its seed was planted. Participation in the *Giornate del Cinema Muto*, the premier international forum for the rediscovery and study of the silent film heritage, made us realize that a new audience is raising questions too often avoided by our own community – a new generation of viewers with fresh ideas, a great deal of enthusiasm, and a growing impatience towards what they perceive as hesitation, dogmatism, or a paternalistic attitude on our part. When asked why we bother insisting upon the projection of 35mm prints, when digital projection "looks better", without scratches on the image, we don't know how to explain persuasively the difference between the two media; on the other hand, when we argue that the digital era opens up a number of ethical issues in our domain, we are exposed to increasingly vocal allegations of arrogance or nostalgia. We're tired of this. In the absence of a frank discussion on these topics within the organizations where we would have expected it to occur since the dawn of the Digital Age, we have decided to make the debate happen among ourselves.

We are presenting our case in the form of conversations instead of formal essays, very much in the spirit of our first meeting in Vienna. We agreed at the outset that we would not be afraid of contradicting ourselves, of disagreeing with each other, of repeating the same concepts when we felt compelled to do so. Redundancies, paradoxes, and incongruities often represent hidden intentions; as we have nothing at stake but the desire to bring dilemmas to the surface and explore their implications without

reducing them to mere technological issues, we opted for leaving our viewpoints in their rough state, even at the cost of making the reader feel at times dazed and confused. Under the current circumstances, we prefer chaos to the polite sterility of consensus, the work print to the polished final cut.

We belong to three generations of film archivists and curators. Some of us have lived in a mostly "analog" world and are now facing the challenge of the digital paradigm shift; others began their involvement with film archives and museums while the change was occurring, and are now trying to find their way in a plethora of possibilities and constraints. Then there are those for whom "digital" has been in the picture from the start, and yet are keen to understand how this brave new world will reshape the principles and questions raised by the founders of our discipline. All these voices will hopefully be heard in the following pages.

Some of the texts included in this volume are drawn or adapted from works previously published by members of our team, or written by colleagues with whom we found an intellectual affinity. Alexander Horwath's "The Market vs. The Museum" was published in the *Journal of Film Preservation* no. 70, November 2005. Chapter 8 integrates a piece written by Kristin Thompson, "The Celestial Multiplex", published on Kristin's and David Bordwell's weblog (www.davidbordwell.net/blog/?p=595) on 27 March 2007; it is reproduced here with Kristin and David's kind permission. Paolo Cherchi Usai's "Five Scenarios" at the end of Chapter 7 is adapted from his speech to the students of the L. Jeffrey Selznick School of Film Preservation at the graduation ceremony held on June 23,

2006. His "Charter of Curatorial Values" was first published in the *Journal of the National Film and Sound Archive*, vol. 1, no.1, Spring 2006; the glossary in the Appendix is reproduced (in abridged and revised form) from the National Film and Sound Archive of Australia's *Collection Policy* (2006), pp. 55–61. Both are reprinted here with the kind permission of the National Film and Sound Archive of Australia.

Chapter 2 contains – as a prologue – an edited transcript of the initial conversation between the four authors in Vienna on December 31, 2005. All other chapters are a montage of a series of conversations – via telephone, Skype, e-mail exchanges, or in actual meetings on four continents – among the authors, with editing kept to a minimum in order to preserve the liveliness of the dialogues. These conversations took place between 2006 and April 2008. Our thanks go to Edith Kramer and Livio Jacob for their support and advice throughout the book's gestation. Teresa Devlin patiently transcribed most of our discussions, and encouraged us with her feedback to our initial discussions. Catherine A. Surowiec tackled the formidable task of editing and styling our avalanche of words with sensitivity, clear-sightedness, and attention to detail, miraculously transforming our exchanges into readable prose while retaining our individual voices and conversational tone. The design by Gabi Adebisi-Schuster interprets the spirit of our project better than we could have possibly hoped for. We would like to express here our gratitude to all, and happily take responsibility for any failure in conveying our thoughts in an intelligible manner.

Chapter 2

Prologue: The Vienna Sessions

December 31, 2005

___AH: How we can structure this? Paolo wants to be expansive at first, and try to cover the whole terrain...

___PCU: I would suggest that at first we do not put any limits, we just let ourselves go, let the juices flow. And then, when we feel that we have warmed up enough and have enough topics, then we begin to say, "OK, what do we do with all this?"

I thought a good way of getting the ball rolling would be to discuss among ourselves the reason why we are meeting, and the reason why this idea of Alex's came up. When I first read the first message from Alex, really, within ten seconds, I felt I understood...

___DF: Absolutely.

___PCU: ...I understood what this was all about, because I felt that the reason for such a book, or whatever this is going to be, is that there is a perceived need to re-discuss, to re-evaluate, the notion of curatorship in moving image archives at a time of quite spectacular change. And this need seems to be dictated by the fact that, while we have spent a long time in the past few years discussing the technological implications of the transition from analog to digital, and the fact that the very notion of "Moving Image Archive" has to take into account a new economic reality which reflects society, what has been left aside

has been the core of our profession: us as curators. So there is a profound gap, which is demonstrated by the fact that nowhere in the traditional forums for discussion, such as FIAF [International Federation of Film Archives] or AMIA [Association of Moving Image Archivists], or the other conferences I've been attending, has there been a structured discussion of how we redefine curatorship in this world. Am I correct?

___AH: I think you are, and my other question would be, am I correct in thinking – because I'm relatively new to the field – that in the past 15 years, the issue of preservation was so much at the centre, and so dominated all discussion that maybe we feel the need to rethink, or think in new ways about, curatorial work.

___DF: *(speaking over Alexander)* I think that is true, and I also would like to add that, I mean, the basis of our philosophy is this awful term "Moving Image Experience" *(laughter),* and whenever an archivist is challenged, they sort of retire behind this phrase. It's basically a phrase that really doesn't mean anything to anybody except the archivist. I would like to find a completely new way of expressing that, because I feel that it's almost as if it's our wall that we can retire behind if challenged – but it's a passive response, not an active response. We have to have a more *active* description of what it is that we are trying to preserve and make available.

___AH: What do we mean by that word if we use it? Do we mean the moment of making the film public, the moment when the work or artefact – whatever it is that we collect and preserve – achieves its true reality?

___DF: Basically, we've always said that preservation was only a route to the "Moving Image Experience". But we had to concentrate on it, because the easier it is to make access copies, in some sense then the more you have to concentrate and find a justification for preservation, in order to continue to receive funding for what's an extremely expensive process compared with other media.

___PCU: I agree that the problem with the term "Moving Image Experience", first of all, is that it is quintessentially a defensive definition…

___DF: Exactly.

___PCU: …but it needs to be analysed a little bit. We're saying "Moving Image", and that's our way of saying, OK, it's not just cinema – it is the "Moving Image" in all its forms. It is our way of counteracting the attack of the people saying, "Cinema is *passé* because now we have so many ways, you know. There is television; there is the video iPod; whatever." So we protect ourselves under the term "Moving Image".

And as for "Experience", it is, unfortunately, a sort of almost passive-aggressive way to claim the importance of the act of seeing, as opposed to the creation, preservation, and access to the works. I feel the same dissatisfaction in that this term "Moving Image Experience" may be understood only by us, by the community. But if we use this term outside, people stare at us, and say, "What are you talking about?" And so far, I

haven't found a better alternative other than going to a term which is widely recognized and acknowledged in the museum world as the term that qualifies the profession, which is "curatorship". I sometimes feel, why don't we just reclaim the word "curatorship"?

___AH: Why not actively call it "Film"? Why not call it the "Film Experience"? Isn't this what we are actually interested in?

___DF: It's a smoke-screen. We don't want to openly say "Film" only because outside there are so many people who will then turn on us. So we use the term "Moving Image Experience" as a smoke-screen for meaning, to ourselves internally, "Film", but to the rest of the world showing that we have, you know, an understanding that "Moving Image" is greater than "Film". It's because of our own insecurity that we're using this term "Moving Image", but I think most of us mean "Film". *(Laughs)*

___PCU: I'm afraid it's not that simple. Because I live in a world where the very use of the term "Film" or "Cinema" is perceived as limiting. Automatically. I'm implicitly or explicitly told that the universe of the "Moving Image" as we're experiencing it now has "Film" only as a slice, and that is not where future image-makers are going to go.

___DF: Yes, it's the same in America. Exactly.

___PCU: And we're being told, more or less, "OK, you come from the film generation, but, you know, this is becoming history, there is now much more going on." And in a way, that's the interesting challenge for us, because if we do care about the art of creating meaning through moving images, we should care equally about the way new artists and new film-makers will create new works. So I do fundamentally care about the Bresson of the 21ˢᵗ century, or the artist who will create something with means which are completely different. And my question is, how are we going to treat these works in a museum context?

—DF: But I would prefer to be honest, and talk about – just using the terms at the moment – the "Film Experience", the "Television Experience", the "Digital Experience", and the "Internet Experience", as "experiences"… rather than put them all together as the "Moving Image Experience", because I think the "Moving Image Experience" is confusing everybody. It's giving us a feeling of false security. So I'd much prefer to somehow divide those experiences, because I believe that they are different experiences, and I think we should come out and face that fact.

—AH: So we should at least put it in the plural, and call it "Moving Image Experiences"…?

—DF: Yes.

—AH: I do believe that the title of our endeavour should signal immediately that we're not dealing in a very general way with museums and curatorship, but with those two things in *our* field.

—DF: *(speaking over Alexander)* But is it film? The key thing here is: you could treat it as film alone, but you'd have to signal your hope that this would lead to people doing a similar analysis for other media, for digital, for television, and the Internet… To do it for film would be acceptable, because film is the oldest of those "experiences", and therefore Number One on the list. But I think if you just do it for film, without any reference to the other "experiences", it will not get as wide a circulation and as much interest.

—PCU: OK. So this means we are talking about a fundamental philosophical choice in relation to the focus of the book. Do we want to have a book that deals with "Film", cinematic works originally created or presented with *analog means,* and how these works are being collected, preserved, and disseminated, including dissemination through means other than analog? Or do we want to address this notion on a broader scale, including, but not limited to, Film? I think this choice is inevitable; we are going to come out of this meeting with a choice. I would like to point out some consequences of both choices. If we choose to say at the outset, this book is about a historically determined form of expression called "Film", meaning the analog 35mm or photochemical experience, we exclude works created in new media, and we explain why. By doing so we have to be ready for the fact that part of our readership may, in a kind of crude way, say, "OK, these are the guys dealing with the old, they don't care about where the new world of moving images is going. They are nostalgically or archaeologically oriented people."

Now there may be ways to counteract these allegations, by saying that, you know, it may well be archaeology – so let's take it as such; let's discuss it. But there is this risk. If we take the holistic approach, taking all moving images together, we in one way eliminate this disadvantage. We engage directly with the new generation of the younger curators and archivists, who will have to deal with a world which is very different from what we have been dealing with. There is more hope to have them listening to what we have to say in relation to curatorship of the analog moving image, but the challenge is we may risk losing specificity…

—AH: I'm all for the second path, in a way, but for a specification of that second path. Let's call it, for instance, "Museums, Curators, and Moving Image Experiences", but make clear that the perspective is strongly characterized by the fact that all four of us speak from a film background. And that we are trying to analyse these problems from the viewpoint of the oldest medium in this spectrum. I like the fact that we are speaking to a current scene of curators and people who are working in this field, and who not only deal with film, who work in fine arts museums maybe, but are confronted with the situation all the time. How do curators deal with video works, moving image installations, with "traditional" film, etc.? We should speak to this wide array of professionals and people entering the field, but it should also be an identifiable position. Somebody who has started out, let's say, as a video curator at the Whitney Museum in the late 1970s, would have a totally different perspective in general, but some basic issues could be shared.

_PCU: Then, if I interpret your words correctly, would it be fair to reformulate the concept by saying that we propose to discuss what we'll call for the time being the "Moving Image Experience", in a global way, but we implicitly or explicitly suggest that there are values which transcend the specificity of the medium? I'm simply putting it as a question.

_DF: My concern is this. I believe we should concentrate on film because that was the original intention. The question is, how would you address and show everyone else that you recognize that this is only part of the "Moving Image Experience"? The thing that I would like to do is to challenge the people responsible for the other experiences to initially agree on a formula for discussing these experiences, so that effec-

tively this becomes Volume I *(mumbled agreement)* of a concept. I just went the other week to a lecture by Howard Besser, of New York University, about the preservation of works created on the Internet, and it was absolutely fascinating. The issues involved and the ethics of experimental work which is now created on the Internet. And you realize that our "moving image experience", even in its broadest sense, is now outdated. I think it would be nice to say that we must consider the presentation and preservation of the Internet *now*, not until 40 years later like we did with the cinema. Let's put it on the table now. I see this as Volume I of a discussion. Hopefully you can get some agreement about a broad structure and some sort of commitment from other organizations responsible for doing this in the same way. So we don't hide behind this broad generalization of "Moving Image Experience" – we come out in the open and say, "Yes, we are concerned with film; we are addressing film first, not only because it was the first of this particular family, but because it is the one that is most likely to disappear." So we are justified in doing it as Number One – but we recognize that we should address each of these areas…

_PCU: OK, by all means. In this volume we concentrate on what we call the "Film Experience" in all its ramifications, including the use of new technologies for the access or preservation of this specific manifestation of the "Moving Image Experience", with the understanding that the same kind of discussion should take place in the domain of – for lack of a better term – digital, digitally-born works.

_DF: Or even of television. Because the "Television Experience", the "Video Experience", the

"Internet Experience", are all separate experiences...

—**AH:** Maybe it's different in Continental Europe than in America, or Great Britain, or Australia, but my experience is that people who never had a piece of celluloid in their hands, who work digitally or for television, they still call their works "Film". "Film" is old and "settled" enough to have gained the status of a desirable form of expression. So that even those who technically and materially have left the technology and materiality of film behind, speak of their product as "films".

—**DF:** That's true.

—**AH:** I think that we are already – for 30 years at least – in the phase where film as the dominant popular medium has receded behind other media, but that its status as a concept and as a way to describe certain experiences has risen. Which seems like a slightly paradoxical situation, but that's typical of a mutational period such as the one we're in. We need to find a way of addressing both aspects: that "Film" will not go away, even if film goes away. For the wider public, the idea of "Film" won't go away just because they see *King Kong* in a digital projection.

—**PCU:** For them there is absolutely no difference.

—**DF:** Does this mean that we represent film from its popular current definition, which is, as you say, much broader than celluloid? Or do we say No, we are concentrating on analog, except in terms of presentation, where we're recognizing that there are other forms of presentation? You know, that's sort of the limit of what we're talking about.

—**AH:** What I wanted to suggest was to actively say "Film" or "Film Experiences", and thereby address the wider idea of film as it exists out there. And then, in the book, progressively speak more about the specificities: talk about analog, talk about television, talk about digitization, talk about moving images in museums, talk about the ways in which traditional museums and film museums are working with film, maybe even what traditional museums could learn from film museums concerning the ways they present and curate film.

—**DF:** Ah ha, now you see, that's interesting, because obviously you're thinking of film even in a different way than I'm thinking of film, because you're incorporating within film the other "experiences"...

—**AH:** It's not necessarily my personal or professional definition, but I recognize that it has become the global idea. On the one hand, for *me* film is really "frame, frame, frame" on a strip, you can hold it against the light and project it with light – it's a rational description of the phenomenon. On the other hand, the wider world has this very general idea of film, not related to the physical side of the medium. That's how it is used in language, today at least. So the book could take up this generalized idea as a starting point, almost like "film is everything that moves on a screen", and become more precise along the way. I think it's essential to avoid giving readers the impression that this comes from the corner of some old-fashioned celluloid-cinephiles.

—**PCU:** The "wax museum" syndrome...

—**DF:** I mean, if you take that approach – let us call it the popular meaning of film – then effectively you *are* covering the "Moving Image Experience". I have read so far, probably because of knowing your association with Peter Kubelka and generally, that you were talking about film in an archivist's sense of film – in other words, as celluloid or analog…

—**AH:** I do think the book should also deal with this whole question of the "constant availability" of films and moving images on the Internet and in other media, or the presence of moving images in art museums, in museums that go beyond the film museum.

—**DF:** But you're talking about presentation there – what about preservation? I mean, the theme of presentation has come out strongly from the things that we wrote down at the beginning. It could be a book about presentation. But it would be a bit odd if the preservation part was on analog/celluloid, and the presentation covered everything…

—**AH:** That's why I think it's important to discuss, for instance, what film archives do *vis-à-vis* digitally-born materials. They get more and more of this. Do these materials go into the same collection, or is a separate collection being created? *(Mumbles of agreement)* If so, what would the needs for the separate collection be in terms of preservation, conservation, etc.?

—**PCU:** I also think that the book should not concentrate on presentation only, because, as we all know, the way you present a moving image is dependent on the way you preserve it, and it is dependent, in turn, on the way you decide to acquire a given work. I think one of the imperatives of our profession now is to demonstrate, in a persuasive manner, the importance of an integrated approach to archiving and curating, which incorporates the acquisition process, the preservation process, and the presentation process. Separating them would be lethal for our profession, because it would make people lose perspective on why we are doing

things in the way we do. But in addition to this, I would argue that perhaps what we are debating so far reflects an awareness which is more or less present in our field; which is the fact that, fundamentally, people do not really care much about how a moving image is made accessible. What is so important for us is not that important for most people, including people in our profession. Sometimes I'm startled by people who love, who care about cinema, using the traditional sense of the term, and who are saying, "I'm perfectly happy to see this film in digital form." So this indifference to the way moving images are presented is pervasive; it is even within our gates.

—**AH:** Absolutely. I think one of the jobs of institutions like ours is to enable people to differentiate better; to better sense and understand the differences. They will go on to say "Film" about all this, probably, but this book could still contribute to a better understanding.

—**DF:** But do we have to accept that situation? Who is the book for? When I first read this I said, "This is our last big chance at transparency and honesty in film archiving." Let's not hide behind the generalist terms, let's not try and say we understand, because in the end we've not made a case for the basic preservation of film, and access to film as film. If we take the popular view of film, which may well cover materials which are not on film, I think we're not going to achieve that level of honesty and transparency. But I think it is essential for the survival of the analog film archive in this day and age. So I see this as the last big chance to be absolutely straight and honest, not ignoring the others, but saying, here is what we're really talking about as film archivists. The book is a representation of what film archivists really feel, in the most persuasive manner, to a much broader archive, museum, and educational audience. We never do that; we're always hiding. If there's any confusion in this work, it will not help us at all.

__PCU: This fits in with a term which I heard Alex use in Sacile when we first discussed this, to have a book as a sort of series of statements, a series of position papers, saying that this is the way we think things should be. Then it would be our responsibility to argue for these points as persuasively as possible. But this is our position. And then...

__DF: How do you create awareness of how material comes before your eyes if you use a popular definition which itself does not understand that?

__ML: I've always liked the notion of having "Moving Image Experience" in the title, because it sounds misleading at first, because it's a term that people who deal with film or people who deal with moving image media immediately recognize, and say, "Yes, it's that smoky thing that's everywhere." It's the whole of the experience of seeing moving images before your eyes. Starting out with this term, but then concentrating on what we do best – and we shouldn't forget that the "Film Experience", the analog medium, has been a bench-mark for all the audiovisual media that followed. I mean, just reconsidering what it meant for video artists, or for film-makers who turned into video artists – the art they measured up against, where they tried to do the opposite to find ways of expression with video that they thought they couldn't do with film: it was always Film. And not only the way you produce something, but also the way it's going to be seen, the whole video installation idea, the end-less loop, etc. Digital artists working with non-linear media, what was the thing they went up against? They went up against the linear film script. Trying to take a time-based medium and define time in a new way.

If I go to a fine art museum – they really present *moving images* in a sense, because they don't seem to acknowledge, or there was never any kind of communication from the archival world to correct them, that it's not just images which you can show on any screen, just because your architects say, "We can put a television set in that corner; that would be good." There is a whole set of values, and a whole set of audience situations associated with film, and a different set associated with video. Our profession should also be valued as a profession that can preserve certain ways of how audiences see films, certain practices of dealing with film – the fact that it is recorded life, for instance, that history is recorded here, and how these records were incorporated into our image of who we are, and where we stand, and what the 20th century has been. Preserving certain specific practices associated with the medium, and then comparing different media and different practices, and the transitions where one medium, like film, is translated to another medium, like the way "archive.org" does with moving images that they put on the Internet. To directly talk about which aspects of what you are presenting are dependent on the medium, and which aspects are not. Because if one starts talking about film on the Internet, one has to talk about what is lost, maybe, and also what is gained by putting it into a different context.

When I was thinking about this, I always came back to what Paolo said, to the centre of his arguments: curatorship. Where are the competent people, where are the mediators, where are the guardians – or the people who come up with the terminology for all of that?

—AH: I think this also touches upon the issue of the library function vs. the museum function of our institutions. What does it mean when we talk about our institutions as "libraries"? This happens a lot – in translation at least, at FIAF congresses and in FIAF writings, for instance, when the French term "cinémathèque" is being translated as "film library". Would it refer to the "consultation" of films in other media formats than their original ones? That's something I can understand, and it would be called a "mediatheque", I guess. In the traditional library, the act of book consultation – or copying from the book – is usually not about the artefact in an archival or museum sense. Should we then speak about the "Moving Image Library" as something distinct from the "Film Museum"?

—DF: You see, I believe that both "library" and "archive" are the wrong words, and "museum" is the right word. I've been doing some research into Ernest Lindgren [the first curator of the National Film Archive in London] around about 1935, when he said, "Film archivists will never be accepted unless they use the terminology of an art form that has already been accepted." And he suggested at that time that one should use the terminology of the art gallery. So I think of all the words we've got, "museum" is the best. But we have a problem when, if you look at the title of your organization, the *Austrian Film Museum,* it seems to define the archive; in English the museum can have a separate function from the archive. Whereas I believe it's a totality in your case. So this problem of terminology is

a difficult one. I think why the whole concept of curatorship is nice, is because it gets away from the titles of institutions. But I believe that curatorship should be based on museum terminology. Because the museum itself today is a total experience: it accepts the need to preserve the artefacts, to maintain heritage, but it also accepts the need to present. So I still believe, and I know that I shouldn't be saying this, since film archives have now been going for 70 years in the form we know, one would hope that we've got past this discussion that Ernest was having in 1935. But we haven't. To a certain extent we haven't really faced it.

—PCU: No, but you see in the other arts, you don't have a museum of paintings and an archive of paintings. The Louvre is a museum, and there are huge deposits of paintings which don't necessarily see the light for a long time. No institution in the painting world thinks of itself as an archive. It is a *museum*. In our world there is this distinction: if you decide to collect as much as possible, you are an archive; if you could decide to collect according to selected criteria, you're a museum.

—AH: Well, I think it has to do with the word "muse", actually…

—PCU: Exactly. In your own country, you have the Austrian *Film Archive* and the Austrian *Film Museum*. What does it tell people?

—AH: I think it simply tells the public that there are two different genealogies: one bases itself on the museum model and the other on the archive model. The museum usually relates itself to presentation, and very often to an art form, or to the "muses". The archive does not necessarily refer to presentation or to aesthetic production. The archive is a place where historical documents are being collected, or documents related to the person, the company, the nation which has established the archive in question. And so, for film institutions today, calling themselves either "film archive" or "film museum" would seem to tell us that they either understand themselves as collectors of documents of history, or as standing in the tradition of collecting and presenting artefacts.

___PCU: So should we not use the word "archive" in the title of our book?

___DF: You see, I think the word "archive" to me signifies very little curatorial intervention *(agreement from others)*, and "museum" does. Also, "museum" values the artefact, and one of the problems we're having in film archives is to attach enough importance to the artefact. And that's why we have so many problems today: that we have never really managed to create an impression of the importance of the artefact itself. Again, if we move into the museum field, it is accepted that the artefact is the baseline, and when it comes to funding – and I don't necessarily want to get into funding for the moment – I think that museums don't have to argue the preservation issue, whereas film archives seem to spend all their time arguing the need for preservation. And that's because we've been using the wrong terminology.

___AH: I think it comes from the fact that film is seen as "the reproducible art". I think that's probably the main reason for the relatively small value that the film artefact has acquired.

___DF: But you could argue the same thing with painting, no? I mean painting is reproducible, but the artefact is valued, the original artefact.

___AH: It's seen as a unique original, which, in its copy, has lost all its essential characteristics.

___DF: But the way it's presented to the majority of people is through books.

___AH: But that came later…

___DF: A museum can cope with that kind of dichotomy, and the archives have not.

___PCU: You see, you must admit we have plenty of colleagues in our field who resist or reject the notion of the uniqueness of the artefact. This is fairly common.

___AH: You mean in the film archiving field?

___PCU: In our field, when we claim the importance of the artefact, we still have this ongoing answer: "What's the big deal? You can always reproduce it."

___DF: But again, that's because we've not valued the artefact from the very beginning. If we'd taken the museum approach from the very beginning, we wouldn't be having this argument any longer.

___PCU: But then, what I'm saying is that the first entity, the first people we have to convince, are colleagues in our own field.

___DF: Oh, absolutely.

___PCU: It is there, it is there all the time. As you know I've been taking, intentionally, rather extreme positions to highlight this specific viewpoint, including, for example, gestures such as the creation of the Facility Condition Report for film exhibition.

___AH: And fashioning loan contracts after the model of loan contracts in fine art museums.

___PCU: Yes, and being told, "This is absolutely crazy, this is unacceptable; you're treating film as something that is unique, while it is not." And now new ammunition is being given to the opponents of the moving image as an artefact, with the notion that there will no longer be an artefact, because with the new moving images the artefact becomes irrelevant. Which is a position I still argue against, because I keep saying that as long as the image has to be contained somewhere, be it a piece of celluloid or a hard drive, in a place, a physical place, be it a rack, with four terabytes, whatever it's going to be, that is an artefact.

__DF: But there's new ammunition given to the archivist by the very fact that celluloid's life is limited. Therefore, the viewing print is no longer a replaceable element.

__AH: But a master artefact.

__DF: The master artefact – well, at least a semi-master artefact. And I think we should exploit *that* situation by pursuing the line that Paolo has started in treating the viewing print in the same way as you treat a painting when you loan it to another institution. Now it may make it expensive, and mean literally employing fine art movers to move it in the same way as you would move an artefact from a museum. And I can see everyone objecting to that...

__PCU: You can take that for granted!

__DF: *(laughing)* ...but it seems to be that we have an argument for reintroducing this concept, because we're at a moment when, effectively, the viewing print may not be instantly replaceable any longer.

__AH: And we have to try to do this without giving the impression of élitism, but the exact opposite. It should be a democratic duty to speak like that, and not an élitist game.

__ML: The archivist position that you outlined has an exact opposite... Let's all make up an archivist, who values the artefact, but can't argue why he values it. This is like a quasi-religious...

__AH: You mean the "fetishistic" archivist?

__ML: The archivist who builds a smoke-screen and says, "This is valuable, and it's so valuable that we don't even talk about why it's valuable. The only argument is its imminent death, so we put it away and we never argue the case." Both positions lack any possibility to educate a public about why we do what we do, and why we do it exactly the way we do it.

__AH: There is something interesting to be gained if you look at the private film collector for a second. The private film collector has no philosophy, in a sense; he or she does not know exactly why it's so valuable, but they feel it. It's a fetish. And they don't put it away; they show it in their cellars or custom-built "private cinema" spaces. So, in a way, we return to one of the beginnings of the cinematheque tradition: the collector, who "naturally" senses the specialness of the artefact and wants to share it with others, and in the process tends to destroy it and keep it alive at the same time.

__DF: It's a problem. Because I tend to agree, as a private collector. Here I speak as a private collector, not as an archivist.

__AH: You are a private collector?

__DF: Yes. Not of film, but of pre-cinema material. I was always thinking what institution I could give my collection to. I sometimes feel the only way to guarantee access to the items in my collection would be to put them back in the marketplace and let the next generation of collectors make them available to scholars and other interested parties. I need to keep it out of museums, because museums are now imposing conservation control. For instance – I'll use the magic lantern as an example. The Cinémathèque française, when it does lantern shows, now does them with transparencies of the slides, because they will no longer allow the slides themselves to be used because they could get damaged. Now this means that the future generation, if everything is in a museum, will not see the artefact. Now film is a bit lucky, because it's reproducible. I was brought up in the Lindgren ethics, and was in the middle of the Lindgren/Langlois controversy. I left the archive because I couldn't agree with Ernest's totality of view that you didn't show anything until you could make a duplicate copy.

__AH: That you would not show *anything*?

__DF: Well, you see, in the early days there was no money to make copies, so you either had the Langlois/Ledoux approach and you showed the original artefact, knowing that you were wearing it out. Ernest, on the other hand, said you can't show anything till you have the money to make a copy. Well, clearly that meant that the archive had no way of representing its role in society. So that didn't work either. So, basically, some middle ground was necessary.

__AH: And he accepted this middle ground?

__DF: Well, he accepted the middle ground. This is the interesting thing in my research. If you look back at the early days, 70 percent of the programming at the NFT was done by the Archive. And it was basically Ernest who was doing the programming. But his reputation came from a later period, when he felt that the British Film Institute was no longer recognizing the role of the Archive, because he believed very much that the head of the Archive should be the director of the Institute, because all the other Institute functions stemmed from the Archive. And three times he was turned down, in favour of people who either came from an educational sector or an administrative sector or from a pre-

sentation sector. One was from television, one was an educator, and one was an administrator. And so his reputation as a person who did not show films came from his own retreat from the Institute into the iron world of the Archive with a big wall around it. But in the beginning he was very actively involved in the presentation of films. So it's the later period this bad reputation came from, after his rejection by the Institute. It's very interesting that he was in fact doing the very same things as Langlois to begin with.

__AH: So when he was responsible for 70 percent of programming, he took unpreserved film from the collection and showed it?

__DF: Yes, but only in the NFT, and only in very controlled circumstances.

__AH: Being more conscious than Langlois of the problem of wearing out the films?

__DF: Yes, exactly. And where the Archive fell out with the Institute over presentation at the NFT was the Archive's rule that the film must be programmed 6 months in advance, so that it could be inspected prior to screening, to show that the film print was of archival quality that represented the work of the Archive.

__PCU: Well that's curatorship to me.

__DF: Yes, exactly. And so, this is where the whole thing fell apart. Because programmers were last-minute people, and the relationship broke down simply because the programmers were not prepared to programme far enough in advance for the existing material to be inspected. Because Ernest's view was, if the archive had the money, if the print wasn't good enough, we could make a print for that screening.

~

_PCU: Let me make a few comments on what you have said, because you have opened up another series of fronts. First, what you described about the Cinémathèque française doing magic lantern shows with transparencies – something I did not know about – is something which is likely to happen with film. It's not happening now, but it will begin to happen. There will be a time when we will see a given film in digital form, and there will be a minority of people saying, "But I want to see it on film!" And the answer will be, "Sorry, the print is too fragile; there is no longer a way to create a new 35mm print. For the sake of the print we'll have to refrain from projecting it." Now this connects with another point. When I worked with my colleagues at the National Film and Sound Archive of Australia on redefining the collection policies, I introduced a concept according to which we, the archive, will not grant access to a given print in the collection until preservation is ensured. Say someone wanted to use a nitrate print for a TV programme: the nitrate print would be put through the telecine machine – without proper preservation – and the resulting video would be used for the programme. And I said, "I'd rather have the film available *both* on film and on video, so that the audience has a choice between experiencing it in the original format or in other forms." In a way I guess I'm following Lindgren's path. But maybe what I'm thinking about is that there's a way out, which has been suggested by David: which is to stick to the principle that a film should be preserved before being made accessible, with the proviso that the curator has the authority to make accessible the original artefact, under strictly controlled conditions in qualified spaces, possibly on the very premises of the archive – in a way that guarantees that there is minimal or no wear-and-tear on the artefact itself. So there is a blanket rule saying, "No, we will not make it accessible if it has not been preserved." But the curator can make an exception. The main thing is the prerogative to make an exception to the rule.

_DF: I would argue that that is reasonable. We had in the NFA the print of *The Sound of Music* shown at the Odeon, Tottenham Court Road. The projectionists were promised a bonus if they could complete the whole run with one print. I understand it was screened over 2,500 times and that the projectionists shared a £10,000 bonus. The print was still in projectable condition.

_PCU: I could offer a similar example! In my early days at the George Eastman House, when I was teaching for the University of Rochester at the Eastman House, and therefore was presenting a film every week, I decided to show for undergraduate students *Battleship Potemkin*. It was my first semester, so we put up a 35mm print. And there was this fantastic, beautiful print of *Potemkin,* which had been received from Gosfilmofond back in the early 1950s. I went to the projection booth and said, "I don't think I have ever seen such a good print of *Battleship Potemkin*." And the projectionist proudly said, "You know why the print is so perfect? This print has been shown at least once a year, because all your predecessors have been showing *Battleship Potemkin* to their students, and it is what it is because no one has ever asked to loan the print from the George Eastman House." The print had never left the premises of the institution!

_DF: So I believe that is a justifiable approach, but the question then comes about loans between archives. I'm very pleased that FIAF is going into projection in this way, and is actually considering the importance of projection. It's long overdue. I think we have to be really strict. I mean annual certification of archive projection by a group of three people who are FIAF's guardians of projection, film handling standards. If they don't pass certification they cannot project a print from another archive. *(Grumbling from Paolo)*

___PCU: But that's why I'm sure that my Facility Condition Report has been taken as a provocation. If we mean to do things seriously, sooner or later we're going to get there insofar as we care about projecting 35mm prints – *if* we care.

___AH: Well, one of the points David wrote down before this conversation was, "As it is difficult to explain the difference in viewing experience that occurs between analog and digital projection, archives should consider only projecting films produced on celluloid in their viewing theatres." And you gave the example that there will be times where the museum has to say – like the Cinémathèque française does with the transparencies – "We have a print, but it's too dangerous to show it; we will show it digitally." This is an idea that I abhor immediately. *(Strong agreement from the others)* What if we take the guardian function of the film museum as seriously as other museums do? Would it mean that the scope of what we can show is simply being reduced? Because the loans will become more difficult?

___PCU: Here we're coming to the really hard question. Is there a point at which a museum will accept the idea that if it cannot show a film as a 35mm print, it will not show it at all? Will you go that far?

___AH: Any fine art museum has to accept it.

___ML: Imagine you had a fine art museum show, like the Goya exhibition. You have a Goya picture, and you have a sign next to it: it says the title, the year it was made; there's no information on whether it's oil on canvas, whatever. You don't care whether it's a photographic reproduction, a copy of the image, or the original painting. We had a public debate in the Albertina about the famous Dürer work, "The Hare" – are they showing the original, or a perfect copy? You can easily go to a historical programme, in an art-house theatre or a cinematheque, where you don't get any information on what print it is, what generation it is. Is it possibly shown on video? For a curator, a fine arts curator – it's part of his job, it's part of his ethics, and part of his being a professional, to inform the public about what he or she is showing, and what condition he's showing it in, or why he's showing it in that condition. Let's go back to the Cinémathèque française example. In many cases – if, for example, lost frames from a film are projected digitally with PowerPoint – there may be no argument at all, because as you say the public doesn't care – they want to see the image, they don't care which carrier, which medium transports the image. The next argument is, we can't show the original because this is too costly or too valuable.

___DF: Yes, but you see, a lot of that is a matter of ethics. But staying just for a moment where we are, another failure of the archive movement is to engage with the academic community. And it's a total failure, because any university you go to, anywhere in the States, virtually none of them are showing film in film form.

___PCU: OK, but I need to reiterate the question then of how many of our colleagues will enthusiastically endorse the notion that they will sacrifice the completeness of a programme for the sake of the principle of showing a work in its original medium? There will be a riot if you impose that, and this phenomenon will begin at film festivals. The film festival will be the first place where people will say, "We want to show the complete Manoel de Oliveira. OK, we're going to show it on video, it will still be fine." We can still say, "It's a festival, it's not a museum. They're making their choice, and the audience is free to accept or reject it." And the audience will accept it. Then the same danger will come to the museum. And someone will question the curator, and say, "You're being too strict, you're being a purist, you're preventing people from knowing what film artists have done for the sake of a principle which is becoming untenable."

__AH: It will probably happen like that, but there are two ways to deal with it, both of which may seem debatable at first. One is to follow the model of the fine art museum, and simply not show the one Goya piece – if you can't get it on loan, then you don't show it. That would create a distinction between the museum and the festival, and make clear that the museum is about artefacts, and that completeness is not the point – it never is, in the case of a Schiele or Goya or Vermeer exhibition. This is one way to go. The other way, something that the 20th-century medium of film could bring to the more traditional fine arts museum model, would be to reduce the auratic* aspect of the work, and strengthen the educational or terminological

* *Editor's note:* Auratic: "aura-filled", in the sense Walter Benjamin has described, of the experience of an artwork as being saturated with an "aura", a phenomenon of distance, however close an object might be.

clearness of the contextual elements, by saying, "Why not put a paper or photo copy of the missing Goya on the wall?", and making it fully obvious that it's a photographic "stand-in", not the painting itself. Film museums could, if they treat this actively, say: "We are showing you a complete Nicholas Ray retrospective. In this case it is important to see every single Nicholas Ray film. Among the 26 he made there are 5 titles that are not available for loan in their original form – which is why we are presenting them to you in other ways, as substitutes in the mediatheque, on a monitor, for instance."

__DF: But you see, if you're going to take that route, and I think there's some justification, I would imprint on the digital copy onscreen, and it would come up every so often, "This is not an original film". And any digital copy originating from the archive, whether it's on television or anywhere else, has to have a symbol that is clearly understood, that this…

__AH: … is a reproduction, or a transfer. But if we look historically at the way paper reproductions of fine art works have been distributed around the world, the sad fact is, all the people responsible for creating the reproductions have tried to emulate as much as they could the original artefact. They want to be "as good as the original". In a way, we have to fight this spirit of "coming as close as possible" in the reproduction, and strengthen those who accept and openly discuss the distance between the original and the reproduction.

__DF: Yes, but you see, our real problem is between now and 2050, because by the time we get to 2050, the way things are going, people will be coming to the film museum to see a film projected in ideal circumstances, and it will get an aura about it, the same sort of aura you get when coming to see an original Goya. The problem is this period, from now till then. How do we keep the interest of the public in our work for this period?

___AH: I think it's already happening. I don't think it's a 2050 question. *(Objection from the others)* I think we're starting to arrive at that point.

___PCU: Well, you may recall that one of the points I put in my proposed list of topics is, what will happen in this so-called immediate future. Because I'm not sure what you said corresponds to my way of thinking about it. I do feel that the period between now and 2050 will be the most difficult one *(agreement from David)*, because during this time our view will be perceived as *passé*, nostalgic – you know, "Why are these people bothering us with this principle?" We will be seen as folklore, or as the wax museum: "Come see the way films were shown, once upon a time." That kind of rubbish. It is like the history of antiquarian disciplines. Take furniture. When a piece of furniture is no longer produced, for some time it's just quaint. And then, after several generations have passed, it becomes antique. So, this time will be extremely difficult, because we will be fighting against an overwhelming tendency by which we will be told, "Come on, don't give us this nonsense about 'original experience'. We want to see the content."

___DF: I'm saying exactly the same thing. But the question really therefore on the table is, do we take extreme measures? Our responsibility as film archivists is to create this environment. And we start with this book we're talking about, which puts our points on the table absolutely clearly, transparently, and says, we need to do this if the concept of the film archive is to sur-

vive till that time when it's appreciated because of its unique characteristics.

___AH: I would even say the concept of the film museum, not the film archive, because I don't really believe the latter is endangered so much.

The archivist Nicola Mazzanti is arguing that film museums today have less and less audiences for their presentations. In Bologna, he told me, "How can Chantal Akerman or the Straubs survive – all the great 1960s and 70s film-makers whose works you had easy access to on celluloid, until very recently?" He argues for digital projections as a means to keep alive the most "difficult" types of film art, and to attract a wider distribution for them. This position would be closer to the second path I tried to describe: Yes, we do show digital reproductions. We make this as transparent as possible. That way we can keep the works in circulation. I do not subscribe to this view, but I can understand it as an attempt to "survive" in that intermediary period. Even though I think we'll come out stronger if we don't go that route.

___PCU: And accept the price of unpopularity.

___AH: Which is hard, of course. We all want audiences. If you want the institution to keep or expand its role in society, you need audiences; you need some presence in the public discourse…

___PCU: And you need funding. *(Agreement from others)*

___AH: Because funding is partly, and sometimes strongly, dependent on public attention.

___DF: But, you see, that's only partially true. The funding for preservation in a museum is an accepted part of the funding. To a certain extent, because the artefact has been rated as important, the funding is pretty well guaranteed. Archives have never reached that stage.

___**AH:** That's true. But it's also true that even the big-name art museums have, in the past ten years, come somewhat under pressure to reduce their conservation and preservation budgets, their conservation staff – and to spend more money on attractive exhibitions for mass audiences, possibly curated travelling exhibitions. I think they're not immune to this, either.

___**DF:** Well, you've just said "curated". I mean, this was one of your points originally, and it is one that we should look at. I literally mean a *curated* tour, a tour with the curator present – armed with the appropriate documentation and the appropriate background material about the titles you are showing. It may be that FIAF and archives have to concentrate more on centralized curated programmes that travel with the related material, with the appropriate inspection facilities, maybe even with their own projectionist. The other route is one that we used to talk about in FIAF – the idea of FIAF headquarters being a central film distribution operation for copies. So that, instead of each archive providing a copy, there was a list with a selected number of generally recognized important films. There was one copy held centrally, which was available for all members, and even outside if under certain agreed circumstances for screening. That would reduce the pressure on the individual archives to provide copies. Because one of the problems at the moment is that if you happen to have an important national cinema, there's more pressure on you as an institution to provide copies of that to colleagues and festivals than there is if you have a less important cinema heritage. That was one of the big discussions 20 years ago.

___**ML:** And it's funny if you then again step out of the archival community or the FIAF world,

and look at private industries and how they do it. There is no IMAX cinema worldwide bearing the IMAX sign that is not certified by IMAX and also provided by IMAX. Projectionists are trained by IMAX, sound facilities are regularly checked by IMAX. Even if a multiplex theatre bears the THX logo, they have a certified THX technician coming and checking their sound system. If they don't, they are not allowed to bear that sign. Because people associate IMAX with a certain experience – guaranteed by something, a code of ethics, a code of values, a technical set of controlled conditions. This is something where private enterprise has surpassed the archive community for years.

___**PCU:** Well, as we have hit a sort of nerve in this discussion, something which I think will inform some good part of the book, I need to put two monkey wrenches in this line of reasoning, and see how we deal with it. Because in the spirit of being transparent – when we were talking about being transparent, and arguing that the notion of *artefact* will not disappear in the Digital Age, we are bound to clash against the fact that if I have a hard disk here containing a certain work, the problem with this artefact is that we know that its lifespan is going to be much, much shorter than the lifespan of a 35mm print. Because in a few years this specific piece of metal and plastic will no longer be usable, and the artefact will have a value insofar as what is contained in it can be transferred to another artefact, which will have a museum value, but for a much more limited time span. In other words, this hard disk will be unusable in 10 years.

___**AH:** Will it be unusable *per se,* or will it be because the machine which plays it will not be in use any more?

__PCU: Probably both. Because objects today are being built with a very limited lifespan.

__AH: But is this an essential difference from film, or just a quantitative one?

__PCU: It is a quantitative difference; but how do you make a museum, which is based on the notion of longevity, accept the idea that this hard disk containing the work of so-and-so is a museum artefact? And at the same time, be aware that in five years you are going to migrate the content into another artefact, and this piece will…

__DF: But Alex is actually right. There is nothing stopping you having a *digital master*. In other words, a *digital preservation master*, which has a longer life than a *digital presentation master*…

__PCU: As an object?

__DF: Yes.

__AH: Film is also not as durable or long-lasting as granite…

__PCU: OK, OK. So this brings me to the second point. Are we willing to discuss in this book the moment when… Let me take a step backwards. We have often compared our situation with the situation of fine arts museums, where you have a painting that was made in the year 1500, which can still be shown. This will not happen with film.

__DF: Why not? Projection is a mechanical process. We will always be able to make projectors. I believe that we will always be able to make film stock – at least black-and-white film stock – without any problem. As long as the manufacturers will give us all the associated coding and information and knowledge to do so.

__PCU: I think the book should talk about this.

__DF: So I don't agree with the philosophy that we can't continue, as long as there is a big

enough body of committed people to act as a force in the marketplace.

__PCU: I think the book should have something discussing the notion that 400 years from now it will no longer be possible to show a photochemical work in photochemical form.

__AH: Or that possibly it will be.

__PCU: We have to say it. One of the statements that need to be challenged in the book is the statement that is made not only by the outside world but also by fellow colleagues in this field, saying, "Cinema is dying anyway. Why bother making this effort?" There has to be a statement to this effect.

__AH: I can offer a story which Peter Kubelka likes to tell. He often talks about certain musical instruments from the Baroque era, certain flutes for instance, which were decisive for the creation and performance of important musical works. At some point, these instruments vanished, because nobody cared about keeping this "technology", these tools, in the post-Baroque musical era. And 200 years later, in a period which saw a renewed interest in early music, it became necessary to regain them, to rebuild the tools from scratch, in order to be fully able to understand and perform the music that was made with and written for these instruments. They had not existed as material artefacts for 200 years. He is certain that the same thing will happen for film. I think we can safely say that, historically, film has already proven itself to be one of the really unique forms of expression which humanity has developed, and a specific way of thinking; so if it vanishes, there will almost certainly come a period, in 100 or 700 years, when humanity will feel the need to reconstruct these tools and machines of thought and expression.

Why should we wait for that to happen? Why not act in a different way than in the case of the musical instruments, and keep this 20th-century "instrument" and its products available and present without interruption?

__DF: And also, there's already the experience of museums that have cut-off points. The Musée d'Orsay has an acceptable cut-off. It only deals with, what, 1848 to 1914. And everything it does is related to that period. Why shouldn't there be a museum that deals with film on celluloid, and stops there? This is one of the other issues.

__PCU: Today especially.

__DF: Yes.

__AH: I'm not sure if there's an absolute or "ethical" necessity for film archives and film museums to start collecting digital work now. Maybe this job "falls to us" now simply because at the moment there are too few specifically organized public institutions with the mission to preserve the tools and products of the Digital Age? And if there were, it would be up to them to take care of the digital era. And we would still have this discussion. Those film archives which have a national mission and a legal deposit framework can't even decide the issue for themselves, because the new production for the cinemas is now coming into the archive more and more in digital form only. And it does come into the *film* archive and not some newly created *digital* archive.

__PCU: This is difficult today because... I had some concrete experiences in mind. If you make a statement – "OK, this museum will collect works of the photochemical era" – the predictable and actually frequent answer you get is that you're cutting yourself off from the future, you're cutting yourself off from the digital era,

you're eliminating having a dialogue with the future. Institutions are afraid of this now. *(Agreement from the others)*

__DF: But is it worth fighting for?

__PCU: I would say Yes.

__AH: I'm not 100 percent sure. Is it legitimate to say, "We deal with film in terms of celluloid, and when it isn't being produced anymore, we will stop at that historical point and only collect 'backwards' from then on"? How could the other path be argued? Is there a historical task for institutions like ours to continue collecting works from the present mutational era – like we once discussed with *The Lord of the Rings* – and beyond? If the answer is Yes, is it because we feel more devoted to the social phenomenon of public moving-image *viewing* than to the technological-aesthetic complex of film-*making* and film projection? In the case of *The Lord of the Rings,* what are we supposed to bring into the future? The social experience of seeing the primary release version, projected on celluloid, in a cinema, *and* the experience of seeing the secondary release version, on digital, also in a cinema? Because the films of the trilogy were publicly shown in both versions during the original release. Or is it an issue of the master medium of creation? Would we then have to primarily preserve the hard disks which represent the most original medium of creation, the "first generation" so to speak, since it was on this plane that the final cut and mix took place before the film was played out on a celluloid negative from which the release prints were made?

__DF: But if you take Charles Musser's generally accepted theory that the screen experience is something that started with the Camera Obscura, went through the Magic Lantern, and then came to the Cinema, there is a good reason to say that the cinema period comes to an end and a new experience starts with the representation of images in a different form because, although we are unable to define it now, I think there will be a new experience. That's one of the reasons why I want to have Volume I, Volume II, Volume III…

I mean, the same building that housed the theatre, the music hall, or vaudeville, became a cinema. That is probably irrelevant, that you have the same place. But it was a different product. (I must not use these words like this!) The "Cinema Experience" or the "Film Experience" is approaching an end, and a new "Experience" is coming. And we, as a series of organizations which were tasked with the idea of preserving and making available film, we must start collecting the new media. But separate. In my film museum you would have your Camera Obscura, your Magic Lantern… If you view what happened before the cinema and call it "pre-cinema", you're only looking at it from the experience of cinema. You must look at it from the other direction. Therefore a proper film museum actually traces a history from the beginning of the screen experience, through to the next generation of the screen experience. But it recognizes the stages of the screen experience, even in terms of collections, presentation, etc. It has an ongoing life.

__PCU: To follow your example: As in the fine arts there are museums taking a comprehensive approach, saying, we want to collect art in general, from antiquity to the 18th century, let's say, and there are departments. There's a department of Greek art. This is the Metropolitan Museum approach, or the Louvre. And then there are the museums of Impressionism, or of medieval art. So both models are ok. But this is a measure of, really, institutional configuration – what the institution wants to be. These are equally legitimate claims. And ambitions have to be measured against resources. I can think of some institutions in our field which would be better off limiting themselves to a certain one of these phases, and then there are others who want to take the ecumenical approach, and say, "We are going to follow all the four stages, and take responsibility for it." If they are strong enough to do it.

__AH: So I guess nobody in this room would want to state that one form is "superior" to the other. *(Agreement from the others)* But we *would* want to state that, either way you go, there are very specific terminologies, educational needs, and the need for differentiation, which should all be respected – no matter if you are a "screen museum" that includes all stages, or a museum that deals only with the "film stage" or the "magic lantern stage" in the history of screen experiences.

__PCU: There should be a pre-cinema curator, a film curator, a digital or whatever curator – because it is also true that today it is difficult enough to find a curator whose expertise covers the entire spectrum. Someone who can be equally competent in the analog and the digital. There are art museums with curators of Japanese art of the 17th century, and so forth. Admittedly, this is going a little bit against the grain of what's happening now, even in the fine arts, where I have noticed that the notion of the specialized curator, a curator of 19th-century photography, say, has a problem.

__DF: But, on the other hand, in the academic

world we're getting more and more specialization. I was at a party the other day in Indiana, and I talked with somebody who said, "I teach Japanese medieval history." And he was saying that this is happening everywhere in the academic world. People are becoming more and more specialized, because the more knowledge exists, the more research itself becomes specialized. So, to a certain extent, we may need to look at academia as well as museums in terms of the way we build our structure, because there it's going in the other direction.

__ML: If *we* say there's a danger of being seen as élitist or that it's folklore, and we are preserving a past experience, we must look into the future and say, how will researchers, academia, which also today doesn't really engage with what is done in the archives, how are *they* going to describe the popular audiovisual entertainment of 2050, without having a place to go back and look at what cinema was – we called it cinema, then – not only in the 1910s and 20s, but also in the 1970s, 80s, 90s, or in the transitional period? And I'm quite sure the only place where they will be able to go, not only to read about it, but to get some hands-on engagement with the artefacts of that era, is going to be the archives.

__DF: One of the things archives could do – again very unpopular – would be to take a much more active curatorial role in the commercial presentation of items from their own collection. I mean, at present, we are passive. Somebody comes along and wants a clip, or wants to make a DVD, and we have a passive approach...

__PCU: And if you resist you are accused of obstructing access...

__DF: But if you have an active role, and you make it absolutely clear what you are doing,

i.e., every DVD has a preservation history of the material it includes...

__ML: Controlled conditions.

__AH: That's exactly what we – with our very limited economic means – try to do. Our first DVD release, on Dziga Vertov's *Enthusiasm,* attempts to make transparent that the DVD is a kind of "catalogue medium" in relation to the work that we have preserved and restored.

__DF: It's a curated representation...

__ML: I fought the technicians doing the DVD and those who are partners in the whole project when they said, "The DVD audience doesn't want to see black leader; they don't want to see reel changes. They don't want to see any of the overscan area." And I said, "They probably don't want that because they don't know it." But we have our conditions to show material. If we say we put the Gosfilmofond version, the "original" version on which the restoration was based, on disk, we are presenting it the way I would present it if I showed it at our venue – where I can stand in front of the audience and say, "You are going to see black leader in it, you are going to see reel changes. We include them to inform you about the special condition the material was in when we found it." They said, "This is crazy. You can't do this." We said, "We must do this if there is going to be an edition of DVDs done by film museums. We need to educate the public through these DVDs what film museums actually do."

__DF: I think it will help us resist the idea that we are mausoleums and waxworks if we ourselves are involved in presenting material. We allow anybody who comes along to do it in their way without any contractual control whatsoever.

~

___PCU: I think there is one important principle for the book. I strongly believe that the tone should be proactive rather than reactive.

___DF: Absolutely. We're not defending our position; we are showing our position in a transparent and clear way. We're saying, "This is our position. We are film archivists. We have now 70 years of experience, and this is a collective view. We're not apologizing for it; you may not agree with it, but it's ours. We're not hiding it behind loose terminology; we're putting it on the table.

___PCU: As much as I strongly believe that the tone of the book is going to make a difference, I do not see how we can escape the debate on certain common concepts in our field. I don't know if this is reflected here, but there's a thread, a *fil rouge*, linking many of the topics we have touched upon this morning, which has to do with the distinction between "work" and "content". The word "content" has become quite pervasive. It has entered the world of archives, you know. Even in my own limited experience I can tell that. The distinction between "content" and "work" has become part of the common vocabulary of our profession, and, we could ignore it or…

___AH: No, I don't think we should ignore it. But, if we all agree, I think it should be made clear maybe more than once that part of the position that we try to represent here is that there is no "content" separate from the artefact. Except if we have differing opinions on that?

___PCU: No, I don't think we do.

___AH: If we say we are materialists, and I think we are in this sense, why not make clear whenever it comes up that we believe the material characteristics of every object/artefact to be an essential part of what is being referred to as its "content".

___DF: Are we really saying you can't separate "content" from "artefact"? In other words, "content" doesn't exist on its own?

___AH: It doesn't exist on its own. If an artefact is being reproduced on a different carrier medium, many elements or *aspects* of its "content" may stay the same. But the characteristics of the new carrier medium – and of the transformation process – will, in return, become part of the new artefact and of its new "content". To take the most trivial example, *Casablanca* as a theatrical projection, and *Casablanca* as an experience on television or via video, is a different thing. That's the question. Do we want that basic understanding to characterize the approaches in the book?

___DF: I think we need to take that viewpoint.

___ML: A nice turn would be to say we acknowledge that "content" has become the key reason why people have to turn to archives, or people undertake research into historical film. And we can say, "We can help you with our knowledge and with our specific way of identifying a certain 'content' with its carrier. To broaden the picture you have of 'content', and to enhance it and to help you get a much larger understanding of the 'content' you're looking for as seen through the artefact." So, again, offering competent assistance and taking a curatorial stance towards the word "content". Because I think most people do have a basic interest in film documents, for instance; not only TV programmes – there are audiences for historical footage and for documentary pictures of the world.

___PCU: Well, these are the people who are saying, "No, sorry, I'm only interested in the 'content'."

___AH: And to them we need to say, "Well, if you're interested in the 'content' you should know that this was shot that way, made that way, has existed on this kind of carrier, and was made public that way. Because it tells you more about the desired thing than if you just look at it from your limited 'content' perspective."

___DF: Are we taking this view for all cinema, or do we say, for instance, that it is different for, say, a newsreel?

___AH: It should absolutely include all cinema.

___DF: It's an important issue to raise. I think we can learn a lot not only from museums but also from photographic collections. Because when we think of what is a creative photograph, the only copy people want to see is the one that was actually processed under the supervision of the photographer. Why should the same not be true for film? I mean the argument is, how many actual film-makers or directors cared, besides Kubrick, what the film looked like after it came from the laboratory?

___AH: All the independent film-makers…

___DF: Yes, yes, they care…

___AH: There is always the moment when something is released to the public. Maybe it's the moment after the producer has told the director, "I'm cutting 40 minutes out of your film; I'm making it. I'm hiring this editor to make a different version." The director should not be the point of interest in this, but the moment when something is released from a non-public state to its public state – that's the vintage moment, if you like.

___DF: But there are different scenarios for directors, according to their power. Kubrick may have had the power to control it right up to the projection print, and to reject projection prints, as he did regularly. Orson Welles, on the other hand, walked away from the film even before it went to the laboratory. There are so many different attitudes. You've got to look at the individual creator, or even the creative team.

___AH: Well, that's why I think newsreels are a good example, because in a way they lack the individual author, and for them the moment of becoming public is the "vintage" moment. At least up until the material is changed and a different version appears, with its own "vintage" moment. Vertov is a good example. Certain newsreels or historical images are being put to the public; then they are re-used in different forms. So there is an independent life that images lead through their history. They become part of this first experience, then of another experience, and of a 50-year-later experience. Look at an experimental film-maker today, like Paolo Cherchi Usai, using 1920s or 30s images in an artistic work, such as *Passio*, or many other "found-footage" film-makers… So I think there is an element of non-fixedness. If we talk about the artefact, we also need to acknowledge that, through this history of film, artefacts have…

___PCU: Permutations.

___AH: Yes, have mutated into other forms. But there is always a moment where that process of permutation is fixed in the form of a new work, and it should be preserved accordingly.

___PCU: But I think you have just pointed out another good reason why this book should be perceived ideally as Volume I of a series. We see no separation between the content and the carrier, and we are living in an era where works are being produced for a multiplicity of carriers, where the work is no longer linked to a specific mode of dissemination of the work. Things are done in view of exposure in different ways.

___AH: That's why I think maybe the word

"work" could become a problem. Look at *Greed*. What is Rick Schmidlin's work, whatever you think of it, the 4-hour video reconstruction of *Greed,* where he uses whatever exists of the film plus 500 stills…?

__PCU: It's a different work; it's another work. Why do you have a problem with "work"?

__AH: The question is, would it be possible to say it's a different artefact or version of the work *Greed?*

__DF: It's a different work. I don't have a problem with the word "work". If a film is shown on television in Britain it's shown at 25 frames per second. In America it's 29,97 frames per second, because of the different television standards. So there is a totally different experience. Not only are you seeing it in the light and seeing it on a small screen, but you're also seeing it shown at a different speed. That must have an impact.

__AH: But that's also the case if I show *Blind Husbands* by Stroheim at 18 or at 22 frames per second.

__DF: Yes, but this is a conscious curatorial decision you're making. With television it's a technological requirement. You're forced into a different experience…

__ML: "This presentation has been formatted to fit your screen" – my favourite insert card with all American videos.

__PCU: All I'm saying is that a work manifests itself in a variety of artefacts. Someone will have to deal with the creation of works which have been conceived with the goal of making them accessible simultaneously on a variety of – what they are called today – platforms. They're a different kind of animal.

__DF: But you see, another reason I think this sort of purist approach makes sense is because

of what's happening now, in the digital environment. There's no sanctity of images. You can superimpose, change beyond measure. So one thing that's even worse now than presenting a film in a substandard format on video – that at least copied the continuity and form of the original, even with its technical limitations – now, you have total ability to change images. The only way to protect the creative achievement of the team that made the film is to consider it in artefactual terms, not in content terms.

__PCU: Fixed in time. Something fixed in time.

__DF: Nowadays it literally is possible to do anything with an image. And people will. More and more.

__PCU: And this will present a different curatorial challenge.

__AH: Do we agree that this is the essential difference between the photochemical film mode and the digital mode – that there is no longer the certainty that it refers to something that was materially fixed, and now every pixel can mutate in any way?

__ML: Not only every pixel. The second cultural movement that has taken place is from audience to user. There's a whole different idea of how a person who sees a work of film art or something on video considers him- or herself a user, because that's what's so fascinating about commercial DVDs.

I'm not talking about the Criterion Collection, but, for instance, *Final Destination 2*. A Warner Brothers B horror movie, presented in a 2-DVD edition, where you can not only see the film in the Director's Cut with the missing scene seamlessly spliced into the film, but make up your own Director's Cut. For the last 60 years there have always been virtual films – for instance, you might know if a whole set of scenes had been kicked out, but you could never see them; maybe an archivist could see them. Now, as a user, you have the power with the push of a button to see the complete version, and also the other one…

There was another interesting feature on this DVD. Not only was there a director's commentary, but also a little feature shot on video, where they had university students watch the film, and measured their responses (brain activity, and heart activity, and if their hands were sweating), to determine how a horror film effectively affects your body. Something that academia has been doing for 40 years, and the military has been doing. The DVD itself implies that you have at the push of a button all the knowledge appended to the film – film studies, archival practices, how the restoration was done, how some shots were done, what camera models were used, etc. So you are in the position of virtually having control of the whole body of knowledge associated with the film as "work", like the complete "work".

__DF: The control of the original is not in the hands of the archive, so it may or may not be accurate. I'm worried about the fact that in future any image can be distorted in any manner possible, and I'm looking for justifications for us going back to a purist approach; a statement of what we are. We can no longer protect the creative integrity of the product except by associating it with the artefact.

__ML: Or the historical accuracy of something. Just to make it clear, I'm exactly of your opinion, because I think that this whole cultural fantasy of the user being in power over film history, or over a certain work, is a false impression…

__AH: I want to make two comments. One is that Michael just introduced another decisive element of separation between two stages of the "Moving Image Experience" – the possibility of home recording and easy home intervention. The VCR was the first moment in film usage when something that was thought to be essential suddenly changed – that there is a certain duration, a beginning and an end, and although you can come to the show or leave it whenever you please, you cannot change the progression and continuity of the film as it moves along. With the VCR, you can record from TV, you can acquire the "film" for home use, and you start to be interactive. The "user" starts to be a co-author of the work; you can go back and forth, you can do time-lapse, you can speed it up, fast-forward, you can stop in the middle for a day or two… And these kinds of film usage expand further and further, up to the present day.

This way of "working the film" in every which way, on the part of the viewer, is a decisive difference to the previous stage. The other aspect is the integrity of the artefact, which to me is not a "fetish", but a human-readable trace of history. And that's probably where the debate needs to become political or sociological. I think that the rhetoric of digitization, and this quite incredible process that we're experiencing, that everything, every kind of artefact, be it an oil painting or a book or a film, is put through digitization, aims at putting everything on one level. All these very different kinds of artefacts, in their physical shape, which have come into existence through very different processes of treating materials, all these are now, at least in the impression of half the world population, levelled to one and the same kind of carrier... Maybe "carrier" is the wrong word – "experience", namely that of the computer, that of digital availability. Which might erase any understanding of the differences, the very *concept* of difference almost. It tends to erase the in-built "resistance" that each physical shape provides. If it's all boiled down to this same cultural level of Digital, it feeds into the fantasy that everything is available all the time, and that we are closing in on a reproduction of the world, just in a better or easier "format". I'm aware that I'm sounding like a Philip K. Dick novel, and I don't want to appear paranoid...

__DF: No, but if you read the mission statement of the Internet Archive, that is almost what you're describing. Their aim is to make all knowledge available to all people. I believe our very existence is endangered by us not having strong principles. The only reason for us continuing is to ensure that people understand what cinema is. And unless we make a clear statement at this time, at this turning point, and it's absolutely clear, and all the basic members of our fraternity agree with it, then we will be unnecessary.

__AH: And we will have missed the chance of at least saying and representing in as clear as possible terms why we believe – especially at a moment when this levelling is taking place – that the differences, and precision, are so important.

__ML: This is not about being part of a race. Or about going into total dissemination of content, and helping to build the fantasy of total availability. It's not saying, OK, we want to be on the train too, so let's jump on it and get more and more special added value, and say, "Please take us with you on this big ride into the digital fantasy." But, on the other hand, if people experience film more and more as something that can be owned and bought – not only the experience of seeing something, but all the knowledge associated with it... maybe we should go back and say, "If you look at the artefact, if you look at the work that has to be done to preserve it, if you look at 70 years of experience, and practice, the best practice and ethics in preserving film, we can tell you film is not something that you can own, it's not something like a pet, it's not something you have, contained in your carrier, but it is something that was fixed on a special place in the world, in a special time." And, on the other hand, as public educators, say, "We don't want to take away all your Director's Commentary, and all that is available if you browse a film on the Internet Movie Database. You can read lots and lots about it. We don't want to put a person in front of you who tells you the same story again and again, because that wouldn't be a reason to go to the cinema either. But we *can* offer you something special. We can offer you the experience of a work within controlled conditions that reflect upon the history of its production and the history of its original presentation. And thus we can educate you about things the industries, for example, won't ever educate you about."

__DF: But you see, I think that the thing we have got to be careful about is not to be against broader dissemination. The more control archives could actually gain over this broader presentation the better. It would be wonderful if we could do more so that we could have some sort of standards in the broader representation. It seems to me all the things that are happening out there are the reason why we should be thinking the way we are and doing what we're doing. In my opinion, this is the last chance of defining what a film archive or a film museum or whatever we call it is, and what its role is, why it needs to exist in the future…

__PCU: Well, I think we have found a good argument to answer the question we originally asked ourselves, about what the book should cover. Because we have identified the need to make a series of statements about how we think a specific, historical period in the creation of moving images should be handled in a cultural context.

__AH: In a changed or a changing cultural context.

__DF: And in a changing technological environment as well.

__PCU: So, ideally, the book should end with a sort of invitation. What we do should be an implicit invitation to the curator of digital works to think, "What would you do? What are you going to do with these different kinds of works, which set different kinds of challenges?"

__DF: And how are you going to prevent people presenting false digital works? There are going to be the purist digital creators, and then there are going to be a whole number of people who are presenting false digital works. So they are going to have the same ethical and cultural and technological problems that we're facing.

__PCU: The curator of the next generation will have to ask himself or herself, "How can I make sure that a digital work produced in the year 2010 will be accessible in the way it was made in 2010 a hundred years later?"

__DF: Exactly. Or 5 years later! *(Laughter)*

__PCU: It will be much more difficult. It will be infinitely more difficult for this person to get a sense of history from an artefact; from a work which may take such a multitude of forms, in a way that it may become really hard to figure out "how was this seen in the year 2010?"

__ML: And, additionally, such a person could ask himself, when thinking about how it will be seen in the future, where does my set of criteria – how I want to have it seen today – where does it stem from? And they will arrive back at cinema, I think.

__PCU: In a way, I also think that our task is comparatively easier.

__DF: Oh, much easier than theirs.

__PCU: Yes, because we are dealing with something that, because of its linearity, because of the fact that there is a first frame and a last frame, is a point of reference, despite the fact that we know the work changes its forms over the years because of the material nature of the work itself. For a digital curator this is going to be a whole different kettle of fish.

__ML: But also with the way a digital film feels like. I had one experience a couple of weeks ago that really was puzzling, and still is. I was at a press conference of the association of distributors and theatre owners which combats film piracy in Austria. And before they started their presentation they showed a trailer on the largest screen they had, and it was a digital projection. They started out with an image in the middle of the screen, which was set to CinemaScope. It was a small 4:3 window with pixellated video, with the heads of people visible in it. They said, "This is the film, but this is not the theatrical experience." Up goes the screen, and fully digitally was presented a trailer for *Harry Potter*. And so, "This is the film experience." *(Laughter)*

__DF: But they were doing this digitally?

__ML: Yes! I can still remember two years ago, when I was at a digital cinema testbed, where companies presented their digital cinema projectors and servers to convince theatre owners that they should switch to digital. The representatives were really struggling with the problem of presenting a technology that needs to emulate film to link into peoples' impressions of what a real film experience should be like. For example, digitally rendering "grain" into the images; or introducing motion blur, something that is completely absent if you shoot digital. They put immense effort into degrading digital technology to make it look like film, because film, something that is obsolete, is still the bench-mark for people, for what they experience as "cinematic".

__DF: But part of that is that they were worried themselves, as property owners in theatres, that people will say, "Why go through the screen experience? Let's go straight to the DVD." There may be a few years when archivists and film producers might actually be on the same side of the table, because we're both trying to defend, or trying to retain, an experience.

__AH: But what they are trying to retain is the big screen experience, not necessarily the film artefact.

__DF: No, they are not interested in the artefact!

__AH: One of your questions was, how will archives deal with the huge influx of prints at the moment when major producers and copyright-owners think they have enough good digital masters that they can get rid of the celluloid stuff? Do you really think that the majors will try to find storage spaces for the celluloid?

__PCU: I'm afraid they will destroy them.

__DF: Well, I don't think they will. I mean, they may destroy multiple copies, but they're insecure about this whole new technology. Look what's happening already in digital projection. It started off at 1.3K; that's now outdated – we're up to 2. We'll be at 4. I don't think the cinemas, outside the major cities, are going to be able to cope with the cost of changing their digital projection all the time. And I think some of them are going to say, "Forget this! We're going back to film!" *(Laughter)*

__PCU: Unless the price decreases dramatically. And even if it does, the fact that you have to renew the equipment…

__AH: But what's implicit in this insecurity is that the studios or copyright-owners will always keep the celluloid master, to always be able to strike whatever is the current need for a digital master to make a new one.

__DF: But, internally, they're going to have the same problems as archivists. Because they're going to go to their board, and their board will say, "Why are you keeping all this film? Why have we got all this stuff in a mountain? We've gone past that."

__PCU: "Didn't you tell us this was no longer necessary?"

__DF: Yes, exactly. So what they're going to say is – they're going to look for an out, and the "out" is the archival movement: "We'll give it to the archives – "

__AH: "…and if necessary we can access it anyway…"

__DF: Exactly. "– and it will give us great prestige in terms of heritage. Here we are, giving the public the heritage."

__PCU: Unless they create their own storage facilities, which they have already.

__DF: Well no, I think that their own boards are

going to say, when they look at the cost of maintaining these storage facilities, "Why? You're committed, you're saying this is perfectly satisfactory, you're saying that all the projection is going to go digital. Why are we spending all this money looking after film copies?"

—AH: Well, the answer could be, to be on the safe side. And the question is, will the board accept that?

—DF: Well, I'm not sure the boards will accept it, because *our* boards are not accepting it as film archivists. Why should it be any different in the commercial area? *(Laughter)*

—ML: Another way this could evolve, but it's a bit more frightening for the archival community, is that they understand themselves as content-owners, and that they actively pull prints out of archives, or start doing this. Or enforce copyright legislation to make it virtually impossible to show the film prints because they want to sell their new digital editions. That was one thing that was rumoured at this conference two years ago, where they said that certain U.S. major studios would not be striking any new prints of their 1940s classic films, to push their digital cinema editions.

—AH: I think that moment is historically over. There was a moment when there were some attempts to get the prints out of the archives, but now it seems to be a very different relationship.

—DF: Well, it depends on each archive. This is where I object to the Ledoux concept, which is still practised in Belgium.

—AH: The Ledoux concept?

—DF: Yes. Because I think Gabrielle Claes [Director of the Cinémathèque Royale de Belgique] is in the weakest position in many ways, because she still feels that companies might take back their films. I know that we rejected that possibility a long time ago in England, and said to the companies, "No, you can't do it. You may have legal rights, but you try it." There are still certain archives which take this very secretive approach, because they still feel there's a danger that material will be pulled. These are just the archives which are making themselves liable to such practices, because they've not come out in the open and said, "Try it. You can't do it."

—AH: So, what we have, for instance, is a number of deposit agreements with majors, which of course state that if the company wants to take it back it can.

—DF: Well, you just say *No*.

—AH: Yes, well, that never happened, and I hope it won't.

—DF: It happened with Disney. They tried to remove their films from the archive in London.

—AH: But which contracts did the NFA have with them?

—DF: Oh, they had total rights – in those days – to all contracts, so they could pull it. I just said No. And the answer was, "Well, we have the right." I said, "OK. Exert the right. Fight it; take it to court if you want to. You're fighting the British Government. Do you want to take the Government to court?"

—AH: Well, if it's a state archive… You were in a better position than we are!

—DF: Well, no, back then the BFI wasn't a state archive. But we said, "Take it to court. This is heritage. We have been around for X number of years; we have established the film as part of our cultural heritage. You, in creating films, have a responsibility. Try taking them away." And they said, "Ah, but these are American films." And we said, "Ah, but that's as much British heritage, because the language is the same, as they are American heritage. You can't take them away. It's our heritage as well as the American heritage; it's an English-language heritage that you've created."

___PCU: So, explain again what you think puts the Belgian archive in a weak position.

___DF: Well, they are still frightened; they haven't come out in the open and said, "Don't you dare." Canal+, for instance, still seems to have a power over them. I've said to Gabrielle many times, "Don't take this attitude. It's over. We've coped with that. The time is gone. The archive movement is now accepted. It can fight. We don't need to talk to FIAPF, the Fédération Internationale des Association des Producteurs du Film. I think we should not even consider that as anything that can happen in the future."

___AH: But talk to our colleagues in France – it's certainly a problem right now for the Cinémathèque française and for the CNC; the bigger libraries like Canal+ and Gaumont exert power over what they see as their assets, which are in the archives, which have partly been restored by the archives.

___DF: I know. They must resist this. Every archive must totally resist this. And that of course comes to the whole issue of whether you can accept commercial archives like Gaumont. Gaumont is the best of them in some ways. Because Gaumont realizes they need the archive movement in order to get back their own films. But to what extent do you allow them to participate in archival issues?

___AH: The funny thing is that on another level, in terms of screening films on their premises, archives sometimes take another position and show what they have in their collection, be it de-posited or non-deposited prints, without necessarily clearing rights.

___DF: Yes, but that's because the whole concept of the design of a place like the Belgian cinematheque was that you pay entry to the museum, and the screenings are free.

___PCU: It is a concept which is becoming increasingly untenable. It is something that archives have tried to do, and the more successful they have been with their programs, they have come under siege, blackmailed by the companies.

___AH: Well, whenever you need a print from outside, of course, you are required to pay steep fees nowadays.

___DF: But you see, Gabrielle doesn't lend prints on the grounds that this would endanger her screenings on the premises. I think it's an untenable position. The Library of Congress's view is we just clear them. We send a letter every time we screen a film. We don't ask their permission, we say, "We are notifying you that we will be screening your film on such and such a day."

___PCU: But in most archives it's even worse than that. Archives that have been trying to enforce this kind of natural right, you know, saying, "We are going to show films in our collection without clearing rights," they have been strangled gradually.

___DF: Really?

___PCU: Oh, yes.

___DF: So what are they doing?

___PCU: They pay, and when they don't, and try to say, "This is our heritage," companies don't even have to sue the archives. What they do is say, "Fine, you're going to show this film owned by this company without even clearing the rights. Next time you try to get a print from anywhere else, you will not get another print, ever again."

___DF: But that's why the archive movement must stand together.

___AH: That's interesting as a position – you're saying that, in terms of returning films that the rights-holder wants to pull, to take on an absolute stance of refusal? Why not do the same thing in terms of screening them?

___DF: Because I think that copyright is a different situation. If they have legal copyright, I think you have to acknowledge that in some way. Our way of acknowledging it is simply to send a letter of notification.

___PCU: This is a privilege that only a few archives can afford.

___DF: Oh, I realize that. I know the Library has a unique position, because nobody would challenge the Library of Congress. But you see, I don't think royalties should be paid.

___PCU: I don't think they should be paid either, but I have the feeling that any attempt to do so has failed except in the places where the archive represents a government. And even the corporate owner didn't dare…

___ML: Can we imagine a future scenario where archives will not be regarded as custodians of works that would otherwise have been thrown away or have decomposed over time, but have the status of pirates, in the sense that the industry feels that every screening of films, or giving access to a film work which doesn't conform to their understanding of controlled conditions, is illegal?

___PCU: I think that archives have overall lost power in the past 20 years. And I think – and this is also because the very notion of public do-main is becoming an endangered species – films which nobody would even bother paying attention to are becoming an asset. Films where even the production company would say, "Why are you asking us? We don't care!" – gradually all those are becoming the objects of potential revenue.

___AH: But some arguments go that archives have gained power because they have the films that the industry wants to use.

___ML: The physical assets.

___PCU: But what is the point in having a film, if you cannot show it?

___DF: And also, the archives, for their own survival, have been giving back to the industry in one way or another. The studios now have most of the material which has real commercial value, so the archives' power has gone. The power they had to resist.

___PCU: I do recall a case of an archive holding a certain title for years and years. All of a sudden the production company paid attention to this title, and said, "We would like to create an element of this film for further distribution." The archive said, "OK, let's make a deal. What would you like to pay for this?" And the production company said, "No, we want to have an element of this film because it is our film. And if you don't…" Again: "If you don't…" While the company would not sue the archive, the company said, "Be aware that this is going to have negative consequences on your future business." Which meant that until the archive gave up, the archive was no longer allowed to show films from this production company on its premises. The company just said, "No, you don't have permission to show this film."

___DF: Well, once you've paid fees, you can never

go back. There are a few that have survived by one means or another. Either they're too small and unimportant, or they're so powerful that they can determine their own course of action.

~

__PCU: How is the industry dealing with those strange analog artefacts called 35mm prints still held by the archives? How are they going to keep them under control? Either they are marginalized by saying, no, this is low quality; this is the wax museum kind of thing...

__DF: Well, if you look at history, new technological change to create a new market is driven by the idea of higher quality. And we haven't yet reached the potential resolution of a good 35mm negative. So we are going to be in demand for some time to come.

__PCU: Is higher quality the criterion? I didn't think so.

__DF: Oh no, it is. Because each time new technology for the home market comes along, the only selling point...

__PCU: But VHS won. And it was not the best quality...

__DF: I agree, but that was a market force that did that. But what's happening now is the next format, DVD, came along, and it had the opportunity of extra material. The next home market format that comes along will rely on going back to the higher quality of the image again. And as we've not yet got the maximum resolution from the potential 35mm negative, they're going to come back to us again, in cases where we still have the best master material.

__PCU: OK, we're talking about films originating on celluloid?

__DF: Yes. So the archive is not yet in the stage where it'll be marginalized. It's still important, at the moment.

__ML: But the presentational side, as Paolo said, I think will really become a problem. Because I have at home the 1996 decision of the DVD Consortium of what the next generation home-video format should look like; what features it has to have. Apart from all the technological companies, all the majors were in this Consortium. And Point 1 of the majors was, the image quality has to surpass VHS. Point 1: image quality. Point 2, since the image quality is so good, all means must be taken to protect the content from being distributed freely. It's exactly the same with the HD formats. Now the quality must be better than DVD, but it must not be as good as digital cinema, and it must be protected by all means necessary.

__PCU: But don't you think that the moving image – the film – industry will eventually take the same approach taken by the music industry? Instead of fighting the lost battle of trying to counteract piracy, they will basically try to make piracy irrelevant by making moving images accessible at such a low cost...

__DF: Low unit cost?

__PCU: Yes, at a low cost. Why bother pirating something that you can have for 99 cents?

__ML: They learned with the whole iTunes Music Store that people happily accept the quality being a tad lower than on the CD if you can have instant access to it. I mean the other thing with digital cinema is – you talked about the thing with 4K – it doesn't really touch upon 35mm, and 4K is far away. But when I look at television I see a battle that the consumer decides, of either having 10 channels of high-quality television signal, or 99 channels of bad-looking, heavily compressed satellite television. Most people go for 99 channels of bad-quality television.

___DF: I don't think the consumer has much say in this. The industry is determining what they think the consumer wants.

___ML: Let's say a consumer who is not educated about the true possibilities, for instance, of what an image could be. We can probably imagine a situation where in maybe only 6 or 7 years a lot of medium-sized to small-sized screens show films digitally in a reduced format because they can't afford 4K projectors. They may not even want to afford a true 2K projector for a screen that is only 5 metres by 3.5 metres. And so they just decide to show the low-quality version, because it doesn't really make any difference in terms of audience interest. It keeps the cost-per-unit down because people will mainly go for the DVD, and only go out to the cinema if they're on a date. And the cinematheques or film museums can then show this film in the true beauty of a 35mm print that has been well preserved…

___DF: If we can survive this lean period I know we'll come out in the end with enough public support for a quality film museum presentation. But it's this period in-between. We have to state what we want to survive during that difficult intermediate period.

___AH: Let's assume the iTunes model works out for film, in terms of commercial viability, and as an endeavour parallel to what you've just described. We'll have a situation where, on the home computer, people can watch a wide range of films, more or less for 99 cents, and this will be an even bigger difference to the cinema. It will be by far the most common way to watch moving images, and there will be an obvious and clear distinction between this and the original experience…

___DF: But will there? If I look at my kids, quality is immaterial. They don't notice.

___AH: Well, the same probably also goes for how your kids look at Raphael. For many people it's OK to look at the history of fine art in catalogues, in books. I have no qualms with that. But we all know of the moments in many people's biographies where there is a sudden, or not-so-sudden, intense understanding of being in the presence of a work as it was made to be. As opposed to being in the presence of various forms of reproduction. Won't that be the case with these millions of reproductions of films on computers?

___DF: I doubt it, personally. It's only a small percentage of the population of every country that has access to a gallery that's going to show an important original work of art. And the same with film – even if you had the number of film museums that you have in the United States, you're still going to have one-half to three-quarters of the population who are not anywhere near one of those places.

___PCU: Or the vast majority of the population, because cinema is a form of mass entertainment. They will be perfectly happy to look at their films on their computers.

___AH: Of course! But what I was driving at was that we will probably have the same situation that exists already in the world of the fine arts. Only a certain limited percentage of the population ever comes in touch with the originals of fine art. Most other people, if they ever come in touch with art, do so in the form of reproductions.

___PCU: The difference being, however, that there

is a market – an art industry, an élite market, aimed at bringing someone in front of the original Picasso or Leonardo. It will be much harder to create such a market for cinema.

___AH: For bringing people into the presence of Hitchcock or Murnau – or the way Hitchcock and Murnau originally worked.

___DF: Or bringing people in contact with an original Technicolor print, or a nitrate print.

___AH: But the fact that over the 20th century, the history of art got reproduced in an exponentially wider way than ever before actually helped the popularity of the museums. It did not make the museums less interesting, but much, much more interesting. I would assume that a similar process comes into play with moving images. The more people see *Vertigo* on their home computers in that way, they need to see it…

___DF: But I don't think that's going to be true, because I don't think that we've created the same artefactual concern for film.

___AH: Isn't that what we're working on? Creating that understanding?

___DF: Exactly! In order to do that now at this late date we have got to be prepared to be totally unpopular for a period of 20 or so years. And the question is: can you survive economically in a situation where you are taking up a sort of purist position? The sad thing is that we didn't do it earlier. This is the problem. And I think the real reason is, people say the archives started in 1935, but they didn't effectively start until the mid-1970s. If you want to be realistic, the archive was not really doing much except collecting or showing, depending on its philosophy.

___PCU: Until the mid-70s.

___DF: So the archive movement really is only 30 years old, or perhaps 35 years.

___AH: Then it's more normal that we're only doing this now.

___DF: But while we're trying to spread the idea that there is a long heritage of archives, we're suffering for the fact that it isn't true.

___AH: I shouldn't be trying to make too many comparisons – but maybe it's not so different from the history of museums. Museums, as we understand them now, are also a relatively young concept. There used to be the *Wunderkammer,* the "Cabinets of Curiosities", for centuries. Only in a relatively late stage during the 19th century did the concept of the museum as a public institution take hold. So the film archive era between the 1930s and the early 1970s is maybe more like the *Wunderkammer,* or those kinds of private collections, and only since the mid-1970s would we even be able to talk about a modern museum type, or even real archive functions. Isn't it comparable to that?

What I'd be interested in as a further historical question, you were saying before that in 1935 Ernest Lindgren proposed to deal with film the way art galleries dealt with artworks. What, in your opinion or experience, led to that position being marginalized? And which forces during the development of, let's say, the 1930s to the 60s or 70s, led into other directions that did not care about the Lindgren perspective?

___DF: The Langlois perspective was more attractive; the idea of seeing the material. And because his philosophy was so prevalent, Lindgren realized that he was in a losing battle, because he followed museum practice, treating the artefact as an item that had to be protected from wear and tear. So, to a certain extent, he was defeated by the very success of Langlois and Ledoux and all the others who showed films. It is why there's no biography of Ernest Lindgren, and we get Langlois biographies every year. And, you know, because basically it was a populist approach. I am convinced now, looking back at Lindgren, that it is absolutely remarkable what he said in those early days. There's a leaflet that was published in 1935. If I put it on the table, and took the date off it, you would say, "This has come out of the Technical Commission of FIAF." It's unbelievable. None of the other people were thinking about these issues except the Imperial War Museum and the documentary archives. They were the only archives that were really thinking about these issues. The archives that I would call cultural archives, which is the tradition of our archive movement, were not interested in that at all for many years, except for Ernest.

__AH: But then Lindgren, as you said, was interested also in showing, and keeping alive, and presenting, so he could have followed the art gallery approach simply by putting money into preservation, creating…

__DF: But there was no money!

__AH: There was no money?

__DF: When I first went to the archive in 1959, Harold Brown's printer was the only printer, and that was probably one of the first printers ever in the archive movement. This was a home-made printer, a step-printer. It had been copied by a local engineer, so it was slightly better than the original by the time I went there…

__PCU: I saw it in operation. It was made with pieces of Mecano – yes, the construction kit which used to be so popular among kids – pieces of Mecano were actually used in the construction of the printer!

__DF: And in the archive, I think, when I was

first there, the total budget for preservation was £3,000 a year. *(Silence)* It was not the same world at all.

__AH: But when we walked over here, you said 90 percent of the American collection at the NFA was preserved.

__DF: That was done later, particularly in the period after 1974. I was there as curator. That year there was a big fire in England at a chemical works in Flixborough, and it had an impact because a lot of people were killed. The Government said you cannot store flammable materials, or inflammable materials as we call them, in areas where there is housing in close proximity. And therefore the archive will have to move their collection. So we said, "OK, we'll move it." We had to agree to move it in one year. We had to build nitrate vaults in Gaydon, which was an old airfield. But we said, "The way of getting rid of this problem altogether would be to duplicate the film," and the Government said OK. Our staff went up three times, and the budget went up, so that we were able to copy 5–6 million feet of nitrate a year. We had this thing called the 24-Year Nitrate Preservation Scheme, which started in 1976, which was designed to copy all existing material held by the archive in '76 by the year 2000, and for that whole period we had this money. It was still there in 1990 when I left, but sometime very soon after the money dried up and the process stopped.

__AH: Between 1976 and 1990 you followed the plan, and you had the money to do it?

__DF: It was a plan that was accepted by the Government as a way of getting rid of this problem of inflammable material.

__AH: So it was no museological or…?

__DF: Oh, it never is. It never is. You have to use

any methods possible. I mean, we're talking about survival. Talking about the right thing to do is not necessarily the way of achieving the right thing, unfortunately. During that period there was continual copying. And that's why during that period most films of any importance were copied.

—**AH**: The very last question on this topic: why didn't the Government force the Archive to then get rid of the nitrate?

—**DF**: It tried. I mean, this was the deal originally: I had to sign so I'd get rid of it.

—**AH**: It sounds like, "We get rid of the nitrate; you get the money to copy it."

—**DF**: Oh well, I had to sign an agreement, but then I just refused to do it. *(Laughter)* In the end, because time had gone by and the Government changed.

—**PCU**: Things are forgotten.

—**DF**: Yes, we started creating a new philosophy. Because civil servants change, they didn't know and they gradually accepted the new philosophy, and forgot the original deal. "The ends justify the means." Otherwise you won't get anywhere.

—**AH**: But that also allows our "opponents", in a way, to say we have the same ends as you do, we just have different means. There are a number of people who say, "We have the same ends. We just think that going actively into digital, showing films digitally, is another means to achieve these same ends." That, I think I've realized in a few years, is also one of the problems. You rarely find people you speak with who state very different ends. They mostly agree with you immediately on the ends, but there are variants in how to go about it...

—**DF**: In that case the end is purely "content".

Our end is different. The trouble is that to the uninitiated the ends seem the same. This is why we have to make the distinction very clear. The end is the protection of the creator of an artistic work.

—**PCU**: And the protection of the way in which it was experienced.

—**ML**: I would even extend it to non-artistic works like newsreels.

—**DF**: Oh yes, you should. Well, I think the answer is, we're saying all film is artistic. The straightforward act of putting your camera up, going away, and letting it run...

—**AH**: ...is an aesthetic act.

~

—**AH**: It seems to me that the word "curatorial" or "curator" has slightly different meanings in the English-language world and in our world. A *Kurator* in German, as the term is understood in the world of art exhibitions, museums, and festivals, is not necessarily tied to an institution; it's not necessarily someone who's guarding objects, but the person who is the mind behind an exhibition.

—**PCU**: So the Rubens exhibition has been curated by...

—**DF**: But this unfortunately is certainly not the way, for instance, the National Film Archive worked – the curator was the director of the archive. And in the museum world, too. In Britain, some museums have a "director", particularly the bigger museums, because finance is more important than culture. In the smaller ones the curator is still the leader.

—**PCU**: And then there are institutions – maybe the majority – where there is a separation between the curator and the director.

__AH: But they're on the same hierarchical level?

__DF: No, the curator is lower.

__PCU: Or there is at least a clear separation of responsibilities, in that the curator determines the intellectual policies of the archive, and doesn't have a portfolio…

__DF: Unless – and I dread to say it – there's no money to do it.

__AH: But do I understand correctly that this Anglo-American or English-language use of the term "curator" includes to the same degree the care of the objects in the collection, and the making use of the objects by presenting them?

__PCU: This is one reason why my paper on curatorial values has been revised so much. There was a fierce debate in my archive about the definition of "curator" versus the definition of "archivist", because archivists were saying, "We do that as well! We do interpretation as well." Well, the truth of the matter is that, as David put it, whether archivists like it or not, the archivist is more like the guardian of the collection, and the curator is more like its interpreter. And there is a dynamic between the two, where sometimes the curator tries to breach the archival rules in the name of interpretation, and the archivist says, "No, you cannot do that."

__DF: The original concept in Britain was that the curator was also the director, because the cultural decisions had to be made at the highest level. It's only in the days when governments stopped funding museums in totality that the curator has been replaced by a director. So what happened in the early days, certainly in Britain, was that the government took responsibility for cultural institutions; for national museums, any museum that had a national perspective. In these cases you had a curator as head because

there was no fundraising element. There was only an intellectual policy, and therefore you had a curator. That has changed, and more and more museums have to rely on private funding, non-governmental funding; you have a director above the curator.

__PCU: The curator says, "I'd like to do A, B, C, and D, and I'm making a case for doing A first." And I talk to the director, and the director says, "I think we have only the money to do one of these two…"

__AH: "And I may find a sponsor for B, but forget C and D."

__DF: But if you look at the Library of Congress, the curators are quite a long way down the ladder. They are the subject specialists responsible for interpretation in specific subject areas. One of them is responsible for film and one for audio, but in an institution where you have 150 million artefacts, then that is a tiny proportion of the whole. So in terms of the administrative structure, the curators are quite low. But I think they're in the same position as they would be in a free-standing film archive, or a free-standing audio archive.

__AH: But leaving aside the question of who is the head of the institution, in terms of the relationship between curator and archivist the way Paolo has just described it, was it already that way in the 1960s and 70s at the NFA?

__DF: We didn't use those terms. There was no such thing as "archivist"; "curator"' was the only word. "Archivist" was associated with paper documentation, not audiovisual material. The way we divided responsibility was "curator and guardian of the collection". It's the same philosophy, but there was no word for the guardian of the collection.

__AH: But they are different professions, in a way?

__DF: Well, there were no professions. There was no training associated with film archives. The only training that existed was general museum, general archival, or general library training. So they weren't *professional* positions, because there was no professional qualification for a film archive curator. There was a curator of a museum, but not of a film archive, an audiovisual archive. There was really no professional base.

__AH: But 30 or 40 years ago, weren't there also people who had no task to interpret the collection, but had the task to look after the collection's well-being, and others whose task it was to make exhibitions?

__PCU: There were institutions where what we call today "interpretation" was reduced to a minimum, if anything.

__DF: You're absolutely right. At the time when I first came in, the idea was that an archive was an *enabler*. You were collecting the raw materials for *researchers* to interpret.

__AH: But if the National Film Theatre existed from a very early stage, what were the criteria by which Lindgren or whoever decided what would and what would not be shown, and in what context it would be shown?

__PCU: You're opening another front here which is another interesting topic – the fact that the very existence of the term "film programmer" in our world was seen as something *distinct* from "curator". When I redefined the position of film programmer at the George Eastman House as "curator of film exhibitions", it was a new thing. Because a film programmer was always perceived as something else, something different from "curator of exhibitions"…

__AH: An extra-institutional person?

__PCU: No, a staff member. But this person was deliberately not called a "curator". The "curator" was dealing with the collection, and the "film programmer" was a sort of glorified festival organizer who happened to work in an archival or museum institution.

__DF: And who was very influenced by other film programming in the rest of the world, and by the need to keep getting audiences. Curating is necessary if you have a collection which you feel is not satisfactorily known. This is an interventionist approach. You'll spend money on making copies available; you'll spend money on publications; you'll risk the fact that the first time you present the films in your film theatre they're going to get poor audiences because it's not an area that is already well researched. That is curating. Whereas film programming is taking established knowledge, including the cultural imperative and the financial targets, and coming up with something that is nowhere near as interventionist as the sort of curating you are talking about.

__AH: Well, the funny thing in hearing all of this is that I find what we do here at the Austrian Film Museum is a real mix of all this. Because there is a side to it that resembles what you call "classical programming". For instance, this institution has a collection which has certain strong points, but doesn't hold everything that you would want to show as a film museum in terms of representing film history. So there is programming with outside sources, and in relation to what other fine art museums or other film museums do, working with what is available in the outside world. Then there is the element of strongly thinking about the assets or the specificities of your own collection: how to deal with them; how to represent them in new ways, other ways; how to create publication formats around them; and sort of accepting the fact that in some of these cases there are different audiences. That element I know also. And both stand in relation to the archivist or guardian function, which is more or less not thinking about programmes or creating a public, but thinking "how can this be treated in the best possible way". So it's this kind of triangle almost. And I was wondering if, in terms of terminology, we should try and define it. As I said at the beginning, in the non-film museum world such a thing as a programmer doesn't really exist. There is the *Kurator,* which means, obviously, both the independent person who puts together exhibitions without being tied to any collection, and also the curator or "custodian" *(Kustode)* of the Egyptian collection in the art history museum.

___PCU: You curate a collection, you curate an exhibition – you can do both. OK, the reason that there is such a distinction in our world comes from the fact that, for the majority of our film archives and museums, what you programme is to a large extent material which does not come from your archive but what you get from somewhere else. This brings your curatorship closer to the curator of an exhibition. And to make this distinction clear the use of "film programmer" became common.

___AH: But my question is, do we want to, shouldn't we try to bring it together again under the word "curator"? Would that be an aim of this project also? To find the best expressions for every activity that is concerned with interpretation, contextualization – making available

works in an educational and contextual way?

___PCU: Yes, at the minimum there should be such a thing as a "curator of film exhibitions".

___DF: But why should it just be film exhibitions? I think that the archives neglect film-related materials and other associated documentation. I like the idea of a "curator of collections".

___PCU: Yes, but if you say "curator of exhibitions" today in the film world, people will think that you're curating exhibitions of posters, photographs, and artefacts, not film. And I have to say, "Hey, I'm talking about film as well." So there is still this sort of prejudice.

___DF: Well, I'm not saying "exhibitions"; I'm saying "curator of the collection".

___PCU: But then sometimes there are institutions where there is a separation of roles. I was a curator of a collection, and I was delegating to someone else the curatorship of a certain component of our activity, which was exhibition. I would have loved to do it, but I did not have time. I was discussing with my curator about the exhibition, but he was in charge of it because I did not have the opportunity to…

___DF: You were Senior Curator.

___PCU: I was Senior Curator, yes.

___DF: There are so many different uses of the word.

___AH: Since we're putting it in the title, at least preliminarily – and I would argue for keeping it there in the title of the book, that's why I was bringing it up – shouldn't we clearly think about how we use this term, and what we mean by it? Or do we even propose a different or a more holistic reading of that term?

___DF: I think we are proposing that.

___ML: It also comes back to what film museums present. It's the question that I'm mostly asked if I'm downstairs in the lobby. People come in and say, "Where's the film museum?" "Where's the exhibition?" There's one standard answer, that's printed down there on the glass frontage: "The Austrian Film Museum is a cinematheque; our exhibitions take place on the screen." Which is not a satisfactory answer for many people, because they come expecting a museum...

___PCU: The camera, the poster, the artefact...

___ML: Whereas I'm completely with you that one shouldn't reduce film museums and archives, or the functions where an archive and collections and exhibitions collide in one institution, only to film. The question is still the focus of this book. We've found out that rather than "moving image experience", all of us would prefer to primarily talk about film. So probably we need to make a decision to look also at programming, presentation, and exhibition, if we use the terms in relation to curatorship, to film.

___PCU: One thing that makes life so interesting is that sometimes when we try to strait-jacket words into what we want them to be, reality takes over.

___DF: But one thing that I think we're saying is, if archivists are to blame for anything, it's allowing *too many* aspects of curatorial work to leave their own control. We have to pull curatorship back inside the institution. We have to become involved in everything. The curator *has to have* an involvement in screenings, in publications, in exhibitions of physical objects, even in the way in which material from the archive is presented externally by third parties. To me the curator should be making all these decisions, in order to ensure there is an *overall clearly visible policy* for the institution.

___AH: Which means that by reinforcing these aspects, you want to recapture the "director is curator" or "curator is director" format, a holistic approach which used to be the case, and which in smaller institutions like this one, can somehow still be practised. I must admit that this is more or less what I feel I am, in this job. It is not called "curator", but "director", because in our region of Europe the word "curator" is not used that way anymore. But I now remember that, in the early days at least, the founders and my predecessors at the *Film Museum,* Peter Konlechner and Peter Kubelka, had the word "curators" [*Kuratoren*] on the letterhead. It is exactly what you were saying, as an ideal at least.

___PCU: Don't forget that at the other end of the spectrum there is the other danger, that sometimes there are curators who feel so committed to what is called "programming" that they identify their leadership as a leadership in programming, thus neglecting everything else. So you can make the word "curator" to be what you want it to be. You can be the curator, and actually the programmer of a theatre. You can be the curator, and be an archivist. You can be the curator, and be a scholar. Well, we are looking at the curator who has the *authority,* but also the *stamina,* to cover *all* these components, and to keep them in balance. Yes, as much as I love programming, it's only part of the story, because the risk if I do just "programming" is that I will become weaker institutionally on the other fronts.

___AH: That's such an essential definition of a process. That should be part of our initial discussion, if we put the word in the title.

___DF: What did we say at the beginning? What was the title?

__AH: Well, Michael suggested: "Museums, Curators, and the Moving Image Experience".

__PCU: No. "Museums, Curatorship…"

__DF: Ah, "Curatorship". You see, I would not say "Curators". From the discussion we've had, I would prefer the word "Curatorship" as the philosophy of being a curator. It's longer, and maybe the word is not in the dictionary! *(Laughter)*

__PCU: There is even a book, a *Manual of Curatorship…*

__DF: Is there? So it's not an invented word?

__PCU: No, it comes from the museum tradition.

__AH: By saying "museums" instead of "museology", we're naming concrete institutions or buildings. We could also say that we mean a concrete profession or a concrete activity by saying "curator" and not "curatorship". By using "curatorship" – what do we gain, in your opinion?

__DF: We are searching for a definition of "curator". We're looking at the *range of activities* that the curator does and calling it "curatorship". I don't mind that they're not in the same category. The "museum" is what we're following as an institution; "curatorship" is what we're suggesting as the philosophy.

__AH: I think the book should be called "Film", and the subtitle is "Museums, Curatorship, and the Moving Image Experience". *(Laughter)*

__DF: We'd like to do that, but we might have to put "Film" underneath… *(More laughter)*

__AH: It would be so preposterous… No, "preposterous" is the wrong word. By doing it like this, we'd say, "Now is the time when this is finally becoming a discipline. Our book is a book that describes the discipline. The discipline is called 'Film'. This discipline has museums, involves activities that are called…"

__DF: I like it!

__AH: By calling it "Film", it's almost like there has been no book about film before. It sounds so childish, but I think it might also represent in a way what we feel is necessary.

__DF: No, I like it! I think somewhere in the introduction one does have to encourage other people to do similar things for other media…

__ML: I think the discussion on what the book is going to be called must be in the transcript of the discussion.

__DF: I like it as long as we've got some opt-out in small print somewhere, so that if anybody accuses us, we could always point to the Introduction and say, "This is a challenge to other audiovisual media to…"

__AH: Well, by naming it "Film", and including the "moving image experience"…

__PCU: The title could be "Film. Museums, Curatorship, and the Moving Image Experience".

__DF: I like it! I think it's "in your face".

~

__PCU: Let's pick our brains for a little while, and review what we have been talking about in the course of this day, and just put down key words in no specific order.

__DF: I think that's a good idea. Well, "curatorship" is probably the thing we've devoted most time to. "Presentation" is probably one of the next.

__ML: And then the question of the "moving image experience".

__PCU: We have been talking about legal rights, or the relationship with the industry.

__DF: Well, the *relationship with third parties* is the biggest issue…

__AH: The issue of how we can use means like DVDs to actively shape these fields.

__PCU: OK, then. We have been talking about the reasons why we care about the presentation of film as an artefact… We have also talked about "content" a lot.

__ML: We talked about the relationship with "academia".

__DF: And of terminology in general.

__ML: And of education. One phrase I liked a lot was "controlled conditions". That came up a lot. "Controlled conditions", in our own way of presenting films, as well as in relation to third parties.

__PCU: OK. We have been talking about behaving like a museum. Why don't we do the same things as museums do?

__DF: I think the thing that Michael is trying to say is really "controlling the conditions". We must control more of the ways in which we present ourselves.

__ML: It came up three times. First, in regard to ways in which we can control the presentation of film as film. Secondly, how we can control the conditions under which our materials are presented by third parties like TV. And the third was the industries…

__PCU: And we did talk about creating the "moving image experience" after the transition to digital.

__AH: It's always called "mutational phase" or "transitional phase". If we already feel that we can honestly call the historical phase we're in now a specific era, then it should be addressed as a topic, I think.

__DF: Yes. We're talking about the time before. There is a small but loyal audience who will come and see films presented as films within a film museum environment. Then we talked about "projection".

__ML: The issue of "quality" came up a lot, as something that is often seen as a criterion that film archives can guarantee. A certain quality of… Not just of projection, but maintaining standards.

__PCU: Well, we already have about more than a dozen topics here. There may be some repetition here, but we wrote down: *curatorship, presentation, the experience of the moving image, relationship with third parties, exploitation, cultural/economic exploitation of museum holdings, legal owners, artefact, content, academia and relationships with educational institutions, terminology, behaving like a museum, controlling the conditions, what do we do in the transitional era?, projection, image quality, moving image archive has to guarantee quality…*

__AH: And what ideological concepts do we deal with in a phase where we are still part of a living culture, and already part of a somewhat obsolete culture?

__DF: And the last two points we agreed on were the financial considerations, and: what is film, what is digital? We said we'd come to those at the end. What we're aiming for is *totality*, something in the end which is a coherent totality. So the questions have got to build on one another. Like "curating" or "collection policy". We've talked very little about "preservation", which will be the big change in any FIAF document. In the past any document produced by an archive has always started with preservation.

__AH: It should be a book that does not radically leave preservation out, but that is not about preservation; it focuses on a different framework.

__DF: Exactly.

__PCU: We don't want to add another piece of technical literature.

___DF: You could say, "Preservation is now a means to an end…and the end is curatorship." Whereas before, in earlier days, we had to concentrate on preservation.

___AH: As an end in itself?

___DF: As an end in itself. I think that the change that's occurred is that we're moving away from preservation as an end in itself. Preservation is simply one of the stages that you go through.

___AH: That's a very interesting aspect, because the commercially oriented institutions or people will say the same thing, but we would want to give it another inflection. They also say, "Preservation cannot be an end in itself. It's all about distribution, making available, servicing the market." And we say, "Yes, preservation is not an end in itself, but we interpret the new end very differently." We give a cultural meaning to this, not a commercial one.

___DF: Exactly. This constant contemplation on preservation meant that we were often defending something which we *knew* was only a means to an end. It was never said because nobody ever dared say it.

___AH: And now somebody has pirated it!

___DF: It's a tricky problem. Do you keep close to the terminology of your enemies, but provide a different explanation? Or do you try and create a totally different set of terms? We're not disagreeing with the words; it's just that we interpret them in a totally different way. That's one way of doing it. The other way is to try to get away from the whole language that they are using, back to a language which is more directly associated with *museum operations*.

___AH: But still, in the end, it's not just about preserving, it is about keeping culture alive.

___DF: But what we are saying is, it's not about preservation. The *artefact* is Number One, and the *curatorship of the object/artefact* is Number Two. It's not the issue of preservation *per se,* it's *the increased importance of the artefact*. One of the ways that ensures the continued existence of the artefact and the availability of material that can be presented is preservation. We have to start with the artefact, because that is what is missing in previous documentation and discussions. And we try to ask questions about why the artefact in the film museum or archive is different from the artefact in the National Gallery.

___ML: We can ask really simple questions, in the sense of a children's book: "How do you curate a film artefact?"

___DF: The artefact has to come first, because that is the new thing we're introducing. We need to look at it as a museum would look at it, as a traditional art form would look at its artefacts.

___AH: We're addressing basic issues, and we're implying that they apply to film as much as for…

___DF: And the reason that they haven't been addressed before is that we're unique in that our artefact is 35mm film, and it has been in existence for 100-plus years, whereas in pretty much every other field there's been no such continuity. So one of the reasons we haven't addressed the issue before is because we've been fortunate enough not to have been *forced* to address it.

___PCU: OK. We have a strong topic for the beginning.

___AH: Many things become clear automatically when you start with the artefact. *(Agreement from the others)*

___PCU: Should we change the title of the book to "Film as an Artefact", or do we want to keep just "Film"?

__ML: Let's just stick with "Film".

__PCU: OK. Well, we already have a subtitle that's eloquent enough!

__AH: Especially as we will deal with presentation, and with the experience of the artefact being "performed".

__PCU: But we are presenting an artefact.

__AH: We are presenting an artefact, but the experience of witnessing the artefact does not include, in a funny way, the artefact itself, because as an object it's hidden in the projection booth. It's not like in the traditional "object museums" – in our case, you don't get the experience of the artefact by looking at the object. We are mediating the artefact within a special setting.

__PCU: The more we talk the more I feel that we should hold interviews among ourselves.

__DF: Sorry for this sidebar thought. But in Japan in the early days of the film archive, about 20 years ago, I was asked to offer advice. The archive had just started putting films in its new vaults. All the archive had in them was prints, no negatives. I said, "Where are the negatives?" They said, "Oh, the negative is not important. The print is the artefact," because they related film to painting. They said, "The print is the one that has the creator's signature on it, not the negative. The negative is a purely the source of the print."

__AH: Oh, like with a woodcut? They were referring to the graphic arts.

__DF: They were saying they didn't keep the negative. The negatives were kept in the laboratory. The print was the archival artefact. It was one of those difficult moments. The comment had logic, but it was alien to anything I had ever considered. It's difficult to disagree with the concept in many ways.

__AH: But in our case, the print does not necessarily have the "creator's approval".

__DF: In the case of the experimental film, the negative may well contain material that doesn't appear in the print. That was their argument. The print as shown at the original public presentation was what an archive should be preserving. In the future, because the print will have additional value, because of the greater difficulty of reproducing it, we will then have to think of the print as similar to the negative…

__PCU: In a classical archival world we always thought that if we could have the camera negative that would be great. And the print has always been seen as something disposable: well, if it's scratched, we'll make a new one. This rebalances it a little bit…

__AH: And it does not mean you should not make a preservation negative from this.

__DF: But if you're starting with the concept of the artefact, preservation is only a means to an end. You could argue that the print, which is what you actually show, is the artefact, as long as it is as close as possible to the original. This would make it easier for us to incorporate museological practices.

__PCU: It's a very daring idea.

__ML: The first time in my life I understood this was when I reviewed a nitrate print from 1911, and I put the print in and started it. And I looked at it and said, "Right now I'm looking at a print, and it's on the table." And then I was listening to the sound it produced. And this particular print was shown in a theatre in 1911…

__DF: That's what we always said – the glory of nitrate! If we dared to go this route, it would make it much easier for us to justify the argument of association with museums.

__ML:__ Sometimes talk comes up like, "This film is worn. It's got scratches all over it. DVD is better; it's so pristine." We sometimes show historical non-fiction films that are like that, and I like to go up in front of the audience and say, "You are going to see an archival copy, and every scratch here you see is part of its history. You're looking at a print that was struck 50 years ago. So enjoy all you see of it!" And I found out people are proud of that thought, that they are attending a unique performance.

__DF:__ In the future, when we are undertaking quality control by comparing a nitrate original and a duplicate side by side, we could screen the original artefact for the public.

Chapter 3

What's the Problem?

___ML: I think that at this particular moment in history, the profession suffers from a perceived lack of definition. It's still called "the archival community", but do we perceive ourselves as archives, as museums, or as libraries? How much has this blurring of borders between the distinct functions – preservation, presentation, and making accessible – been with the community from its beginnings? Or is it only an effect Digital has on our self-image?

___DF: I agree with your first statement, and it's been a great concern for me for quite a time. I had hoped that the coming of a new century, and of course the challenges that the archive movement is facing, such as not only digitization in terms of preservation, but also the fact that the collections are no longer as unique as they used to be, because more material is available on the Web in various sites, which you would have previously only been able to find in archive collections… that all these things would have an impact. The first was the FIAF Code of Ethics. One of the reasons behind that was that hopefully we could increase the range of our membership. And, you see, I'd always felt that FIAF itself was a rather élite club. And I know the reasons, and I could explain the reasons why this came about. And they were justified up to a certain time. But what I felt we lacked was

what other organizations, like the Association of Moving Image Archivists (AMIA) had, a broad membership, not only including archives themselves, but including individuals, and any organization that utilized the material. The idea behind the Code of Ethics was that as long as an organization actually agreed to the Code of Ethics, and agreed that if the Code of Ethics were breached they would be responsible to the entire membership at the General Assembly to make an explanation, then this would broaden the base of the archive movement; bring in people who are utilizing the material, bring in museums, and other ancillary players… And I was even happy with the idea of certain limited access to industry archives, because that's been very successful in the Association of Moving Image Archivists, to have the members of the industry present at discussions. But, unfortunately, when the Code of Ethics was finally put together, the Statutes and Rules remained unmodified. And so you still had these pretty restrictive Statutes and Rules, *and* the Code of Ethics. The Code of Ethics was intended to replace all those Statutes and Rules, except those that were necessary to establish one's legal position in a country. So the Code of Ethics didn't work. Membership hasn't substantially increased. And therefore I believe we haven't benefited from a lot of other organizations who utilize film in one way or another, who would perhaps be able to help us have a discussion about our future. So that was Number One that didn't work.

The other thing I was hoping when the new century came – always when a new century comes you tend to look back, and hopefully look forward – was that FIAF's Second Century Forum would specifically address major issues, and as a result of this we would be putting on paper material that would eventually make up a sort of new manual or a new *modus operandi,* but again this hasn't happened. What tends to happen is you get one person giving their point of view, and a very brief discussion, and no follow-up. There is no way in which the material is assembled in a logical manner, and, in fact, now I think it's just another event at the FIAF Congress. So these were two possibilities that I hoped would change the situation, but they haven't. So in answer to your introductory point, I believe there is a lack of definition. And I think certain people are aware of this, but are not really sure how to change it and how to initiate a serious discussion. But you've then extended this to "What do we perceive ourselves as: as archives, as museums, or as libraries?"

—**ML:** Just to explain why I have come up with this follow-up question – because you mentioned commercial archives or industry archives – I think this lack of definition has to do with this big question of what does "access" mean, the way archives or museums feel that they are a service to the public. There seems to be an increased perception that archives must react on demand, and I think one of the key differences is that FIAF archives – and I use "FIAF archives"

to speak about the whole community of traditional film archives – perceive this demand as something that aggressively forces them to react while commercially-oriented archives or footage libraries always have perceived themselves to be in a service to the client or to proactively make materials available. So this is one of my observations. Would you agree from a historical perspective?

—**DF:** Well, I don't know; it's not been my experience. You see, when the archives first started, they were really started by private collectors, and the aim was simply to acquire material, so that they could show this material to other people who were interested in the history of the cinema. They weren't thinking of the researcher particularly, they were thinking of the individual enthusiast. That was the main audience. Now, when the second-generation archivists started to take over, they obviously started to think about what they'd inherited, and what was the purpose of the archive. But they didn't have the confidence to say A was better than B; so they tended to collect everything. The idea was to collect as much as possible, and leave it to the researcher, to the user, to decide what was important. And that, certainly at the National Film Archive when I worked there, was the concept. Nobody wanted to make selections, because they didn't know how to defend selecting, and also they didn't feel confident in saying A is more important than B. So, at the National Film Archive, the aim was to collect everything. Now we did have Selection Committees, and I think that was a thing that no other archive had. Every month, we had a History Selection Committee meeting, a Science Selection Committee meeting, and a committee that considered feature films, and one that considered television. And they looked at all the materials that had been released or transmitted during the previous month, and decided what, in an ideal world, we would have in the archive. But, as there was no way of acquiring this material, to a certain extent it was more an exercise that helped us think about archiving and think about the shape of our archive. In reality we had to take what we could get, and that may or may not have included the material we selected. And we certainly didn't reject material if it hadn't been recommended by the Selection Committees.

So, really, while I was at the National Film Archive, the aim was to collect as much as possible across as big a range as possible, so that when the serious study of cinema improved, we could make available the materials required. One has to realize that the level of research into cinema history and culture we have today was unthinkable in the 1960s even – there just weren't people writing in-depth books – and so we at that time had no idea what would be demanded of us. The way of coping with that was always to keep everything. We were happy to react to demand. The basis, the way in which we judged our success, was by how many people came to look at the films, and what came out of these researches, a book or an article, and one of the conditions always was that if someone used the collection they had to donate a copy of any work that came out of the research. And we also used to have on our Steenbecks a little box, and if people found mistakes in our cataloguing records, or if there was information we didn't know and they knew, we encouraged them to put this information in this box. The cataloguers used to look at it once a week, and modify our records, so that we also benefited from the researchers. So, certainly, at the National Film Archive we actually liked the people who used the collection. That's what we wanted, and we encouraged it.

Now it's a slightly different thing when you're talking about the commercial use of the collection, because of the copyright situation, which I think is the single biggest problem to the development of film archives. Maybe we can get to that later. Obviously, you could not let filmmakers use material unless you could actually prove that either it was in the public domain, or you could find the owner and the owner was prepared to enter into a commercial agreement with the potential user. A lot of film-makers resented the fact that we attempted to trace the copyright-owner a long way back, because we felt that the whole success of an archive depended on its scrupulous observation of copyright. And if we could not clear copyrights then we would not make material available, because we were afraid that one scandal could completely upset our ability to acquire material.

_ML: Which in fact makes you appear passive, defensive, to the public, doesn't it? In two fields in particular: on the one hand, the relation with copyright-owners and the film industry, and in regard to making films accessible to the public either theatrically or in other formats – video, DVD, books, catalogues, etc.

_DF: You know, I saw an archive as a passive operation which is providing the material as a service to research. I think today we should be considering ourselves museums, because I see the museum as taking a more proactive role, being concerned with context and presenting its collection to the public.

The question of libraries is a little difficult, because the concept of a library in many ways is that you can loan the material, and for a number of reasons (copyright, technical, etc.) we cannot loan the material in our collection. We can, to a certain extent, make it accessible on our own premises, but we can't loan it. I think that the library concept doesn't really fit in with the archive world. So I think you're either an archive, or a museum. I believe today we should be a museum. The word "museum" would be a much more useful word to attach to what we do than the word "archive", although I do understand that the word "museum" means different things in different countries. Whatever term we choose, we're going to have problems finding an identical term to that in all languages.

_ML: Let's go back to the last thing you said. I agree that archives or institutions working in the field of collection, preservation, and presentation of the film heritage should function as museums, because if you perceive yourself as a museum then you do integrate all three of these basic functions. But you do it under strict curatorial rules. You make things available either on your own premises or under your complete control. But I think many of the new models, developed in what I think is a rather defensive action by archives, are related to the library in the sense that all the responsibility of what to do with films, all the judging of what is significant, or who decides what is significant, and what significant elements of films in our culture could be, is delegated to the user. You make things available, either on, say, computer monitors where people can browse them, or you put them online and try to make available only public domain work, or you dare to make available copyrighted works, but are prepared to fight legal battles over it if you only stream them. As long as you do not give users a hard copy, then you're actually not breaching copyright. But you do delegate all the responsibility to the user, more or less what they call "access on demand", a concept which is treated – ironically enough – as an active solution to the problem of selecting and curating for access.

_DF: That was the old archive. A lot of them still do it because they didn't have the confidence to make the decisions. And also because they weren't secure enough in their environments to take on the museum role. But my belief is that now we should be museums; we should be following a new approach where we still provide material on demand, if people know what they want. But, at the same time, we should look at our own collections. We can contextualize them. We make special presentations about elements from our collections, which are curated so that gradually our constituency begins to learn what we hold and why we think it's important. To me that is what the archive should be today, and what it should be doing. And that is absolutely necessary, because so many other people are making available on the Web material that was previously our preserve, and if we do not concentrate on contextualization and on curating our material, in many people's minds there is no reason for us to exist. And we will find it extremely difficult to raise the necessary finance to preserve and make accessible our collections. So we must change. If we don't do this, in my opinion we're dead.

_ML: In a conversation I had with Rick Prelinger I asked him to explain why archives should make things available online. And he said this is simply necessary, because there is this idea in society now that archives are actually an obstacle to access, and not enablers of access. And publishing materials online offers a solution to this misconception.

___DF: Yes, it's all very well him saying this, but then most archives are, in some way or another, governmental organizations. They either receive their funding directly from the government, or their existence depends on their actions. And the copyright issue is a significant hindrance to archives operating in the way that one would ideally like them to. I mean, if you think of the current US copyright law, only material before 1922 is in the public domain. That means that for everything after that, you have to get permission to use it. In many cases it's difficult to find out who the owner is, but you cannot possibly distribute it in any way whatsoever unless you have permission. So we're not free agents. Now Rick Prelinger can happily say, "OK, nobody's going to get upset because I put online a General Electric documentary made in 1935," because probably General Electric would be delighted to have it there. It's free publicity. So he doesn't face the problem, and it often annoys me to hear him talk because he is not facing the problem that archives are facing. He only has a personal responsibility, not a corporate responsibility like archives do: a responsibility as national bodies who rely on government funding, and who have to meet certain criteria. One of the reasons we just cannot at present pursue the ideal policy that we would pursue if we were museums is the copyright restrictions. You just cannot do what you want with your own collection. You cannot make it available unless you get formal approval. Until this issue is solved, archives are going to be seen as organizations which are resisting demand rather than encouraging demand, because I don't think members of the public appreciate the limitations on their actions.

___ML: I don't think so, too. But, to go back in history, when did this change occur? It probably was a gradual change. Starting from the 1960s, starting from your own experience in the field when you worked at the NFA, you said you were happy to react on demand, and the NFA and its staff understood themselves to be enablers of access and integrated their users in the process of contextualizing. When I started out in the late 1990s/early 21st century, there was the notion of archives being closed-wall organizations, and the idea, the rhetoric, of online entrepreneurs was that archives are repositories where everything slowly, gradually fades away from public view, and everything you discover and make available is a treasure, and would have been lost if it had remained in an archive. This is a rhetoric that has developed over the years.

___DF: Well, I don't think that notion has changed. I think you have to look at different countries and different organizations. You can't talk about the archive movement as one movement. There were a lot of archives, and still are a lot of archives, that actually find demands interfere with their daily work. But that was not true of the two organizations that I've worked for, the National Film Archive or the Library of Congress. Both of them felt they had a role to make material accessible within the limits of copyright. Obviously, in the Library of Congress, with a Copyright Office on the floor above the archive, there is no possibility of doing anything that violates copyright. And it wasn't much different in the National Film Archive, because we knew if we did, and if there were complaints from the industry to the government, what would happen is that we would lose our subvention. But a lot of other archives were afraid of people knowing what it was they held, because they were afraid that the industry, the copyright-owners, would come and say, "We want those back." And it was more of a problem in a country where there wasn't a strong film production. I remember talking to Jacques Ledoux at the Belgian cinematheque about this problem, and he was terrified that, because he had a huge collection of American films, the American producers in Europe would come and demand the copies back if he let people know they were there. So he always refused to give any information about the holdings of the archive. In fact, the archive movement as a whole did not issue catalogues because they were afraid that the copyright-owners would find out what they held. There was, when I first came to the Archive, one book called "The Black Book" (or EMBRYO). It was only available in the archives, and it had to be kept under lock and key. That just gave information about the holdings of silent films in other archives. Even today it's extremely difficult to find out on a worldwide basis what exists in archives. Part of this stems from the concern that some of the materials come into archives through the back door. There are archives which are still concerned that they are not strong enough to resist an attempt by a film production company to take the material away.

I remember particularly a situation at the National Film Archive. The Walt Disney organization came to us and said, "What Disney films are you holding?" Now the normal reaction at the time would have been to say, "We don't have

any." But I just turned around and sent them a list of every Disney film we had. Of course it was greeted with some shock. As a result there were some legal exchanges, but, in the end, they accepted that we had this material. And it gave me an opportunity to talk to somebody senior in the Disney organization, and explain what archives were all about. So, to a certain extent, by being terrified of providing information about your holdings and not entering into a debate with the producers, you are continuing a problem that I believe could have been ended in, let us say, the mid-1970s. In other words, after FIAF as an organization was 40 years old, we should not have been concerned about producers coming and trying to take away the films in our collections because they were the copyright-owners. Now it has happened since, and it still does on occasion, that they try and do this, but if we had been much stronger earlier on, and we had come together and agreed an international policy on how we'd react if a company approached us and demanded material back, then I think we would have been able to produce international catalogues more quickly, and we would not have suffered so much from the idea of the archive as a fortress, and not as a resource.

But each archive was different. Certainly, at the National Film Archive, we had the view we were happy to say whatever we had regardless, because once you overcame each hurdle, each individual company, and they knew what you had, there was no problem in the future. And, in reality, they knew that they could not take on the government. So, as long as you didn't breach any agreement you had, I think you were secure, and there was no reason you shouldn't say you had a given title.

__ML: And this is also the reason why you could with a certain confidence, for example, screen films to your audiences without, say, paying a copyright-owner for the screening?

__DF: Well, this was another big issue. A lot of archives felt that if they ever started paying... that they should have a right to screen on their own premises their collections to a non-paying audience. Again, going back to the Brussels situation, the reason that the Musée du Cinéma was established was so that you paid an entrance to the museum, but the screenings were free. The museum was always open at the same time as the screenings, but there was no charge made for the screenings themselves. In this way Jacques Ledoux could say, "No, we're not making any money out of these screenings." And so he never paid a copyright-owner, or asked their permission. The situation in London was very different, because the National Film Archive did not own the facility where films were presented: the National Film Theatre. This was a separate department within the British Film Institute, and only a percentage of the films they showed came from the Archive. And they, from the very beginning, paid a fee for the screening of a film. It annoyed me immensely that they paid the same fee if the print came from the National Film Archive as if they had hired it from a distributor. Because I said, "Look, one of the reasons you're paying a fee is for the maintenance of the material. We here have maintained this material at government expense, and we're going to have to pay the same copyright fee as if the print was hired or loaned from the distributor." And this was a big argument that went on a long time, but as I was not in charge of the NFT there was very little I could do about it. I think nowadays most organizations pay for screenings, and one of the reasons for that is that most of them also charge an admission fee. But there was a very, very strong view in the earlier days that it was vital that you did not pay, because the only way you could establish your role as an archive was that you had a right to show your own collection on your own premises, providing you made no money out of it.

__ML: Were there discussions within the archival community on how to circumvent that fact that you would probably have to pay a fee? Or who does pay, who does not pay, who's afraid of copyright-owners, who's not afraid? Were those open discussions where you had a committee that openly discussed it, or were those things you'd rather talk about in secrecy, and not make a lot of fuss about?

__DF: Well, to a certain extent, they were hardly talked about at all. They certainly weren't talked about openly. If they were talked about, it was between two individual curators over a glass of wine. So it was up to each country to decide how far they could go, and it depended on how much control they had over their venues. Were they physically in the same buildings as the screenings were held (so you could really say it was on your own premises)? Were they prepared to show the films without charge? There were so many issues. It was really a decision made by each individual archive.

__ML: So, from the point of view of a person who's been in this profession, this community, for so long, do you think it would have been impossible, because of all those differences between the institutions, to talk about it in public? Or do you, if you look back, regret that on a large scale, like on a FIAF level, similar to what the International Council of Museums (ICOM) have set up as standard procedures in showing objects from their collections, no open and no proactive discussion took place?

__DF: Well it's slightly different in most museums, because a lot of the material that they hold is no longer in copyright. So they don't have to ask anybody's permission, because either they have, under the terms by which they acquired the material, they have acquired the right to do certain things with it, or because it's out of copyright. It's because of copyright and its restrictions that archives are perceived as fortresses to which it's difficult to gain access. I don't know how you can explain to the public at large what you can and cannot do as a film archive. I mean, certainly, if you talk to an individual person who's making a film, they're nearly always angry because you won't give them free access to somebody else's films. When they go away and talk about you, they talk about you in negative terms, because you were unable to satisfy their own demands. I don't know how you can cope with this. But again, you see, one of the things I would have always wanted FIAF to do was to spend more time engaging with the issue of copyright, to see whether we could come up with any solution which would allow us to show films in certain circumstances without having to clear each individual film. There have been lots of discussions about this, but it's never got anywhere because I don't think FIAF was ever strong enough to engage with the international production community.

__ML: Has there ever been something like a public declaration by FIAF on copyright being the single most important issue in this respect? I ask because I've now, during our conversation, opened a document that was emailed before the Tokyo conference – the FIAF "Declaration on Fair Use and Access".

__DF: Well, this is exactly what I was going to say. There were two presentations in Tokyo. One by Pat Loughney on behalf of the discussions which took place in São Paulo, which was coming up with a "Fair Use" document. Now it's a pretty innocuous document, until you get to the last paragraph…

__ML: Paragraph Number 10.

__DF: Yes, all the meat of it is there. But it's a start. I found the other one much more interesting, which was the presentation that Gabrielle Claes gave about the discussion the Association des Cinémathèques Européennes was having with FIAPF – the International Federation of Film Producers Associations. Now, all the time I was an archivist I was very much against talking to the producers, because I felt if you were a large archive it would lead to more restrictions, rather than less. For a smaller archive, there was some value talking to them, because you might gain more than you already had, but for a larger archive you were likely to lose. But in recent years, in these discussions, things have changed. There is an interesting reason why they've changed, because organizations like Microsoft and these large corporations want material to make it accessible. So they've suddenly become supporters of the archive view. And because of that, in the last couple of years Gabrielle has managed to make significant progress in an agreement with FIAPF, because she's been supported by large corporations who are very powerful, and of whom the actual film producers are afraid. So the paper that she presented at Tokyo was a very, very interesting paper, which I believe has made significant progress in respect to the use of FIAPF's members' films which are deposited in archives. Originally she was doing this on behalf of the European archives, although of course FIAF is an international organization. So if FIAF felt that it was worth adopting this as a whole, the discussion would be a satisfactory basis for doing this.

Now, let's go back to the second part of your Question A: "How much has this blurring of borders between the distinct functions – preservation, presentation, and making accessible – been with the community from its beginnings?" That's a difficult one, because in some ways they were blurred and in some ways they weren't. I believe they were blurred politically, intentionally, because the archives were always concerned to say you could not make a film accessible until it was preserved, because that was the way of getting money for preservation. Nobody, no government, would give money for preservation if they thought they didn't have to. And so from the beginning archives were mainly talking to governments, not like it is today, where they're talking as much to private individuals. And the argument they made was Yes, of course, we want to make this material available; we understand the educational use and importance of our collections, but we can't do it until we have preserved the original. And so the archives themselves blurred the boundaries, because they wanted to assure absolutely that the total package was funded: the preservation of the original, the making of an access copy, which was all part of the same process. I think that's still true today, but I'm not sure it's sustainable any longer. People are still using that

approach, but we need a new one. Because if you're absolutely honest, I think you could say now that digital techniques are almost at the point, maybe in the next four or five years, when you could use digital techniques for preservation at an economic level – and that's an important thing. Archives are thinking in the long term. I think that if you are ever discussing archive policy the minimum period you can discuss is a hundred years – I'd like it to be 200 years. If you take it over a hundred years, you have to look at the total cost of safeguarding a film for the next hundred years, if you are taking a photochemical approach, or a digital approach. We're not yet sure, because we don't have a hundred years in the digital environment to know what the actual costs will be of maintaining that material over the hundred-year period, because we don't know how many times we will have to transfer it or refresh it, or what we will have to do in the digital environment to ensure that it's still freely available in the same quality at the end of the hundred years. The trouble is that funding agencies always think in the short term, and so they say, "What are the actual costs now for copying this material?" And if you take that alone, you're looking at a cost... The digital cost is cheaper than the photochemical cost.

But I don't think it's sustainable as an argument any longer to insist that we can't make material available unless it's preserved. We have to think of another approach. And this is where we come to the question of the artefact. Because the one thing that museums have succeeded in doing is making it clear to the public and to funding agencies that there is no substitute for seeing the original artefact. Now as far as archives are concerned, unfortunately, as they haven't stressed the importance of the artefact, they're unable to use this argument. Now if they had followed the same process as museums, they would not have to argue for the preservation or the long-term care of the original. Because that, in the museum world, is now an accepted responsibility. So I'm very keen on ideas like Paolo's, of treating the prints that we loan as important museum objects. Of course I realize that this will cause considerable concern among archives wanting to borrow that material. But why it's really being done is not trying to restrict access to other archives; it's trying to increase the importance, the recognition of the film as an artefact. Maybe some sort of compromise is necessary – for instance, if one has done a full-scale restoration, then you apply these new rules to just that group of restorations, so that you have the ability to build up an understanding of the film as artefact on objects, on films which you have spent a lot of time restoring and bringing back as close to the original as possible. But you don't do it for all films, because if you did it would have a backlash within the archiving community. So it's a difficult one, that. The reason why Paolo wanted to do it was just to increase the recognition of the film as an artefact. The whole start of our original discussions, and Alex's intervention in FIAF in the first place, was our failure to use a language associated with museums, rather than a language associated with commercial exploitation. So if we are to become museums, we have to start using a language that is understood in the museum community, and not words like "access" and "content" and all the other things that we do use. We have to make significant changes, and some of these changes are going to

be difficult for us to accept, because in some cases it will restrict access. But we need to do that if we are to raise the status of what we are doing. And, of course, there are other things that help us do that. There are a large number of film schools that are giving an MA or whatever in Film Archiving; it's a help. Because before there was no professional qualification. Immediately you start having professional qualifications and you find that a large number of the archive staff have those qualifications. They start getting together and insisting on standards, because they want to protect the qualifications they have. But that hasn't existed in the past, because nobody had a professional qualification; they mostly came to archives as enthusiasts for the cinema. So going back to the original question, I'm not sure whether there is a blurring of the borders. There is a blurring to a certain extent, but I think it's purely for political purposes. For, let's say, normal archival purposes, there's a distinct difference between preservation and presentation, because, traditionally, it's always been thought that you must preserve a film before you make it accessible. And that was the big issue that highlighted the so-called Lindgren-Langlois debate: can you show the original, or should you put the original away if you have a single copy, until you can afford to make a copy you can screen so that the original is secured for future generations? It's really whether an archive is working for today's generation, or for future generations.

—ML: So let's talk more about the notion of us as "museums". Did anybody at any time during the last five decades attempt to invent original criteria for a "museological" treatment of film? And if Yes, why is there still so little consensus?

I think your article in the *Journal of Film Preservation* [No. 71, July 2006] on Ernest Lindgren and the early years of the NFA in Britain is a revision of that popular notion of archives always having been only fortresses, and only digital access now making films available. You make Lindgren's approach look like a very modern approach.

__DF: Well, the only reason why Clyde Jeavons and I chose to do pieces on Ernest – we saw another book on Henri Langlois, again saying he was the father of film archives, and there's never been a book written about the work of Ernest Lindgren. And yet the person who's being praised, Henri Langlois, is responsible for the loss of more films than any other archivist in the world. But because he had the support of the *Nouvelle Vague,* who were a powerful creative force, his policy of showing the original was looked upon as a forward-looking policy. Nobody realized the long-term results of this, which would be that a lot of films would not be available now that were even available in the 1950s. There have been several major fires; the generally bad way in which the Archives have been run was responsible for a lot of losses during the Langlois period. The reason that we've put pen to paper is because, first, the conflict was a false conflict, and, secondly, if you do look back at Ernest's early writings, you can already see that. You say, "Has anyone come up with a museum treatment of film?" Well, to a certain extent, the article Ernest wrote in, I think it was No. 5 of the *Penguin Film Review* [January 1948], which describes a total archive, which in fact is more like a museum than an archive, still remains one of the few places where someone has defined an archive, designed a film archive.

I think that both Clyde and I were concerned that this was totally forgotten and neglected, and that the later part of Ernest Lindgren's life as an archivist, where he retired into a sort of fortress, was the period which was being remembered. And the creative thinking that he'd engaged in, in the very early days of the archive movement when nobody was thinking about what an archive was – they were just collecting film – had been neglected. I would like to see us looking at the people from the past in terms of how we move forward, not continually going back and looking again at the relationship between two individuals [Langlois and Lindgren].

__ML: I have met young students who are very interested in the "foundational period" of the movement.

__DF: Well, I'm pleased with this, because FIAF has been particularly bad about keeping its own records, and so have a lot of individual archives, and I'm hoping that student interest, undergraduate student interest, in the early days of the archival movement will help the archives to look into their own history, and ensure that that is adequately kept and available. But I would prefer, I must say, students to concentrate not on the individuals or on history, but on the actions of archives, what they have done in looking after their collections, making their collections available, etc. I have a friend who's just completed a Ph.D. on this very subject. Pretty much all the books on the film archive movement are based on personalities. They're not based on what archives have actually achieved or not achieved, and what they should be doing, etc. They're just, I would say, biased histories based on individuals. And that's not very helpful.

_ML: You said that Ernest Lindgren's paper was published in the *Penguin Film Review.* There seems to have been, at least in the 1930s, debates on what is the role of an archive for society, what is the relation of film archives to current film production, what are the functions in the service of future generations, in the service of national film production, etc. There was a public debate, because you had a film press that was engaged. In the Soviet Union you had a number of journals dedicated to the debate of what is film history's service to future generations, or to the formation of society. I can't think of a situation now where you have, say, issues of *Film Quarterly* or *Sight and Sound,* or any magazine in Austria or Germany either, discussing film heritage from the point of view of archives, seeing them as partners in the formation of our view on film history or the history of our society.

_DF: Absolutely. Part of that, in my opinion, is our failure to have a closer relationship with organizations like the Society for Cinema and Media Studies, because these are the serious users of our collections. The academics who use our films in film studies courses – we should have a very close relationship with them. But we've never managed to establish that relationship; we've never managed to involve the academic community in both an understanding of the issues of film archiving and in helping us develop our archives in a way that will benefit future study and research. We just cannot seem to engage with the academic community. I think this is a huge mistake.

_ML: And why is that? What are the historical reasons, say, for the period when you started to work at an archive?

_DF: Well… That's a difficult question. When I first started at the National Film Archive, it was an age in which the main cultural viewpoint was a semiological one, which, to a certain extent, was more talking about the films, and was relatively uninterested in the film itself. I know this sounds strange to say.

_ML: Not at all!

_DF: But quite often the people in the BFI Education Department would be very happy with relatively poor-quality film – the film was almost ancillary to their discussions of the cultural implications of films. And so it was not a good time to engage with academics. But today, where I think there is more concern with representing the film as it was made by the original creative team, there's more chance of serious engagement with the academic community than there was then. And, of course, the academic community is better organized itself. They come together regularly to discuss issues associated with film scholarship. But I would like to see a joint congress between an academic body, say the Society for Cinema and Media Studies, and FIAF. And to establish a programme that would help to have the sort of discussions that I think we as FIAF members need to have. Now it may be that we would get nowhere, because we seldom do at a conference. Most people want, when they come to a Congress, to talk to one another, which is very valid, because obviously the unofficial side of getting together is very important. But it's very difficult to get members to engage in a serious discussion about what we should be doing in any particular sphere. So I haven't an answer to how to do this. But I do feel that the failure of FIAF to have these discussions is leading to more and more people attending what is really a local

Northern American organization like AMIA, because they find the discussions there more satisfactory.

—ML: Actually, all of the things you said do work towards the notion of our community taking on the model of the museum and the artefact.

First, the Langlois-Lindgren debate: I think this in a way puts cinephilia into perspective again. Because if you do screen originals, and even destroy originals, without the notion of those films as artefact, but rather as content or as treasure, you do give away the whole potential a museum has to exhibit an artefact under controlled conditions.

Secondly, in regard to access and digitization: at a recent lecture a historian made an interesting observation: he said he had studied archaeology and ancient history, and in these fields there are two distinct approaches to how you engage with the object of your study. In archaeology or in history, say, pre-1300s/1400s or pre-13th century, your whole approach on working with your materials is artefact-orientated. If you have, say, a stone artefact, a prehistoric artefact, this is not a text *per se,* but an object, and this object needs to be restored, then exhibited in a presentation. You can, on the one hand, make accessible the artefact as an artefact, but you also have to provide contextual information on how this artefact was used – what was its original purpose, what was the use associated with the object – and you can always use technologies, even digital technologies, to simulate the original form it had. That would be the second approach – and the two exist side by side without much conflict. When I was at the British Museum a couple of months ago, there was an exhibition of art from Polynesia and the South Pacific, with totems and religious objects related to the concept of taboo, and you saw what museum presentation, traditionally good museum presentation, can be. You have an object that has been preserved, and restored to a certain degree so it can be made accessible, and, next to it, you have a demonstration of the restoration techniques, and you have a simulation and description of what the object might have looked like, say, 400 years ago. This is a museum approach, in a way. This takes away a lot of pressure.

Finally, there's academia. From what you said, film studies – those with a semiological approach, more oriented towards textual analysis of films – do not care for the material character, because of the way they perceive the film as content. And so I think right now there's a chance to strengthen the relationship between film museums and academia, because film studies are at a crossroads again. Either they can use the opportunity of the availability of materials in digital form to completely perceive film as content, as something that is available as information, whether it be on DigiBeta, VHS, DVD, streaming video, or whatever, or they can turn towards a more object-oriented, or material/artefact-orientated approach. Because now the chance offers itself that film as an artefact becomes a valuable object again, valuable in the sense of knowledge associated with film as cultural practice and film as a material artefact. This is what I have been seeing with many young students. They come from film studies classes but have an immense interest in the foundational period of the archive movement. They deliberately choose approaches where they come into contact with film preservation techniques, with film as material; they know more about film formats, about the history of the film material, about film handling, than their professors do. You can easily go to a film studies conference and not see one piece of celluloid film projected, even if it takes place at a cinema.

—DF: Well, this is the terrible thing, which I call "moving wallpaper": that film is moving wallpaper in museums. I had an endless battle with the Library of Congress, which I eventually won, saying that if you want film from our collection we must get the same credit for it as you would give to the Manuscript Division. We are not moving wallpaper in the background; we are central to the exhibit, and should receive the same credits. And eventually, after two or three years of arguing, that's what happened. But I agree with you; everything you say is really saying, "Look, we must make ourselves more like museums." Museums are, to a certain extent, artefact based.

—ML: Oh, yes.

—DF: But if you for a long time have not valued your artefacts, as we have in film archives – or not valued it in public, maybe only valued it in our own institutions – it's very difficult to change that perception overnight. And I'm not sure how you do it, unless you do some things which are pretty drastic, and which are going to be unpopular. One of them, as I said earlier, is the proposal by Paolo to treat a loan copy as an important artefact that has to be handled in a particular way. Another one might be to say to the film departments of certain universities, "Look, the archive movement is prepared to offer more help and more opportunity of access to you, providing you agree to establish a certain environment within your university where the film can be screened, and provide a certain contextualization which you work out in conjunction with the archive. And if you agree to this proposal we will make accessible to you material which we cannot make accessible to anyone else." Hopefully, if one can do that worldwide, we can re-establish the idea of film being treated as film, and establish the importance of – it may not be the original artefact, but an artefact representing the original – film as always central in film studies. But this will be very unpopular, because a lot of archives have relatively low standards of projection, and are not as careful as they should be. I think a lot of museum curators in traditional art museums would be rather appalled if they visited film archives, because they would feel that the handling of material was not up to the standards that they would feel desirable for objects of historical importance. So I think there are things we can do, but they're going to be unpopular among our members, and they're certainly going to take time to have real effect. And of course the real time that concerns me is *now*. Once film is not so much on film, a time will come, probably 50 years from now, when we won't find it difficult to get audiences to look at film projected in the traditional manner, because it will then be an unusual experience. We know that people always like to see things that are unusual, and they will come to the archives then. But it's this period of in-between, where you have two or more technologies running side-by-side, and there's no particular excitement in going to see a film projected, when you can go to a local cinema and see an image which, to all intents and purposes, looks very similar if not sometimes better. It's only when the photochemical technology has passed, and is something historical in itself, that interest will revive in seeing films projected by traditional projectors in an archival environment.

__ML: Every projection will be an exclusive event. But you must make sure not to confuse your presentation with what is called "art-house cinema" presentation. Can you imagine going to a museum where an object is exhibited, and there's no caption next to the artefact or work, no contextualization at all? For instance, a caption that tells you this is made from this and that material, it was preserved using this and that element, and so on. Say you have presentations where the person presenting the film says, "what you see now is a contact copy made from a nitrate original by our archive" – you have the obligation to inform your audiences about what they see, because all they see is immaterial shadows on a wall basically.

__DF: You were talking about the idea of restoration, where you don't necessarily fill in the gaps that are missing. You may keep them as blanks or black spaces. And an audience that understands what you're doing will start to accept that a film is like the Venus de Milo – a film is not always all there. That doesn't mean you make it all there, you just indicate where there's something missing. All these things, I think, are essential. This is the only approach we should have in today's age. Otherwise archives will disappear; they will no longer get support; and they will become musty vaults to which the key appears to have been lost.

__ML: The key is a certain knowledge, not only about film history, and not only about 'content,' but also about the particular material and its

relation to, say, a certain mode of production, a certain mode of exhibition, a certain mode of distribution, and a certain audience. There was a beautiful paper Alex and I read in a German magazine by Heide Schlüpmann, a German film historian; she has in a way written a manifesto against the predominant mode of media studies in Germany. It is entitled – what is the best translation into English? – "Film Studies as *Cinema Studies*". In it she reclaims the act of moviegoing and the cinema experience as a social experience *and* as an aesthetic experience. You know that a particular film has been seen by living people 80–90 years ago, that it was threaded in a special machine, and this machine was set up in a certain venue, which was visited by a certain class of people, coming from a certain economic background, living under certain political conditions, etc. It's not solely a cultural studies point of view, which is only interested in the economics and sociology of the audience; she's trying to establish the film projection as the point of convergence for all those practices – contextual analysis, political reading, technological point of view, aesthetic considerations.

__DF: I agree. But there are various problems with this. Obviously, it would be nice if an archivist, an archive staff member, says something before the presentation of any film on their own premises. And that the history of the physical material shown is recorded both verbally and in the programme. But often in an archive the programmer is not a curator; it's a separate post. For some reason programming has become separate within the archives. It is not the responsibility of the curator; it's become the responsibility of a separate individual, who is not part of the core archival team. And I think this is sad. I think it is the responsibility of the curator to do the programming. To ensure that it is contextualized adequately, and that there is always someone at the presentation to whom you can talk afterwards about the issues associated with that film. Of course you can't do as many screenings if you take that approach, but to me it's more important for an archive to do fewer screenings, but contextualize them more and engage the audience more in the whole background, not only of the film but of the physical material, than it is to show large numbers of films. That can be done by somebody else; it can be done by a film festival, etc. So, again, it's all about our own presentations; it's quality more than quantity. I always remember one thing after Kevin Brownlow finished the restoration of *Napoleon*. We had this huge event; we did the first screening in London, a film of 5 hours, with Carl Davis and the full orchestra, and of course the ticket prices were high. And for that whole reason we got a new audience; the audience that had previously gone to opera or concerts came to this particular performance. It was people we'd never seen before, seeing a film. Because the event we'd created was a different sort of event. It was not going up to a small hole in the wall and getting a ticket. It involved an interval in the middle for 2 hours for dinner; people came to the event dressed up in evening clothes; there was all sorts of documentation, a full programme of about 40 pages, with all the background material about the film, the restoration, the music, etc. And suddenly you changed the film experience totally, almost into a live performance, and you got a totally different performance, you got a totally different level of respect. I mean, *Napoleon* is not a great film, but

when it was presented in this manner, it was a major *event,* which we repeated again and again and again. It was because of the contextualization and the presentation of it, that it became something other than just a film screening.

__ML: I do agree completely. In the current landscape you have basically three types of organizations dedicated to film heritage and screening historical films as something special, not a commodity: film festivals, film archives/museums, and cinema clubs/film societies. I think film festivals and film societies are pretty quickly going to make the transition to digital projections, and screen what is available in digital form, because they can't afford the costs anymore. If we as archives and museums are more restrictive with the way we loan copies, and with the way we want our films to be presented, they are pretty soon going to switch to digital anyway, because they are solely interested in the availability of certain films, no matter what the form is.

__DF: Exactly.

__ML: Which, I think, is going to make their survival pretty difficult, because if you treat film only as content, and an event only as the occasion to see something, whether it is projected from tape or from hard disk, in 16mm, in HD, in 2K, whatever, in a way it doesn't matter who does it, because you're all basically on he same level again.

__DF: Well, I don't totally agree with that. I mean, I have a particular experience. Now I'm living in a small town in America, where there's no possibility of seeing anything in 35mm. But because of the availability of digital material, for instance, just before I left we went to a screening of *Die Abenteuer des Prinzen Achmed,* with a really good pianist, an excellent critical introduction, but the film was on DVD. Now, it would not have been possible to present that in this town on film. So, I see in some ways as a reverse possibility that actually being able to have available the DVD, and being able to show the DVD in a space as opposed to a cinema, you can then revive the original associated contextualization – the original score and the introduction – in places where you would not have been able to do it in the past. So it works both ways. In some ways, if harnessed by the archive movement, it could actually increase our constituency to areas which have never been able to see the material in the form in which we hold it. But again, it needs to be done in a controlled manner. This performance was a model in every way, because the pianist was superb, he was playing the original score; the professor who introduced it knew both the film background and also the political background. The DVD looked pretty good on the screen, and it was on a big screen. And I felt – well, you know everything I say against this – if handled in the right way, this actually can increase access. But there needs to be what we call "archival" DVD screenings.

___ML: That's exactly the point I tried to arrive at. Because the one opportunity of digital technologies, which in a way is a danger to archives who are not engaged in curating their programmes, is that the film enthusiast, the people who not only want to screen something for the screening's sake, but who want to pass on knowledge about film history, they probably will not become staff members of an archive, but will rather found their own film societies or film clubs, or will be free curators moving from the fine-art world to the academic world to the art-house cinema world to the festival circuit,

etc. So, in a way, I completely agree with you that this is a good opportunity. In London we presented our Vertov book together with Michael Nyman, who had composed a new score for one of the newsreels. The organizers, a local art-house cinema, wanted to show *The Man with the Movie Camera* accompanied by the Michael Nyman soundtrack, but for technical reasons they couldn't show a print, so they screened the film with the pre-recorded soundtrack from a Betacam tape loaned by the BFI. Which was, under these conditions, perfectly OK for me. Alex said he wouldn't do it on his own premises, but I said it's the theatre's responsibility to their customers if the image quality doesn't hold up to their standards; it pretty well did. And I could not only contextualize the film, but also talk about the fact that it was being projected from videotape, etc. And this was perfectly OK, because the people were informed.

___DF: Well, I agree with you. But I have some reservations. I would like to see presentations controlled by archives. For instance, in certain places there's no excuse not to show a 35mm print.

___ML: No, not at all.

___DF: But, if it means you can extend the work of archives throughout the world by using new technology, so that people in places who don't have access to a 35mm screening facility can have an experience which is pretty close to the experience they would get if they were in a big city, this is marvellous. The difficulty is how you stop it being a cheap and simple substitute in places where it is perfectly possible to show the material in the form in which it was originally shown. And all this depends on archives retaining control of the material. Now this is a big issue. And it came up very fascinatingly at the National Film Preservation Foundation in America, which is issuing these DVD sets of films in archival collections...

__ML: *Treasures from the American Film Archives.*

__DF: Yes. And they are now concerned that people are pirating their material from these DVDs. Now it's a difficult situation, where you have archives saying, "Look, our role is making things available, but we don't want you pirating things that we've made available." In order to get funding to do this in future, you have to have to show some sort of income. So archives are becoming copyright-owners and are taking the same measures to control use as the film industry does itself. And this is a difficult thing to accept. But, if we are to ensure that presentations take place in the best quality available depending on the location, then it does mean, perhaps, holding back on material that you would otherwise make available. I think the archive world's in a very tricky situation, because if it makes all its holdings available then it loses the opportunity of being able to contextualize presentations.

And this is a very important part of the debate as to how you present this situation to the public. As I said earlier, it may be that you select certain films, certain restorations, for a particular form of treatment and presentation from other material in the collection. You say, "Look, we've expended a lot of effort and money to make this work; we want to ensure that for the next 3, or 5, years it is only presented either in the original form, in other words on 35mm film, with the right contextualization, or on a DVD made under our supervision from that original, also presented in a certain contextualized manner. Now, at the end of that period this will be freely available for everybody, but at the moment it's on restricted availability, because that is the only way we are able in this new environment to show what it is that we can do that other people can't do."

__ML: This makes perfect sense, because you redefine 'restrictions' not as something that is contrary to cultural demands, but as something that enforces the notion that your presentation is special.

__DF: It will still meet resistance when put in place. But one just has to cope with it in advance by making certain that there is a clear explanation of one's policies.

__ML: And it also, in a material sense, is one way to proceed. Because when copyright-owners talk about all the restrictions built into their new distribution models, say, digital rights management and the server-based showing of films, all the watermarks in the films, copy protection, etc., their argument is that they need to protect their investment, which is a pretty plain explanation. On the other hand, isn't the same argument true for the archives? If you say that the safeguarding of the original, the contextualization work, the preservation work, the restoration work, and the production of a new master, the production of a DVD, etc. – simply on an economic level, there were thousands of dollars or euros, and specialized knowledge, that went into producing this new artefact. So it's the safeguarding of our investment, the investment of public money too, in the sense that if we can educate the public that film is not generally available, and it's a free-for-all, but that it's cost intensive, and that it's specialist knowledge you need...

__DF: I would like not to use the economic model if possible, but to say, look, the reason we do this is that in order to demonstrate our importance in society as a cultural institution, we have to make restrictions, so that people can see what we are really doing, which isn't being done by any form of commercial distribution. But I'd like to avoid doing this on the basis of economic investment, because then we're coming back to talking the same language as the industry. We have to put this in a cultural environment, not a business or marketplace environment. I think if we can do that successfully, this will help us achieve our aim of protecting the work of the creative teams that made the films.

You see, I think, going back to where we started, FIAF, as an organization, is not an organization consisting of like-minded people or similar institutions. It's an amalgam of people who are, in one way or another, interested in cinema, and trying to protect it and make it available. But most of them are using whatever works in their own environment to achieve this. You get some very interesting models. It's quite an interesting thing, to look at the models of archives. If you go to Montevideo, to Uruguay, the archive there is the central distribution agency for all important films. It runs all the country's cinemas.

__ML: This is unusual!

__DF: And, when it takes on the distribution of a film, it orders a negative, which is then deposited in the archive. So it has a fascinating collection, because it runs the cinemas in the country, which show non-standard release material. And it has the right, as a distributor, to order a negative. Now, economically it doesn't make sense that they have their own negatives.

But because it's a function stemming from the archive, it is a way of feeding the archive's collection. Now that's one model. If you go to Istanbul, the Turkish archive runs a state-of-the-art laboratory, one of the few in that region. It operates the laboratory commercially in the morning, and with the profits made from the commercial side of the laboratory it does archival restorations in all the down-time. You could go on almost forever looking at different models of archives, which they've had to adapt to their own environment in order to survive. And I think that makes it very difficult to have international discussions, because, first of all, archives are in very different stages of development. A lot of smaller archives coming to a FIAF conference just throw up their hands and say, "Look, all this discussion is so far away from the basic daily problems that we face, and it's meaningless to us." So I think, really, FIAF itself is not a useful forum as a complete organization. It would be useful if there were some groups within FIAF who could discuss some of the issues we're talking about, and that they could be incorporated into an overall FIAF policy if possible. I mean, in other words, if a country has a possibility of acting in this way, this is the way it should act. But we can't have a discussion which in the end has to be voted on as FIAF policy in the General Assembly, because there's far too wide a range of archives in FIAF.

__ML: You'd never get a consensus.

__DF: You'd never get a consensus about anything challenging at all. So the only way really is sub-groups. But, of course, in an organization which meets once a year face-to-face, and where everyone is so busy, virtually it takes years and years to get anything decided by informal groupings of archives. So I think probably what one has to say at the end of the line is that it is not a suitable forum for innovative thought. One has to find another grouping of people to achieve this. I mean it's sad. I would be very interested in looking at other international organizations to see whether they themselves are successfully, let's say, establishing priorities for their members, operational policies for their members, or cultural policies for their members. I don't know whether any international organization can do that satisfactorily. I don't think it's just a failure of FIAF. I think we may be expecting too much from FIAF.

The really good things are coming out of individual archives. I mean if you look at Paolo's curatorial paper, which I think is marvellous, that comes out of an individual situation. And maybe this is the only way things are going to happen and change. So, in other words, rather than trying to start centrally, you have to start at a level of small groupings of archives, and then get what they produce to be accepted centrally.

__ML: One issue we should probably also discuss from a historical perspective is the question of the preservation of the original in relation to the concept of the artefact. Now, as we move into digital preservation of film, what should the contemporary lowest common denominator for preservation work be? Am I totally wrong in assuming that preservation – film preservation, preserving film on film – has always been based on the assumption that good, active preservation is a *facsimile* of the original?

__DF: That's been the principle, but not in the practice. My big problem with the whole concept of preservation, and it was revealed very much... Paolo had at the Eastman House a series of what he called "The Glory of Nitrate". We spent two days looking at nitrate copies, and occasionally we interspersed a duplicate an archive had made of one of these films. And the big thing you realized straight away when you were looking at it was that it looked totally different in terms of texture, in terms of contrast, because the base of nitrate was effectively so different. So what we're doing, we're not really making an exact duplicate of the original in any preservation except in terms of its content, but not in terms of what it looked like on the screen. And I think this is a big issue.

Going from that is the other question, of what you're preserving. There has become a tendency – what I call the "completist tendency" – that exists everywhere nowadays, like that you have to have a complete retrospective if you're a programmer. And, if you're a preservationist, you have the "completest" copy possible. But if that copy was never seen by the public, basically what are you saving? I mean, you are saving content that was created in the process of making a film, but you're not preserving the film. So, before we discuss how we preserve film, we need to have a much clearer idea of what we're preserving. If you're talking about showing people a film in the version in which it was originally seen, you have to define that. At the very minimum, it has to be a real, public projection print, and hopefully one that was seen not by a first-night audience, but in its initial distribution. If you have additional material, that may be interesting in the context of the film's production, but doesn't represent the historical experience of that film, it's additional information which is interesting for the historical study of the film by a researcher. So, the first thing I would say is that archives have got out of sync, because they haven't decided what they are actually preserving. So one of the things we have to define is what the "experience" is. For me the "experience", if it is a popular art form or mass culture, should be a version seen by the masses. And other versions which may have been preferable to the director or pre-censorship, they should be available, but they're not the bit that you should be showing directly as the "experience". They're like additional elements which you could see if you wanted to, but they shouldn't be included in the "experience" as seen by the mass audience. So, before one starts talking about what preservation is, I think we need to say, "What are we preserving?" I would make a definite distinction between what was actually seen by a mass audience, and what other material is of interest to someone who is studying the production of a particular film, or the work of a particular director, or the question of censorship and what was cut out, or the question of distribution censorship. These elements we need, but they're separate from what I would call "core activity". They're like the extras you would get on a DVD in some ways. OK, once you've said that, the big question comes in: if you define what you're preserving in that manner, can it only be preserved on film?

This is a slight side point, but when we were doing the Museum of the Moving Image (MOMI) in London we had long discussions about how you show the public – and hopefully you do it properly – that you are not cheating on them. All our projections were on 35mm film – and the projection box was glass-sided, so that you could see we weren't swindling them, because they could actually see the 35mm film going through the projector. And that was a museum object. And I think this goes into what Alex was saying a bit, that the film is an artefact, but also the method of projection, the method of producing the experience, is something that should be visible as well. In this age of technology you can do almost anything, so you want people to have some idea that what you're showing them is authentic. Now, of course, everybody knows that even with a system like that you could cheat, but we found that the fact we were showing a 35mm film, and the fact that when they came out of the theatre they could actually see the film being projected, were ways of giving them confidence in the museum's presentation role. But that of course in itself determines that the presentation should be film. What I get worried about is, if you go away from film, and you can produce a preservation-quality… I mean, there's no doubt about it, today if you have the money and resources, you can make a copy that 99% of the population is going to consider to be as good or better than the projected 35mm film. But the problem with the whole digital world is, unless the copies actually are made under the direct supervision of an archivist, one will find that the digital engineers will want to improve or remove artefacts. And that's one version of the word that wasn't included in our discussion: the "artefact" as a scratch, or something like that. It's too easy to improve a film digitally. So my big worry in the whole digitization process is, unless you have archivists trained as digital engineers, or you have a very close working relationship between a curator and an engineer, it is much more difficult to control the preservation process than it is if you're doing an analog copy from film to film. Although in the end, if you did side-by-side screenings achieved digitally, where money was no object, even an archivist would not necessarily be able to argue that the digital copy was not a representation of the creative team's work. So my problem is, almost, that you can do *too* much, and I don't know how to stop people doing too much. One of the advantages of the analog system is that you cannot improve it; you cannot make it better that the original.

__ML: Exactly.

__DF: I know it's a strange argument, but I believe that's a very important thing. If you're looking at the cinema, you want to see what was achievable at a certain time. A very good example is something like *Snow White,* an animation film where you have a lot of original faults in the film because of what you could achieve in animation at the time it was made. When it was first digitized these were removed. And in many cases they didn't want to remove them, but they didn't find a way of doing a digital master which didn't remove them. So my main objection to preservation in any other way than a photo-chemical copy is that I believe that's the only way I can ensure things will not be put in technically. Then you have the issue of things put in culturally. My great example is Kevin Brownlow restoring *Napoleon,* because I was working with him, and we came to an edit, and Kevin had changed the edit. And I said to him, "But Kevin, that's not the way it was in the film." And he said, "Well, Abel Gance would never have made an edit like that." And I said, "I'm sorry Kevin, the evidence we have in front of us is that the edit was made in this way, and you cannot change it because this isn't *Napoleon* by Abel Gance and Kevin Brownlow, this is *Napoleon* by

Abel Gance. And you may well be right, that something had happened since the time that this copy got to us, and this edit wasn't there, but you have no right to change it." So you have the technical control with the photochemical route, but you don't have the cultural control.

__ML: And your scruples in introducing changes are lessened by the fact that it's so easy to do it.

__DF: Exactly. I mean, part of my argument against digitization is that it is much more difficult to ensure that what has been done did not change the original in a way which impacts the experience. So it's not a doubt about the technical way to do it, it's about the huge technical resource you have and the much easier way of cultural interference.

__ML: That's very, very interesting. You said that, on the one hand, in digital there is this fantasy of preservation as going back to a "virtual state of completeness" of a work; on the other hand that analog preservation has always acknowledged entropy and the loss of quality, the loss of definition, a certain loss of elements you couldn't salvage from, say, a damaged nitrate original. But wasn't one of the big mistakes the profession has made – I'd say probably deliberately – in pushing preservation programmes past their administrators and past the public to say that analog preservation, the mass copying of nitrate stock to safety film can exactly achieve that? That if you manage to copy as many feet of film as possible, you can put an end to entropy.

__DF: Well, that's partly true. Certainly the first thing you say is true. Every time you make a copy, obviously photo-chemically, you're going to lose a significant amount of the potential quality. We know that. You also know, as you said, that if there was a significant tear in the original, or a missing frame, there's nothing you *can* do about it photo-chemically. Well, if there's a known missing frame you can't recreate it so that the experience is not interfered with, which you *can* do digitally. I think there are definite weaknesses in the photochemical process. The question you have to ask is, are those weaknesses compensated by what you can do in the digital environment. I mean to me, as I said earlier, if digitally I was better able to represent the appearance on the screen of a nitrate print, I would be very interested in that. But I haven't seen that, and maybe nobody's done it particularly: a side-by-side presentation of nitrate and a digital copy made from the same print.

___ML: No, I've never seen that.

___DF: But that to me would be very interesting, because the other big loss, besides the loss of definition, would be the ability to give the feeling, the texture of the nitrate on the screen. Thas's one of the things I'd love to do, using a specific print which you're prepared to project and making a digital copy of it, projecting those side by side. That would be to me another major aspect of digital preservation, if you could do that…

___ML: Is this difficult cultural situation archives are now facing, when they still demand to do analog preservation, probably based on the necessary action they had to take in, say, the 1960s and 1970s, when they *promised* to their administrators and to the public, that by mass copying of nitrate to safety stock, they were saving the heritage, in its completeness?

___DF: Well, I think some archives said that. The attitude that we always had at the National Film Archive was that what we were doing was not total preservation, it was interim preservation, because the stock qualities, the speed of stock, etc., were improving, and there were other technical improvements even in analog preservation that would mean we would be able to make a better copy again in the future. This wasn't saying in this way you could ensure the long-term preservation, it was saying that if the nitrate disappears, because it deteriorates, we have got the best copy we could get now. But we kept our nitrate in the best possible conditions, because we knew that in 20 years' time we wanted to have another go at it. And, of course, it's very important that one's done that, because if we do undertake digital preservation, we still need to go back to the best generation of material. There are the organizations that said, "We have done this," and then got rid of the original. Unless the original itself could no longer run through the equipment that would enable one to copy it, one shouldn't have got rid of it. One should continue to look after it, at the best possible standards. Some archivists at different archives had to say they would get rid of the original in order to get the resources to make the copy. I was supposed to do that at the National Film Archive; I just didn't do it. We never got rid of the original. I know in organizations in America, particularly like the National Archives, they got rid of all the nitrate when they copied it, and they went one stage worse, they only copied onto 16mm (as did the Library of Congress in its early days), and they threw away the original material. So not only is there no chance of going back to a lot of material, the copy that you made was nowhere near the best you could have made at that time. I'm able to look back a bit with hindsight because I've been through all the periods; I mean, you had to make that argument to get money. The question was whether you were forced to do what you had agreed to, because the only reason the governments would give you large amounts of money was to get rid of the issue of nitrate. Archivists had created this picture of nitrate being akin to gunpowder, and the most dangerous thing in the world, and they'd done this very specifically to sort of panic people into giving them the resources. But basically, if it is that dangerous, you're forced to get rid of it immediately. And that was the only way, because unfortunately the number of countries where government funds would be given because of cultural importance alas is not very many. I think to a certain extent that was possible in France, because in France film was up with the other performing arts, such as opera and theatre, etc. In very few countries has film been on the same political level as the performing arts or major art galleries and museums. It's been regarded as the product of an industry, and the only argument you've been able to use is not a cultural one, because, on the whole, governments didn't think that cinema was of cultural importance. It was a mass entertainment, produced by a wealthy industry. So I think we had to use the "panic argument," and it is, to a certain extent, still around our necks. But I think it was right to use it at the time, because that was the only way you could have made, not what I would call a "totally preserved" copy, but the best one you could at the time.

—ML: I like the word "interim" preservation that you used to describe your policies at the National Film Archive, because interim preservation tells you that the active approach of striking a safety negative is one critical step to ensure that future generations can again access the film for their cultural strategies in the future. What I see now is one logic, which I'd call the logic of content retrieval, and another logic I'd call a museological approach to film. Would you agree that currently we face a situation where a younger generation of archivists, content providers, and researchers says, "OK, you have preserved for the last 50 years. You have preserved all those films. And now we demand, since we are two generations following you, to have access to that work, to incorporate it into our contemporary cultural logic." And this logic is largely based on the logic of content retrieval.

—DF: I've just been to the opening of the Library of Congress facility in Culpeper [Virginia], and it is incredible, because not only is there a fantastic photochemical laboratory, but there is also an amazing digital server storage system. In principle, the way it's described by the manufacturers is that it actually will make copies itself when necessary, without the intervention of a curator or person. In other words, there was a time when one of the big worries was supposing when it's time to refresh a digital file, there aren't the resources available. You can't leave it that long before you do something. So you're continually going to have to demand, maybe every 5 years, a year with an extra budget that enables you to refresh your holdings. Or you've got to space out that refreshment over each year so it's a standard amount. But, if you genuinely can have a system which, in its normal operating mode, continues to refresh, I'm less and less worried about the concept of the costs involved in preserving digitally as opposed to preserving photo-chemically over a period of 100 years.

Archivists can't think in less than 100 years in my opinion. I'd prefer it to be 200 years. If you're saying that it has to be refreshed every 5 years, that's 20 times staffing costs and additional costs of the refreshing process, as opposed to the operational cost of the equipment. That's an extremely worrying situation, when you've been associated with government-controlled cultural organizations, because often you can't get the money at the time you need it – you have to wait. Luckily, with film and good storage conditions you can afford to wait. So to a certain extent that was one of the issues why I was always against the concept of digital preservation, because I was afraid that there would be too many times where you would need additional money to ensure the long-term existence of the preservation copies you'd made digitally. Now I'm not sure. Maybe in the end one shouldn't make a radical decision on digitization on that basis until you've had 25 years' experience of the whole further system and how well it self-perpetuates the material that it's holding. At least if you put away a photochemical copy in a good storage environment it will still be perfectly usable in 100 years' time, and it will be possible to project it, because basically the projector is a mechanical device which can be easily reconstructed at any time, whereas an obsolete digital system is probably going to be impossible to recreate easily. So there are other reasons. Even if, in every other way, you could create, as far as the presentation in the museum was concerned, a copy which was a very close approximation of the copy as seen by the masses at the time of original release, then you're still worried if technology will prevent that being done at some time in the future because of the lack of resources or technological failure. And, you know, we've got 100 years' experience behind us of film. At the National Film Archive they began copying nitrate to nitrate, because safety film hadn't come in. And so one has examples of nitrate films that were put into perfect storage immediately after they were made, that have had no time to deteriorate whatsoever. The whole digital world worries you, because you don't know enough about it, and about how the technology will play out. But more and more I'm beginning to believe that if you had the right checks and balances culturally and technically, and you could effectively ensure the long-term existence of much more material than you could by the current photochemical group, so that one would have the opportunity of both researching and making available more images, then I would seriously consider that we should have at least a programme of digital preservation in certain areas. I would start with the material which is less important – and, of course, immediately when you say "less important", it means that archivists have to start making selections...

—**ML:** Which is a curatorial intervention.

—**DF:** ...and traditionally they've always said, "It's not up to us to make selections. You know, we're only there to satisfy the researcher." And to be honest, that has been a great failure, because it's made people think about film archives as repositories, and not as curated contextualized institutions.

—**ML:** Exactly.

—**DF:** But if you are prepared to make selections – and I don't believe archivists can not make selections any longer – then I would start assigning this 25-year-or-whatever period to see exactly how the digital environment survives. I would start with material that is less important for various different reasons. One, culturally or content-wise. Two, films where the archive knows that the material it has is not that good to start with, and there is a possibility that someone else has material which may be better, but continuing the photochemical approach for national production, which is considered important in a specific country because you know that other people will not do anything to look after that. This is the way Culpeper has been built; it's a dual facility. It's up to the curator whether they use the photochemical laboratory or digital server to preserve the material. So, again, as everything we're saying, it's putting much more responsibility on the role of a curator in an archive, which is what I think we all believe is vital if archives are to be taken as seriously as national museums and national art galleries. So really, I think I would like to accept that certain material is only preserved digitally in the future, but that's after very careful consideration of that material in relation to your collection and the collections of other people.

—ML: Obviously there's a need for a "museological" concept of preservation, which includes that you do make very strict choices of what you preserve in terms of what the cultural significance of a certain work is, and whether this element is the element the film should be preserved from. On the other hand, if you do preserve something, you decide whether you do it photo-chemically, as a deliberate choice to stay in the same medium because you want to preserve the texture, you want to preserve a certain cultural/historical practice of projection, etc. Then, if you do preserve something, you need

to be very, very discriminating about producing documentation of all the changes you've made to the original in the process of copying. This is an area where "digital preservation" so far has only been thought about in terms of technical problems, and not the possibilities it offers. This is something I'm discussing with Paolo – if you preserve something digitally you really need to, in a way, preserve your digital mindset. If you digitize film, you turn something physical, an object, into information. Furthermore the non-hierarchical order of information gives you ample opportunities to not only preserve the images but preserve meta-data with them, in the sense of the protocol of the changes you have introduced to the original, all the contextual materials you have, etc.

—DF: I totally agree. I think that the whole digital approach gives you opportunities you didn't have before. But another big worry for me is this: The Library of Congress is digitizing everything, and not just film. I went to the Head of the Collection Services Department, and I said, "Look, you have shifted your responsibility as curators to ITS, the technical department, because everything is kept on their server. We're used to having material in our hands, and ensuring that it is not mismanaged or mishandled or misused. Now you have completely switched that responsibility to a group of people who have no training as curators." Now how do we integrate, which way do we go? Well, we have three approaches. You either have to have full-time curators in your technology section, or you train curators in digital technology or digital technicians in curatorship. But, at the moment, having the two separate functions, where one does not understand the other, means that there is no way of exerting adequate control on what happens to the material afterwards. Even if you successfully ensure – because of the relationship between the digital engineer and the curator – that the material is preserved satisfactorily, you have no long-term ability to control what happens to it in the future. It's possible to change the nature of it even in a transfer. Even the server, which is automatically copying from A to B, is probably going to have a new control system that may do more than was possible before, and may even do it automatically. And you may not want to, because that may be changing a decision that was made curatorially, simply automatically. All these issues are so complicated, and difficult to understand. But there's no doubt about it that the digital environment gives you opportunities you didn't have. The question is, does it give you problems that you can't cope with as well? And that you can't control? It's very difficult to get answers to these sorts of questions, because you either hear from someone who was trained in the digital environment, or you hear a view from someone who was trained in the photochemical environment as a curator. And of course neither of them knows enough about the whole subject to come to conclusions which are convincing in their own right. What I'm really trying to say is that I'm extremely worried about making a move into the digital environment, for the most important reason, because I think there are a lot of issues that need to be solved before one makes a major step like entrusting your national/international film culture to the digital environment.

THE MARKET VS. THE MUSEUM
Alexander Horwath

The following statement was given during the "Open
Forum" session on Friday, 10 June 2005, during the 61ˢᵗ
FIAF Congress in Ljubljana. It was written on the spur of
the moment, as a somewhat unguarded reaction to the
presentations and debates on Wednesday.

Since the first comments following my statement
were extremely "controversial" and wide-ranging, I
would like to stress again what I expressed when intro-
ducing it last Friday: that I was speaking in the spirit of
the polemic, to stir up debate; that it was probably an
"improper" thing to do (considering the diplomatic nature
of most FIAF proceedings), but that I felt it to be neces-
sary all the same. For reasons of brevity, I didn't touch on
many important issues relating to this topic. Also, I am
well aware that the oppositional paths which are evoked
in the latter part of this text cannot in any way do jus-
tice to the panoramic variety of institutional models that
are represented in FIAF. But just as most utopian visions
of "our digital future" have never (and will never) really
become a reality, my own "dystopian vision" is very much
a stark and admittedly unsubtle projection of certain vis-
ible details onto a wider and darker horizon, hopefully
never to be realized.

Since he is the only (living) archive person mentioned
by name, I should also add that Nicola Mazzanti – who
was sadly no longer present on Friday – is no stranger to
polemic himself, so I took the freedom to respond to his
"invitation". I do, however, look forward to continuing
this debate in a more extended and less pointed fashion.
In the end, I am most interested to find out which image
we – the members of the FIAF community – have (and
want to have) of ourselves; and what our perceived role
in society is, as curators and museum directors, program-
mers and archivists, as "techies", "politicos", and
"passeurs".

I have not revised the text since Friday, but I have tried
to straighten out some bad English (of which there is still
certainly enough).

Alexander Horwath, 13 June 2005

Thank you for the opportunity to be polemical and to
give you some observations and critical remarks about
what I perceive to be not just a shift, but a "neo-liberal
turn" in film archive and film museum politics. We are
currently witnessing this turn or are ourselves part of
it – and I think there are good reasons to oppose it as
far as one can.

My examples do, in some way, relate to the workshop of the Technical Commission on Wednesday
morning, but the language, rhetoric, and ideology
which were partly expressed there are in no way singular
cases. I have heard them over and over – and more and
more vehemently – on many platforms and in many contexts over the past few years. I think that it is necessary
to look at this rhetoric more closely, in relation to the
unique abilities of the museum as well as so-called
"market realities".

On the surface, this is a debate or controversy about
Digital vs. Film and about the question *What is Film?* I
do not want to engage in this debate here, even
though it is far from clear, and is getting increasingly unclear every day. In our context, I think that the *Digital
vs. Film* opposition only cloaks the real opposition,
namely *The Market vs. The Museum*, and that behind the
question *What is Film?* one may find the question *What
is the Museum?*

I would like to name just three examples of this
shift – three terms which, parallel to the development
of Digital rhetoric, have massively entered our language: *content*, *access*, and *user*. Of course, all three are
very innocent terms, and they signify a number of positive things – for instance, certain democratic, anti-
élitist forms of behaviour, and the "opening" of formerly

"closed" institutions. I would, however, like to draw your attention to the way in which these terms are also being used to install a market logic at the cost of the critical and political functions of the museum.

Firstly: *content* – in other words, our collections. This rhetoric doesn't say *artefacts*, but *content*, much like the Hollywood industry uses the word *product* for films. In this sense, *content* is a combative term to somehow get rid of the material artefact with which every content is irrevocably joined. This use of the word *content* desires a kind of "free flow" of content, much like the "free flow of capital" in contemporary finance capitalism.

Secondly: *access*, meaning the way in which archive and museum collections are being presented to the public and are enriching public knowledge. The way *access* is being used in the neo-liberal rhetoric, it mainly means *consumption*. Not creating and curating various forms of engagement with the artefact, but turning the collections into image-banks for intermediary dealers and end-consumers.

Thirdly: the *user*, meaning the person who comes in contact with our institutions and our collections. By *user*, market-style rhetoric does not really mean the interested citizen who is met at eye-level by the museum and who in turn is called upon to meet the artefacts and collections at eye-level. Quite the opposite – in this rhetoric, *user* stands for the disinterested consumer, or the overly-interested intermediary dealer or "provider". The consumer plugs into our image-banks to graze on them like a cow grazes on a meadow, whereas the intermediary dealer or provider plugs in and grazes on our image-banks like corporate raiders graze on various smaller businesses, inhaling them in the process.

The ideology which lies in this specific terminology was best expressed on Wednesday morning when Nicola Mazzanti presented his vision of the future work of film archives and museums: nobody needs pro-grammes or educational presentations anymore, nobody needs exhibitions curated with a specific knowledge, from a specific position. All forms of making-the-artefacts-public, of communicating them, of passing them on, will be "user-driven" – just like the market usually is (or, rather, seems to be). In this vision, the museum is either obsolete or it becomes something like a "server of the world", fulfilling every conceivable need. The user creates his or her own programme, just as it is done everywhere else on the audio-visual market. We are therefore speaking of *content-on-demand*.

At this point I should make clear that, in my book, a museum is a very different kind of place and space, a different kind of social practice. The museum is a critical, ethical, and political tool, which stands in direct opposition to whatever social mood or climate or ideology is hegemonic at a given time. The museum does so in many ways. For instance, by simply reminding the visitor of previous and alternative forms of social and cultural organization; and thereby reminding him or her that the current social and cultural climate is not the only one imaginable. That the dominant forms are never "natural", but historical and man-made. Furthermore, the museum is a different kind of social practice because it offers unlevelled, unaligned *difference per se* through the material shape of its artefacts; it offers specific and accountable viewpoints and arguments about culture and society through curated programmes and exhibitions, by communicating with the visitor from an identifiable and transparent position.

The museum, as I understand it, is also a space in which one can find respect. Respect both for the artefacts that are collected, preserved, and exhibited, and for the person who views them in order to engage with them. The museum collection, finally, is not an image-bank created by chance, but an active and poetic process, which should be presented just as actively and poetically.

All of this, by the way, does not prohibit a museum from fulfilling additional services to commercial or non-commercial users – e.g., to make a DigiBeta of a film in the collection, to create a data-stream of certain of its holdings, or to sell a clip to television – if it chooses to do so and is in a legal position to do so. It's just that this is definitely not the *main* social function and mandate of a museum.

The neo-liberal rhetoric attempts to paint the museum in a very different light. Since the Market always needs to portray itself and the unrestrained flow of capital and content as the most natural and desirable of all things, every space or tool which functions as a critical reminder of alternative options must be presented as an obstacle. This is where the image of the "dusty" and "musty" old museum comes in, an image that was used quite frequently on Wednesday to convey the contrast between the bright and light world of free-flow Digital on the one hand, and the heavy, dusty, old-fashioned world of Film and the Museum on the other.

In addition, any supporter of the Museum as an ethical or critical tool is swiftly deemed to be "conservative" or "naïve". Along these lines, one would actually think that the term *Archive* should evoke even stronger images of dustiness and mustiness. At least, that used to be the prevalent image of archives among large parts of the population. But the *New Archive*, in neo-liberal terminology, is not at all dusty and musty – because it is the image-bank, the valuable asset, the bright and shiny server of the world.

By painting the dusty old Museum as conservative, and as an obstacle to the New Archives' swift conversion into the servers of the world, and by painting dusty old Film as an obstacle to the Digital regime, neo-liberal rhetoric functions exactly the same way as it does in the social and political arena: Whatever rules and regulations the social state has implemented to protect the rights of workers and employees, or the soli-darity between generations, or fair access to health services, and so on – all these rights and regulations, and the groups which represent them (such as unions), are now being painted as "backwards", "conservative", "defensive", and "naïve", and as obstacles to the free reign of the so-called market forces which one is supposed to join offensively. As an ideological tool of Cultural Darwinism, the current use of the term *Digital* in a certain cultural context mirrors the use of *Market Forces* as a tool of Social Darwinism. The *free flow* which is invoked by both terms attempts to separate itself from – and get rid of – material objects and the material relations from which they both derive.

I would also briefly like to point out that the neo-liberal rhetoric of Digital often comes with a rather specific tone and aesthetic of presentation which seem to give it credibility because they are so wonderfully ironic, and, you know, *seen-it-all, know-it-all*. A certain sarcasm or cynicism that is even likely to resort to parodies of the bad English spoken by others. As an homage to its preferred presentation tool, I would like to call this type of speaking *PowerPoint Speak*. It borders on a kind of postmodern propaganda language, because both technologically and in terms of visual aesthetics and intonation, this PowerPoint Speak leaves very little room for reflection, pause, eye- and ear-level communication, and critical understanding.

I feel that we are in the middle of a process which might actually show that FIAF contains two very different types of thinking, or even consists of two very different types of organizations. As far as I understand the history and the identity of FIAF, the idea of the film museum, the cinematheque, as a critical and ethical tool stands very much at the centre. At least that seems to be the legacy of people like Iris Barry, Henri Langlois, or Jacques Ledoux.

In the past two decades, the questions of archiving, conservation, and preservation have become much more prominent than they used to be, and rightfully so. But we might now find ourselves at a moment in time when the newly professionalized archive leaves behind the idea of the museum as a critical tool and turns into a digital image-bank, riding on top of perfectly managed cold-storage facilities for untouchable nitrate and acetate films.

At the end of such a process, this kind of archive would be fully aligned with and affirmed by the market, and would therefore represent a kind of nothingness. In political terms, it would be the actual conservative – or better, neo-conservative – place.

The other type of organization would be an archive which is also a "critical museum"; a confrontation of concrete artefacts and social practices; an actively and poetically constructed collection; a place in which curatorial thinking and work can be felt and argued with. It would stand counter to the ideology of the market.

I must admit that the latter type of organization will probably bring a lot of grief – the grief of having to endure, engage with, and survive current cultural politics, which run on the fetish of the Digital and Digitization. On this point, however, I would like to quote William Faulkner, by way of Jean-Luc Godard: *Between grief and nothingness, I will take grief.*

Chapter 4

Film as Artefact and Museum Object

—DF: In "The Market vs. The Museum" you made a powerful argument that by using the word "content" to describe their collections, archivists are failing to recognize the importance of the artefacts they are charged with safeguarding.

Art galleries and museums, however, seem to have overcome this problem. The "content" of a painting can also be separated from its canvas, and like a film reproduced faithfully in other media, yet art galleries and museums seem to have convinced their constituencies and funding agencies that there is no substitute for seeing the actual work of art in a gallery or museum setting.

Photographic galleries and museums, which have much more similarity with film archives, have convinced their constituencies that a photographic print can only be considered an original if it is made from the camera negative by, or under the direct supervision of, the photographer. This gives such prints artefact status, and means that no new artefacts can be created after the photographer's death.

If film archives considered original prints – those made with the approval of the creative team that produced the film – as their artefacts, could they then convince their constituencies that the art of the cinema could only be experienced by attending the screenings of original

prints on an archive's own premises, in a technical environment specifically designed to replicate, as far as possible, the first public presentations?

One would then have to respond to the inevitable criticism that one was restricting "access" to an art form that, unlike most others, was conceived as a group experience and directed towards a mass audience.

One possible response might be to establish different levels of viewing experience. The first would be to attend a screening of the original artefact on the archive's premises. The second might be to attend the screening of a print approved by the archive in the country where the film was produced. The third, rather than be a screening of any film copy, as it would be today, could be the screening of an archivally approved digital copy. If we are honest, good digital copies are a better representation of the art of the cinema than incomplete, damaged, or badly projected 35mm or 16mm prints. This approach would also justify the money spent on the preservation of master material that would not have artefact status, but would be essential for the production of archivally approved celluloid or digital copies.

This scenario is designed to provoke discussion. However, the bottom line is that I would like to know how you would introduce the concept of the artefact into film archives.

~

—**AH**: My most immediate answer would be to turn the terms around: How to introduce the concept (and praxis) of film into "artefact archives" and museums?

This is certainly not a new question, but it seems that with the recent shifts in the museum world (regarding their self-image and new social function), as well as in the culture at large (the "digital revolution"), it has become more – instead of less – difficult to address it and to make oneself understood. I think that in order to reach a better understanding of film's role *vis-à-vis* the museum, we need to (a) look more closely at what film actually is (in itself and in relation to other forms of expression); and (b) to question thoroughly the values and cultural principles that most contemporary museums operate on in relation to reproductive media and popular forms of expression. Which also means to question the ways in which museums are "convincing their constituencies" of what an "original" or an "artefact" or an "authentic artwork" is in the field of reproductive media.

Before going into any further detail, I thought I'd look up what the encyclopedia has to say about the word "artefact". I went to Wikipedia, in honour of the digital revolution. The things I found there are quite interesting, not only in terms of definition, but also for the associative space they create in relation to film. So here are a few definitions from Wikipedia:

"An Artefact is: a human-made object, such as a tool, weapon, or ornament, especially those of archaeological or historical interest."

"An Artefact is: a human-made object that is a prototype or standard of measurement."

"A prototype is an original type, form, or instance of some thing serving as a typical example, basis, epitome, or standard for other things of the same category."

"Artefact (archaeology): any object made or modified by a human culture, and later recovered by an archaeological endeavour."

"A cultural artefact is a human-made object which gives information about the culture of its creator and users. The artefact may change over time in what it represents, how it appears, and how and why it is used as the culture changes over time. The usage of the term encompasses the type of archaeological artefact which is recovered at archaeological sites; however, man-made objects of modern society are also cultural artefacts. For example, in an anthropological context, a television is an artefact of modern culture."

"Artefact (fantasy): in the fantasy genre, is usually a magical object so powerful that it cannot be duplicated or destroyed by ordinary means. In role-playing games and fantasy literature, an artefact is a magical object with great power. Often, this power is so great that it cannot be duplicated by any known art allowed by the premises of the fantasy world, and often cannot be destroyed by ordinary means. Artefacts often serve as MacGuffins, the central focus of quests to locate, capture, or destroy them."

I believe there is only a short distance from the artefact as MacGuffin (in the fantasy genre) to the artefact as it is still understood by most museums today. In both cases, it is the aura, the "great power" bestowed on the "magical" object (and not its documentary, informational, aesthetic, or educational properties), that is supposed to make us hold our breath. I will come back to this issue later on.

As for the other definitions, tool, weapon, ornament, all seem quite valid for film (a technical-cultural tool for humanity to produce new ways of understanding the world; a weapon in terms of its potential influence on individual minds as well as large parts of a population; an ornament in the sense of something that makes the world we live in more pleasurable or beautiful to look at).

The term "prototype" and the description of the "cultural artefact" appear to be similarly valid for film. By touching on the anthropological context, however (and by taking television as an example), the Wikipedia definitions bring us closer to an understanding of why, to my mind, film *cannot be fully understood as an artefact at all* – at least as long as we identify artefact with an object.

So here's my key statement: In relation to film, a museum essentially needs to preserve, show, and interpret *not just* an object/artefact, but a *system,* more specifically: a *working system.*

The terms "object" and "artefact" fall short in relation to what film is, because they only refer to one element of the film equation, namely the fixed element (the film strip). It is a *necessary* element for creating the film experience (if we exclude certain Expanded Cinema practices that do without celluloid), but it is certainly not *identical* with it. The term *film experience,* on the other hand, is not a sensible replacement term either. An experience is something individual; too much of it resides in the unattainable world of the viewer. A museum cannot "preserve" something which, to a high degree, is outside its

influence. It can only establish the conditions for film experiences to take place. A further conceptual step brings us closer to what we're searching for: The film experience is enabled by a *performance of film* – the act of putting the "time-less" film-object/artefact into a machine which (if it works and if the conditions of the screening space are set accordingly) produces the phenomenon we call film. This phenomenon is always (a) an aesthetic one – no matter what type of film runs through the machine; and (b) a durational one. Apart from a few works in history (loops; some installations) which do not have a pre-set duration, all film works (= performances of film) are defined by the specific time they take to appear in full. One might say they are "framed" by their duration (if you accept the analogy to paintings or drawings) – or, rather, "framed" by the last moment in time before they begin and by the first moment in time after they have ended. In the case of a painting or drawing, the work is what's inside the frame (or wherever the paper/canvas ends); in the case of film, the work is what's inside the time-frame *and* inside the visual/aural space created by the joint performance of strip, machine, and operator.

To make that film work, understood in the above terms, fully appear to the viewer is what a museum can do. It is, I believe, *the only way* in which a museum can make the work fully appear to a viewer. There are many other ways in which a museum can make *some* properties or aspects of the film work appear (exhibiting only the machine or the screen; exhibiting the unmoving film strip; exhibiting film stills; exhibiting transmutations of the work on other machines; exhibiting parts of the film in looped form; etc.). But if we expect a museum to make works fully appear to the viewer (as we do in the case of fine art museums), then a museum of film needs to go beyond the concept of the artefact-as-object (film strip) and look into the concept of the system, the system-of-artefacts-and-prototypes.

The museological aim, then, would consist of preserving the "artefactual" and prototypical elements of the film system in such a way as to make that system work time and again, because it is only the performance of the system that produces what we call film. All the elements of this performance contribute to its specific historical "shape"; it is these historical shapes of human activity that museums are supposed to carry through the generations. Vice versa, the historical shape can only be attained, communicated, and understood if all the elements of the system are present *and working*.

If we look at the film work in such a way, and if we agree that it is the museum's obligation to make that work "happen" in a manner which ensures its transparency, authenticity, and "legibility" for generations to come, then it is the *principles of that system* that need to be preserved and performed every time we define something as film. The word "principles" includes both the conceptual and the material elements which constitute the system.

What follows from this is a decisive – and, to my mind, highly productive – weakening of the "single/unique object" concept. It is important, of course, that the various objects, elements, and principles that are in play during a museum presentation conform to the historical needs of the system (otherwise we could not honestly say that we are presenting the system); but it is *not important* that the single film strip, the single projector, the single screen, etc., are in any way unique, limited in number, or especially valuable. The unique properties of an individual film work (= the properties of its performance in a working system) do not emanate from a specific, individual object to which they are intrinsically, materially tied (as is the case with a painting or sculpture). But they can only emanate if all the elements of the system to which the film work owes its existence are brought into play.

What you, David, have described in relation to photography and the museum gives us some idea of the problem we have to address: Like film, photography is a medium that does not exist in order to produce unique objects; it exists to produce many objects of very similar or almost identical appearance. From the point of view of how the medium of photography was and is used in society (its praxis), the matrix/negative is not the desired object. The negative is not even the *unique* object, because further negatives can be made from a positive. The desired object is the positive, the "photo". In everyday life there has never been any problem with the fact that there is (or can be) more than one print of the same photograph. The special (= modern) "magic" or "great power" of a photo does not derive from its being the only one in existence, but from its indexical relation to lived reality. It is only by applying standards derived from older, non-reproductive arts that the issues of "original", "vintage", and "the artist's stamp" come into play.

I think we are dealing here with a two-fold problem.

(A) The museum as a creation of the late 18th and 19th centuries is deeply intertwined not only with the aims of enlightenment and education, but also with bourgeois notions of possession. The value of the objects in the collection is measured not only as educative value (what the object can communicate to the public), but as economic value. In order to be valuable in an educational sense, an object does not have to be unique (but it has to be authentic in the sense that it carries all the characteristics of the historical praxis which it is supposed to demonstrate). To be valuable in an economic sense, however, it *does* have to be unique. As in all other spheres, the uniqueness of an object guarantees that only one person/institution can have it. The status ("value") of museums in a bourgeois-capitalist society is highly dependent on the number of single, unique, "valuable" objects it has amassed. The threat that mass society and mass culture posed to the 19th-century museum model could be countered relatively easily. Since it is still a *capitalist* mass society we live in, the hierarchies of value persist. The products of mass culture may proliferate, but "real" value (meaning "high", "spiritual" value, as opposed to everyday-use value) will be bestowed on one of these products only if there are limits to its reproduction, in short: if there is one or just a few "originals" (artefacts) which were touched by the creator's hand.

Therefore, I would argue that photography has partly undergone a cultural and social process of redefinition which runs counter to some of its intrinsic qualities. In order to "return" photography to these qualities, I think one has to devaluate (or "deflate") the ideology which is at work in (art) museum acquisition policies. (I always liked the example of the Walker Evans and Dorothea Lange photographs, which any US citizen can acquire simply by writing to the government – the "work" is public property, and its countless copies should be treated as having the same value.)

(B) With film, we haven't yet seen that same process of establishing a "museum value" as with photography. A lot of it, I think, has to do with what I described above: the film strip as artefact is very different from the photograph. In the case of the latter, holding the artefact in one's hands and looking at it gives the full experience of the work – *the artefact is the work* (even though there is more than one artefact/copy which gives the full experience of this same work). In the case of film, as stated above, the so-called artefact (film print) is different from the work; it is only part of the work – and little is gained by holding it in one's hands and looking at it (except for the researcher/restorer, of course). Also, the idea of the "creator's touch" and the vintage print, while to some degree understandable (if not inherent) in the case of photography, becomes slightly absurd in the film medium. In most cases, we have no individual creator who could sign off on a print; we have a complex set of relations in regard to authorship, which means that even if we follow an *auteurist* model of interpretation for industrial film, the *auteur*-artist (director) is rarely the person who controls the production of prints, internegatives, etc. The only area where the photography-model could be applied is the field of experimental, "handmade" film. But as this is almost completely a historical praxis by now, nobody will be able to go back and make "vintage prints" out of something that Richter, Man Ray, Brakhage, Deren, Kubelka, Anger, Warhol, et al., meant to be available in many copies for many distribution systems.

All these aspects, it seems to me, can be seen as the inbuilt "resistance" of film against the art-museum-type treatment and evaluation.

What you, David, hint at are the ways in which we could still try and turn film towards such kinds of treatment and evaluation – in order to make our institutions more similar to the existing museum model. In a way, this seems practical (and smart). In another way, it would sadden me deeply. When I think of the museum as a model to base my work on, it is the humanist ideal of the museum, its educational and ethical foundations that I have in mind. The other museum model which is dominant today is something I'm much less close to. I'm speaking of the current type of art museum, which has devised a somewhat "diabolical" double-strategy for itself: adhering to the old hierarchies (the specialness, uniqueness, and high value of the objects on display: "we have them; you don't") and, at the same time, playing the game of pseudo-democratic consumerist "participation" (now everybody can share that uniqueness; no special knowledge needed, we're an "experience" now, "like the movies", or like TV). This mix of "possessive/auratic" and "populist/mass-mediatized" elements has turned large parts of the (art) museum world into a pop-cult industry which is not that different from Hollywood.

If we say that film is much more than Hollywood, then I think we shouldn't base our museum model on the "Hollywood-style" art museums of today either.

If there is a way out of this dilemma, then it may be founded on an irony – that it is precisely the so-called "populist mass-medium" of film which can return us to an understanding of the museum as an educational endeavour. It does so by focusing on a working system, a process, a demonstration, a performance, instead of an object/artefact loaded with "magic", aura, uniqueness. In this, a true "film museum" also goes beyond the technical and historical museums, which, even though they mostly deal with systems, do so either via artefacts or by exhibiting mainly non-working systems.

Since it is not about the unique/valuable/auratic artefacts on display (or in the collection), this kind of film museum (or any "museum after film") can disassociate itself from the hierarchies and ideologies inherent in "owning things of great value". What we do own instead are (a) "devalued" objects of mass culture (what museum X has, museum Y can have, too), and (b) the systems for making these objects speak and become a work or a living document. We have the chance to keep a historical praxis alive, not just the "blind" material remains of what once was a praxis. But we will achieve this only if we do *not* disassociate ourselves from the basic humanist/educational principles of museum work: In prizing the system, the repeatable performance of film, a film museum can focus all its preservationist and presentational energies on making the experience of film as transparent, as informed, as precisely arguable, as intense, and as *truthful* as possible.

Which is another way of saying: You shall repair and restore and take good care of both artefacts and machinery; You shall copy the artefact onto another artefact; You shall replace parts of the system when necessary; You shall repeat the performance as often as you can. As long as you don't lose the ability to communicate and demonstrate the system. Or, worse, replace the system with another. In film, the "artefact" to be transmitted into the future is not just (but also) the strip, not just (but also) the apparatus, not just (but also) the screening space; what needs to be transmitted into the future is *the set of relations between them while they are in performance* – the working system.

~

__ML: David, so what's your immediate reaction to Alex's statement?

__DF: Well, I agree with everything Alex says. Effectively, what you've done so successfully is to build up the alternative to the film experience. It's not really a film experience. It's film, in a way, but it's something else. As you say, in the end the most important thing is – whether it is a museum or an archive, or whatever you call the institution – the ability to continue to create the use of the physical object, the projection, the environment, etc. But we really haven't got a word for what the end-product is. "Film Experience" is the one we've used, but after reading your paper I feel that that is unsatisfactory. I think it's part of it, but there's even more to it than "film experience". I don't know what that is. I haven't got a word…

__AH: A working system…a functioning system…

__DF: The thing about "functioning" system is that it seems a more technical word, whereas I want a cultural expression. But, anyway, "working system" is fine, because that's what it comes to in the end.

__AH: It depends if you include people in the word "system". Whether a "functioning system" would include the person operating the machine.

__DF: It must, because for the total system it's not only the projector that's important, it's the operator, it's the environment, it's the sound, it's the screen – everything. And the working system is a totality which, when you analyse it in detail, may even have 20 or 30 components or more. And some of those elements change. Projectionists can only work so many hours a week, so you're not talking about a single individual. It's not only about getting the ingredients right, it's about ensuring that your ingredients are as consistent as possible, so that, from the point of view of the audience, they come to one performance or another and they don't have a different experience. And that's what we're aiming for. It's quite a difficult thing to achieve.

We're not interested in museums in terms of the museum's handling of the artefact, because effectively the artefact is only one element of the working system. But we're more interested in the museum concept, because they have learned better than we have how to achieve a working system for their own media. And so what we're really looking at is not, as I said incorrectly, the museum's treatment of the artefact, but their working treatment of how they present their areas of responsibility. And I think that is where we might learn something from the museum. But, of course, as you say, very clearly the painting within a fixed frame is very different from a film, which is in a limited time period. It is not like photography either. There you're looking at the complete work, whereas you have to look at a film within a time frame to have the complete work, *and* it has to satisfy all the requirements of the working system in order for you to have that experience.

The real question for me is that we have the

system we have. The museum world we have at the moment is part of a capitalist society, whether you like or not, and to a certain extent a museum's success rests on whether its collection is unique and economically valuable – not educationally valuable. We have to operate within that system. And, if necessary, I think we have to create a situation where we have something that is economically valuable. And one of the problems I think we have is not being able to situate our own medium within that system. Theoretically I think this is absolutely correct. The question is, how do you fit that into a situation that seems to value a unique artefact more greatly than the content that that artefact can actually represent. I haven't an answer for it, but I feel that we can't move far away from the current situation that we have, and find a way of getting the necessary resources to ensure the working system.

—AH: I'm aware that this is a major point relating to the reality of our cultural institutions and of our policies. There are many ways to respond to this. I think one way is to focus differently on the notion of "uniqueness". It should not relate so much to the print, simply because of the fact that photography and film and later media have a different relation to the unique object than previous media and art forms had. If we shift the thing that needs to be saved to the working system, then it's easier to see it as something unique again. Within a certain period of time there won't be such a thing as a functioning system of the film medium in the everyday world. In a strategic sense, therefore, I think we need to start – or should have started a long time ago – to make governments or sponsors aware that it is *this* which we need to preserve. It is an enor-

mous task, and very few places in the world or in each country will be able to achieve this transmission of the system into the future. The other possibility I see is the one you suggest in your paper – to try and deal with film the way museums have dealt with photography. With prints becoming scarce, each individual print of the film could be turned into one of the "remaining originals" of the film. It may seem more realistic that that could happen. Society has shown that it is able to create that aura and that idea of uniqueness in a reproductive medium such as photography. One could say that only a film print made while the artist or studio or whoever produced it was in existence should be considered an original print, whereas the prints we are making now are not. In the larger scheme of things, this would mean to align oneself with the value systems that exist in most museums and societies and try to fit film in, and make it a museum object like others. But we would lose this idea of the functioning system if we only look at the medium as a series of auratic objects. For me, this is not satisfactory. But when asked to give practical advice to anybody, I would probably say: try it that way; your government might like that. Since it's a capitalist system, it still functions on that idea of real or virtual economic value.

But as ponderous as it may sound, I still think our obligation is to strengthen this other idea. Maybe it's comparable with clocks, which only make sense if they run. If a technical museum shows you a dead clock, whether it is beautiful or not, it's not what the clock is about. So to understand and to see how the clock worked at a certain point in time you need a working process. That's what I believe film museums are about. To enable not only present-day viewers, but also potentially the children and grown-ups of 2080 to understand how the system works, or worked, and to share its specific pleasures, even though it might not be around anymore as an everyday medium. To do that you need to preserve the working system. Paolo likes to create scenarios of 2050, so maybe we should write down a scenario of 2050, where the thing we call "cinema" operates in a completely different way, and everybody who wants to understand 20th-century culture, and to experience its original products, will need to find a place somewhere in the world where the "clock" is running. And that may be a very valuable place which governments will be proud of. Maybe they will spend money along the way to have that "Unique Selling Proposition". The problem, if you like to call it that, is only that we need to accept film as a medium of the past – or at least anticipate that it will be understood as one, even though individual artists might go on for quite some time to make celluloid films. In 2050, there will be other forms and new simulations of cinema, and people will still enter auditoria and watch moving images on a mass scale. I am pretty sure of that. But those who are interested should still be able to tap into the history of moving-image media, and experience the qualities and specifics of each older medium – just as we do today with the various art practices of the past that are no longer valid on an everyday level.

___DF: You see, I don't see a problem in 50 years' time, because I think the working system will be an understood phenomenon. It's the change period, the period we're in now that I find difficult, because, as we've seen in the past, when a tech-

nology disappears and you can only experience it in a few places, suddenly there's a resurgence of interest in it, and people feel it's incredibly important to sustain it. So I think what you want will happen automatically in 50 years. Our problem is we're given the role at the moment of guiding archives into and through the change period, and we can't use that philosophy there. Although one should start talking to people and explaining that that is the ultimate aim, it's more difficult to explain it when people still have the experience of cinema – not always well practised, unfortunately. They also have the new environment of the DVD, which gives in projection a quality which exceeds that of a poor 16mm or 35mm print. What I'm really trying to do is, I want to go where you want to go, but I want to go now, because I'm worried about what happens to the elements of the working system in the time between now and the time when that happens. This is for me the major problem.

Going on to some of the other things you said, cinema is a mass medium, and I think the only problem I have with the working system in the long run is that it will be for the few, and possibly for those who are geographically placed or economically able to enjoy the experience. And of course that goes against the concept of cinema itself as it was originally experienced, but we may have to live with that, we may have no choice. It would be wonderful if we could enable people to see with the working system the most important films – that leads us to other problems – and then say, "That is your one opportunity. You will have to experience the film in future on a DVD or some other electronic form. But you have had that experience, so when you use your DVD as a review, effectively you're doing that against the background of having had the experience." It's the best we can do.

But coming back to this more immediate time, what I'm most worried about is that archives have not done a good job in many ways, and so at the moment they're precarious. And although the film itself is only one part of the working system, we do have to safeguard that in this interim period. One always thought the cinema was finite, and so therefore we would be able to preserve it. When I first became an archivist, the idea was to copy all nitrate within 24 years. It was perfectly feasible at that time, with what we had, and the level of resources we had to undertake that task. We could devise the "24-Year Scheme" in 1976 and see it ended in the year 2000, but we have not kept up that level, and some countries have never succeeded in starting. So we're a long way off safeguarding even the material which has survived. We're now in real danger. If you look around the world you see more archives in financial trouble than I've ever seen at any time in my career. Earlier they had less money, but they had regular money and they did not have to raise funds, because film was considered in some sense an art form, and was therefore considered by some governments as part of an arts budget. But now I see more and more governments retreating from that and leaving archives to fundraise. Fundraising always has strings attached. For instance, there is a plan afoot to restore Powell and Pressburger's *The Red Shoes* again. Now it would be better, because techniques have improved since the 1980s, but I would still say that the version done in the 80s from the Technicolor masters, which involved protection masters and a Technicolor print at the end, can't be done do so easily any longer. I would prefer to restore another film that hasn't already been done. What I see around me is that all the money circles around the same things because the sponsor wants a high-profile event, and the number of films which can generate a high-profile event are finite! This is why I see this terrible danger at the moment. I feel that almost anything that helps us get over this period, when it is rare to see 35mm films projected, then preservation and presentation standards will be supported. But we're not anywhere near there.

—AH: It's interesting that you see it from that perspective, because I'm not nearly as worried as you are about the current state. I would have thought that the question of preserving the film strip was not as pressing right now as you describe, because, from discussions about digital work in the past years with the people who oversee the major studio archives, I see a widening acceptance of the fact – even with people who are all for working with digital – that the celluloid film strip is and should be the element that is kept and preserved, because we know that it will probably live much longer than any digital substitute. So companies like Sony, or the Scandinavian archives, some of which are very much into digital restoration, play out celluloid masters on a continuous basis to be kept in the archive for all eternity. What seems more endangered is the practice of making these newly created celluloid objects public again via screenings of film prints. At the moment, it seems to me that the claim of making film works public in their most "original" or "restored" state belongs more to DVD distribution than to film presentation. You make the tinted version or the "restored" version available only digitally, and you send the black-and-white negative to the Polar Circle, where it will be safe for a millennium. But you create no projection print of that tinted or restored film to show it as part of the "working system". So in a sense, I feel that archives today have succeeded quite well in convincing their governments of the necessity to *preserve* film on film as an object. But they have been much less successful in convincing the governments that these preserved films should also be able to come alive in their natural habitat, that projection prints should be made. The view often seems to be: "Yes, we've preserved it on film, but the way in which we make it accessible doesn't matter. As long as we have mediatheques, and people are able to see it on a monitor, on a DVD, or on the Net, that's enough, and that's OK." Maybe it's the hardest thing today to convince our funding sources that this is not enough. They have accepted that copying will go on, and should go on…

—**ML**: …but not for distribution.

—**AH**: Exactly. I think that many governments have accepted that the national film heritage must be preserved, but they feel it's enough if the material lies somewhere safe. I have the impression that they don't yet see the reasons for keeping the working system as a whole. What is going on now is the separation of these elements. If we numbered the elements that go into the working system, I think practically everybody would agree on which elements these are, but they would treat them separately.

—**DF**: Yes, but the problem is – and I don't disagree with that, because I think you're absolutely right – the archives have done one thing: they've convinced the Hollywood studios that

preservation is in their commercial interest. They didn't make that decision themselves in most cases, and that was important. It depends what you see as the role of a film archive. To me the fictional feature film is not a film archive, it's part of a film archive. And because the archives were late in understanding the importance of documentary and the newsreel, avant-garde film, shorts, and so on, they're way behind. First of all, they're way behind in acquiring; it's only recently that they've even started to acquire these collections. They've done virtually nothing to preserve them, and because the only private financial resources are often tied to the preservation of studio films – and this in itself has caused governments to back off a little from providing funding to the archives, because they also think in terms of the fiction film, and see that the work has been done – what we're finding is that private money is going on high-profile projects; government money is less, but the archives are expanding dramatically into areas of non-fiction, amateur film, and all these other areas. Virtually no work is being done at all in terms of making them so that they could be part of the working system. So, to me, as far as Hollywood is concerned, and as far as material to which there is a beneficiary of the rights, the situation is good. But as far as any other material is concerned, the situation has become worse. For instance, in the two organizations I worked for, the government did not question what we spent the money on. But they're taking more and more interest now in what you spend the money on, because they themselves want high-profile events. Take the Library of Congress. The Librarian has to go back to Congress in order to justify his budget request. Congress says, "We gave you money; why don't we have a high-profile event?" And I'm fighting downstairs, saying, "No, we're the only people to get government funding; we must spend money on the orphans, on the films which are not being dealt with elsewhere."

So I'm not disagreeing; all the things you've said are right. The archive has done a really good job of convincing the industry to protect their assets, but that in itself has worked against the rest of the cinema heritage, which in total terms is considerably more. That is more in danger now. I really am concerned with a much broader perspective of the cinema heritage. That's the reason I made the statement I did. If you count footage, the situation is very much improved. If you look at how much of the cinema heritage is being covered, then the situation's going the other way.

—AH: Two immediate things come to mind. You recently mentioned Indiana University and their film collection. You said that in trying to make the university more aware of what they have, you want to keep "value" out. And that very much chimes with what I'm trying to say. Let's not do it the way fine art museums are doing it. Let's not stick a value tag onto a print. I think we have to establish more and more cases of precedence, where things are dealt with in exactly that way. Which leads me to my second point: that "value" is twofold. Value can mean price, a monetary or economic value, and it can mean educational, cultural value. So what you're trying to do with this project is take it away from one value system and make it part of the other value system, where the value might actually increase. In this other area there is also a very helpful development – the continuing expansion of Cultural Studies since the early 1990s. I think we can gain a lot from this strong shift in academia and the humanities. It can sustain and support the types of cinema which are not "assets" in the rights-owners sense of the word. There is no immediate economic value attached to these films, so they might give us an idea of where to push the debate. If more and more groups in society see the non-economic value, the easier it would become for governments to support this other value system.

—DF: Well, I agree with everything you say, but the problem is, it's not working out that way. The universities are using the material, but they are not concerned with increasing the amount of material if it involves expending their money. They are only concerned with consuming. So they have no role – and this is one of my complaints. A university with a big music department doesn't query the acquisition of instruments. Why should it be concerned about getting the projectors in the film department? The projectors or the working system are also an ingredient of the ability to teach the material. There is also a problem with the use of film in other fields, and it's happening a lot, and it's making a big new demand – but there's no way that demand is helping the archives. What it's leading to is what I would call "medium-quality" digitization, without repair and inspection of material. As content is the lead concern, if content is accessible from the copies available, that is enough. And they're putting pressure on archives to make material available in low-quality form cheaply. They are one of our problems. The very increase in demand for material is a problem for the archives. It's desirable. We support it in terms of our desire to make our collections available. But it's not helping us do that in a way that meets our terms of reference, as people responsible for the safeguarding of cultural inheritance.

—AH: Except if we manage to slowly turn around the thinking which is prevalent in universities. Our aim has to be to make the universities aware of that circuit.

—DF: The university is one thing; the academic staff is another. The academic staff view is: "Of course we agree with you, but we have no control over the funding of the university and how the money is allocated. Yes, we'd love to help, but we can't get even enough money to teach the course." They don't feel a responsibility because they don't feel they have any power to do anything about it, and they want to concentrate their efforts on achieving the modicum of what they need to do their work. The trouble with everything we're saying is that you can look at it in a positive way, or you can look at it in a negative way. And I think I'm probably going to the extreme in one direction and you're going to the extreme in the other, and the reality is somewhere in the middle. It's probably not as bleak as I paint it, but it's not as rosy as you paint it!

But to turn to some of the other things you said, one of my big arguments goes back to the idea of value. And this was a big revelation for me. Because at the Library of Congress one day I got a memo that was sent round, saying, "You've got to assess the value of your collection." I wrote back and said, "It belongs to the government and therefore has no economic value. It's ridiculous to engage in this." Then I said, "Why do you think the British Museum stamps its prints in the picture area, however valuable? So that it avoids valuing the collection."

—ML: This is amazing!

—DF: I wanted the Library to do the same. But the reason why this whole thing about value came up was because booksellers were stealing from the Library by cutting out prints from rare illustrated books. I said, "It's very simple. Just stamp the prints with an embossed stamp saying 'Library of Congress'." And we had this big argument about it. Because I would like to do exactly what you want to do. I mean, that's one of the reasons why we always did our level best to prevent films ever getting into the auction house, because we knew that once they became part of the auction environment it would be over, and we would no longer be able to acquire them. So I totally want to keep value out of this. But you have got to have the support of your institutions if you're keeping value out of it, and more and more they somehow see that having an asset with a high dollar currency value is actually increasing their status within the artistic community, and making them more like a body which has art, where each painting is worth hundreds of millions. Somehow that gives them an increased status.

—ML: Just to add to this: a colleague from the fine art world suggested, when we discussed various strategies of getting more government money for the project of our new study centre, to assess the value of our collections. To calculate all the potential licensing fees you can recuperate if you make a collection available.

—AH: Which implies that the cultural minister or city commissioner – in whose mind 10,000 projects compete with one another – is more likely to say Yes to a new vault, archive building, or study centre if the content can be valued at 500 million Euros. Because then he can directly compare it to the other project the art history museum has asked him about. It means crossing the border from educational-cultural evaluation to putting a price on things.

___ML: Even for educational and cultural use, value is assigned to it, because in our society – as we move from the primary and secondary sector to services as a mode of production – knowledge and information have become so valuable that institutions also compete on the level of who's got the potential for generating knowledge. This is the point where archives, or even more museums, are in an unhealthy competition with universities. An archive is seen as a repository, and the university as an institution to interpret the collection, to generate knowledge and to generate value. If an archive now decides it's also a museum which interprets its collections, they enter into a competitive relationship.

___AH: I think that's a very important point, because that's exactly where curatorship comes in. It is a valid strategy to realize the ability to interpret, to create new perspectives. Let's take the place we're sitting in. I guess at some point, the Cineteca del Friuli and the Cineteca del Comune di Bologna were small archives with collections that were probably not seen as very important by most people. The idea they both had was to create a festival, which also meant strengthening the curatorial structure and developing ways of making film history public again…

___ML: …and even to create publicity…

___AH: It brought them into a much better situation regarding arguments for expanded support. They gained authority. Bologna seems to have become one of the best-funded cinematheques, and I believe a lot of it has to do with the festival. So what I'm saying is, through curatorial work, archives and museums can strengthen their role. The value of an institution is then not only the fictional value of the thousands of prints that they want us to assess, but the capacity and competence of the institution to create "stories" and draw knowledge out of that repository, to produce a cultural history.

___DF: Well, I think if we can attach value, and this is rather crude, to the number of satisfied customers – in other words, if you could say where we present value, because cinema is essentially about media, it's actually going to touch far more people than opera – and if you can put a value on the person touched, that effectively would probably be our best route. If you are trying to make well-rounded people, culture is an important part of that. If we are giving X number of hours of contextualized material to X number of people, we're up there, at the front. We're certainly not at the bottom any longer; we're at the top, even above opera and ballet. That's why we should value ourselves by the number of people that we are able to affect culturally.

___AH: I agree partly, because I would always want to qualify the quantity. The danger in this argument is that it can quickly become a quantity issue only, and is no longer about the depth or intensity with which we engage the viewer. You said that the big museums have 3 million visitors a year, but that also has to do with the fact that they have developed forms of channelling the masses through the museum, which make the kind of in-depth engagement one can have highly questionable. I would look for a mix of what you are saying, plus an evaluation of the ways in which museums offer their medium, their area of expertise, the kinds of guided tours or workshop situations – as opposed to pushing hundreds of schoolchildren through a museum in an hour.

—ML: Or, on the other hand, you could make digital exhibitions, curated websites, and say that every person who accesses it becomes a visitor.

—DF: Well, I don't want to get to that, because that's what the Library was always saying. We took the National Film Registry tour to virtually every state. What happened afterwards is that the State Department liked our tour so much that they sent it all over the world. But we did it internally at first, and went to nearly every state. The Librarian said to me, "The number of people you're reaching is so few, compared with the number of people who visit our website everyday." And I said, "What level of involvement are most of those people going to have with our website? They probably won't even remember it was the Library of Congress they went to." So I do agree with you, but I was assuming that we were counting the numbers of people who had experienced the working system and contextualized presentation. I don't want to count people who are just passing by an area with a screen on the wall, or anything like that.

But going back to the thing about education, there is no doubt that education is the focus we need to use in our battle for financial support, because at the moment education is "in" – putting it crudely – and of course the fictional film is not such a good area to use for education as the other elements of our collection, which we're behind in looking after and presenting. So they're working against one another a bit, be-

cause the things that we have in our collection that would be most valuable in terms of satisfying the current directions of educational thinking are the ones that we're least able to…

—AH: Which is a good thing, because it forces archives to put more effort into preserving newsreels, shorts, and various other types of film, and work with them in an educational context.

—DF: Yes, but in terms of finances, they are mostly privately raised. A favourite example of mine is related to a film critics association whose intention was to sponsor some prestige restoration project. They came and said, "Well, what have you got to offer?" And I said, "We've got the complete set of 35mm nitrate of the entire Nuremberg Trials." They said, "You must have something else." I said, "I'm sorry, I'm not offering anything else. This is my next priority on the list. It is decaying. It is an important historic event, and will certainly be researched in the future. It's nitrate, and it needs doing. And if you're not interested in doing that, I'll have to search for somebody who is." It is an endless problem, and it's a similar problem with The Film Foundation. Funds are only offered for films they like. So, while you're still lucky enough to get funding from the state, then you have some ability to preserve and make available non-fiction and silent films. But where you rely on mainly private money, you don't have a choice of using it in the way you want. So I think it is more difficult for the American archives in some ways than the European archives, where there is more of a tradition of giving government funding for this purpose.

—AH: Let me continue to play the role of the fellow with rose-coloured glasses. I'm usually seen as a super-pessimist, so I'm quite happy to be in this position! It's just an informative question, but when I look at what the American archives have presented at festivals like the Pordenone festival, and the three packages of *Treasures* on DVD, and if I look at the UCLA Film Archive's yearly preservation festival catalogue, and their news about acquiring the Hearst collection, I have the feeling that there are less classics of fiction film being "redone", and that the percentage of other types of film is actually increasing – both at festivals for archival films and in the context of archival DVDs. Also, when I look at the National Registry selections, it seems to me that more and more of these other types of films have been included.

__DF: But that is intentional. The Registry was supposed to represent the breadth of cinema culture. We actually made certain that it did include a broad range of films, because we were concerned about that. But the *Treasures* DVDs are a good example. The production of the *Treasures* sets has put incredible pressure on the archives. You cannot afford not to co-operate with the National Film Preservation Foundation (NFPF), because that is the channel at the moment for most of the money available for film preservation. A huge amount of time is spent in providing films; they all have to be newly preserved, and so the real determination of archival priorities is being made by the needs of the *Treasures* set. Archives, however, are on the whole behind the venture, because it is making available an unknown part of the cinema heritage.

__AH: You mean too high a percentage of daily work is going towards that?

__DF: Yes, and we agree with it, because it's doing what we want. We know that this is a

chance to get out our lesser-known collections to a relatively large audience.

__AH: But it means the control over what is being done comes from outside?

__DF: Exactly. We don't make the choices. Scott Simmon comes and says, "I would like the following films." The end product is superb, and they get the films out, but they are putting pressure on the archives at a time when we want to be active rather than passive. We want to be able to say which element of our collection we would like to preserve and make available. More and more we're doing things for third parties who basically have resources or political power. So, again, pursuing the route of the devil's advocate, it is extremely good, but it means we have very little control.

__ML: There's also another twist to it. If you look, for instance, at the model of the "Edition Filmmuseum", our DVD label, there is no third party involved, because all the archives participating essentially run the label. Fortunately enough, the archives cannot spend too much time thinking about what that public would want. There's no marketing agency which says that's what the public wants. The archives can act out of a mixture of their own agenda or out of opportunity. For instance, if television has provided money for a telecine, and it's a work you are quite fond of, the next step is: "OK, we already have that 2,000-Euro transfer, so we can…"

__AH: But this is also a third party.

__ML: But at least it's a mixture. The other problem I see now is, when a *Treasures of the American Film Archives* set with 112 films is released, interest in orphan cinema will most likely focus on those 112 films available on DVD. If you think of university courses on orphan cinema, if you think of cine-clubs showing American sponsored films, whatever, they will always go back to the DVD sets. It's the same thing, in a way, as Google. You can find everything on Google, but everything which is on Page 3 of Google's results virtually doesn't exist, because you browse what is available on the first two pages, and you find so many results that you don't care about looking for the things that are hidden behind the first 50 results.

__AH: But then, what's the way out of this? If nobody started with 112 first examples, there wouldn't be any. In a way there is no way around it, even though it's true; it just means that the next 112,000 also need to be contextualized and made public – and hopefully not just on DVD.

__DF: I wanted them to stop after the first *Treasures* box. I said, "You have done a marvellous job with the first *Treasures*. Now stop. Because basically you have created an interest in an area of cinema that all we archivists wanted to, but we can't go on providing this back-up." We need to take back into our own hands the decision about what it is we're making available, and how we do that, because I think we have to accept now that we will not be able to copy all existing film onto film for financial reasons. So we have to start selection. But, you can't very well throw out material that's in a collection after it's in the collection. You've already spent public money on it. So the sort of selection we have to do is going to be selecting from within our collection. It is the very same thing as contextualization. There are many areas which will be taken seriously once they appear, only if we put them into context. So I really think this is a moment where we need control, and I don't want to have

to do things with a commercial sponsor's money which aren't our priority. I want archives to gain back their own ability to determine their own priorities. That is a thing I think we've lost recently, certainly in America.

You see, when we set up the National Film Preservation Foundation, it was to replace the previous system whereby the American Film Institute allocated money received from the National Endowment of the Arts. Unfortunately, they took a huge cut for doing it. And it was only for the copying of fiction films. When we set up the National Film Preservation Foundation, we said, first of all, it can't be limited to fiction films, and, secondly, it can't be limited to copying, because there are a lot of other problems that need funding in archives. The range of films considered was extended. And you can see from the DVDs that a large amount of the funds is being used for other purposes, but funding for areas such as cataloguing, etc., was not expanded at all. The DVDs are hugely expensive. Now I think the first set covered the Foundation's costs, but not the archival costs, but I am not sure whether the second and third sets even did that.

__AH: You mean the number of copies sold is not enough?

__DF: Well, they'll cover the costs of the National Film Preservation Foundation, but not of the archives. The work of the archives is not taken into account in the budget at all. So it's a net loss financially as far as archives are concerned.

__AH: And none of the money made from the sales goes back to the archives?

__DF: No. It goes back to the Foundation; but I don't think it's ever made a profit. It may have recovered more than its own costs, but, if you take into account all the costs for the preservation work, there is no possibility of it covering them. And that's why I wanted it to stop after the success of the first set. They make the Preservation Foundation look extremely good, and this does help them raise more money, but the archives that provided films for the *Treasures* sets were not in most cases the ones that received significant financial benefits from the extra monies raised. In an ideal world, where there wasn't competition for that kind of money, I would be 100% behind the initiative. But it's taking away decision-making power, and it's taking away resources from the archives that did the work.

__AH: If it enables the Foundation to use the clout of their success to double their yearly budget, and give more money to the archives, then it would be OK.

__DF: That is a good argument, and that's what we hope. That's why everyone's continuing to support it, because as it's on a match-basis with Congress, it means that for every dollar the Foundation raises Congress matches it with a dollar, and the match-base has just been raised significantly. I don't want to be negative about it, but I am worried about this control issue. I agree with what we've said in other conversations, that contextualization and curatorship are essential to giving a *raison d'être* to the archives' existence and for the receipt of significant funds. If we are to achieve that, we have to have the control and enough resources to be able to put into practice this contextualization, which involves the process of making groups of material available which are not available at present in any form. It's a very tricky situation.

__AH: The situation is slightly different in Europe. In Austria, for example, the value put on newsreels is definitely higher. In the two archives in Austria, you certainly can't say that all newsreels produced in Austria have been preserved, but in terms of the energy and work that have gone into this field – especially on the part of the Filmarchiv Austria, which owns most of the newsreels, and can make money from them – there is much more care. The downside is that Austrian newsreel history has become available mostly in a mass-market-oriented fashion. You have a DVD which is called *1935*, or *1971*, etc., with a selection of the "highlights" from that year, and no commentary.

__DF: Talking about TV, at the NFA we always used to record it. I always did that right from the early 1980s. And now they've stopped it, or are thinking about doing so.

__ML: They're thinking about it, and they're looking into ways of selecting.

__DF: We kept it chronologically, so that you knew what was on the other channels. So if you were a researcher, you would not only know what was parallel to it, but have all the introductions, adverts, and everything; they would be there in the sequence they really happened. Because if you're going to study television, you're not only going to study the individual programme, but the whole way the programming was put together. It's a continuous presentation; rather than cinema, which is in finite programmes. I know we're not talking about television, but I mention it because I am far more worried about the preservation and accessibility of television than cinema.

__AH: That's my general feeling. You see it now in cultural policies and comments made by the National Libraries regarding the preservation of what's on the Internet. It's obviously starting to become a huge problem. It's a big radicalization *vis-à-vis* television. And television archiving already was the radicalization of film archiving…

_DF: Exactly. That's why the Library of Congress is preserving every so often the entire output of the Internet that is not password-controlled or pornography, thanks to the Internet Archive, who capture it. Because the Library is worried about leaving the question of preserving the Internet until 40 years from its creation, and thus suffering the same problems as we have faced in safeguarding television and cinema.

_ML: The Internet Archive is an interesting example, because of this software they've developed which is called the Wayback Machine, where you can take, say, BMW.com, and you can see all the iterations since 1996. This is something that is accepted by many people as a necessity, because you need to go back on a monthly basis to actually re-experience what BMW.com was like on 9 October 1998. Who does the same thing for film? If we arrive at the notion of the working system, who takes, for instance, a presentation of *Paris qui dort,* or of the sponsored films Rick Prelinger has preserved, and recreates a space and institution that enables the user to step back in time and see what the working system of 1925 was? What was it like in 1946, when the Cinémathèque française decided to preserve Clair's film? What was it like in 1961, when he re-edited the film? What is it like now, in a digital restoration projected at the film festival in Italy?

_DF: I would like to address the same perspective from a cultural rather than technical viewpoint. You need to look at cinema horizontally, to relate fictional and factual film, and to relate film to other media.

_AH: That would be the Cultural Studies approach. Look at comic strips, look at household appliances, look at films, look at magazines.

_ML: That's what we've tried to do on this *Blind Husbands* DVD, where we don't only show the film, but fast-forward in time to 1948, when Von Stroheim visited Vienna. Which is completely unrelated if you think of "context" in narrow terms. We also provided excerpts from Viennese cinema programmes from the time *Blind Husbands* was playing, so you could see not only in which cinemas the film was playing, but also which films it was competing against. I think these approaches are essential, and they are approaches which only a museum can offer.

_DF: Well, you see, this is exactly the point I'm making. If you want to say, how can we be unique in the contextualization game, if we work together as archives – and that's a separate problem, as I don't think we work together enough – if we supported one another, we would then have a unique position in society in terms of being able to support cultural studies. Which would be very important, because we know that education at the moment is an "in" subject. And we could say, "The Internet can't do that; only we can do that." We not only have the actual film, we have the related materials; we have the curatorial knowledge to do that. But we don't co-operate, on the whole. There's still a private-collector mentality among a lot of archives, which say, "Ah, we've got something unique. You don't have it." And if you ask for it, there are two approaches. Either they want a lot of money for it, or effectively they don't want to share because they need to have a few unique things in order to satisfy their own position in their own environment.

__AH: That's why I think the National Film Preservation model is a good one. Because even though the American archives might still be competing, they are able to collaborate on a different level.

__DF: That was also true under the allocation of the preservation grants from the American Film Institute, because what happened was we all had to respond when someone put forward a proposal. Every other archive had to say what they had on the same film, and what they'd done, and so an archive couldn't go it alone. It was much more transparent; that was a good thing. The Preservation Foundation is transparent. I mean, everything's in favour of it, except the fact that it puts a pressure on us. I don't want to be negative about it. But let's go on to your questions.

__ML: They all refer to the working system, and a philosophical mind-game, and most of it is between the two poles of nostalgia and the authority to interpret and reinterpret history. I understand the question of the working system as Alex has proposed it, since its aim was to preserve a certain historical technique at work in film production and in the public presentation of film. If we talk about the technological aspect, since you said "artefact" as a concept is too narrow, one could go back to the Greek origins of the word "technology" and say it's *techne,* a certain interplay between the materials available and the cultural process that formed the object. But one question that is still unclear to me, because we are always talking about film, is, at which point in time are we entitled to fix a particular notion of what the system is in detail? If a museum must preserve the full working system, then who decides which system to pre-

serve? Film production and preservation have changed considerably over the course of the century, and new technologies in film presentation have not only encroached on traditional notions of what constitutes film, but have probably helped the concept of film to evolve. One other way to put it, to play the devil's advocate, is whether the greatest obstacle to cinema has been film as a *technology.* Of course this is true for all art. There is a constant battle between what is available and what is possible in technology, but what is probably desired is something that is unavailable, or not yet invented.

__AH: What you're saying is: where does one system end, and where does the next begin? On a basic level, I think it's relatively easy to define the borders where one system, let's say film, ends, and another system, let's say Digital, ends. But what is also rightly included in your question are the "sub-systems" or historical stages that add up to become the whole system of film, the numerous historical forms and variants in the system. I think that in preserving the system, archives and museums must certainly differentiate between these variants, and try to be as "complete" as possible in their efforts, at least on a global scale, in the sense of split duties. We should try to have carbon-arc lamp projections as well as all the other light sources, and we should be able to re-stage or re-create 3-D, and Cinerama, and so on; but I also know that at this point in time we have already lost some of these sub-systems.

__ML: Not only the technological ones, but also the cultural ones.

__DF: Well, the cultural ones are as difficult. And I don't know whether one should really attempt that. But I do tend to see the working system as a box of bits, basically. Maybe an *international* box of bits, which will enable us, at least under certain circumstances, to go further than one can with a *national* box of bits. The working system to me is not a fixed system. It's a room with all sorts of things in it. You select the bits that will best enable you to achieve your specific aims: we haven't talked much about experimental cinema, but that is an extremely complicated thing to include in your working system. And it's often difficult to include without the presence of the creator. Once the creator's gone, you're often in a very difficult situation. So I don't see it like Alex; I don't see the working system as a fixed sector. I see it as a box of bits, which you select according to what you're doing, according to your audience, and according to the material you have. But I don't know if we're getting to the basic part of your question or not.

—**ML:** No, this was part of my question. Since, with a very strict version of the working system, one would end up with something leaning more towards nostalgia than real interpretation; where a film museum becomes a place where you can recreate a certain historical situation or historical technique, but has completely lost any connection with the evolution of the technology and its cultural use. Take for instance the film library at MoMA. Many silent films have been handed down as reduction copies in that collection, a collection which was primarily not aimed at representing silent masterpieces in their complete scope, but making them available. If this library were now done away with, there would be two distinct options. On the one hand, one could try to reconstruct the original works as closely as possible to their former

shape. Or one could think about what a circulating film library, a living film culture, is like in the 21st century, and adopt strategies to follow these models of dissemination, of showing films and mediating films to a public that are probably not historically accurate.

—**AH:** I think we're doing that all the time. I think that archives starting to produce DVDs are in some way an equivalent to what MoMA aimed at when they started the circulating film library. Certainly in a different shape, form, and aim…

—**DF:** But it is worth discussing, because I believe if an archive creates a DVD, then somewhere 35mm prints of the same material should be available for rent at a reasonable price. That was the Library of Congress's approach, and that was the Film Preservation Foundation's approach, but it isn't the approach of a lot of archives.

—**AH:** It was the approach of the circulating film library at MoMA, I think.

—**DF:** Well, exactly. So if you're saying, what is the equivalent of MoMA today, I would say it was still the MoMA Circulating Library. I wouldn't want it to rent 16mm copies of films made on 35mm any longer. I'd want it to have 35mm copies. What the Library of Congress used to do was give them a 35mm copy of everything we put on VHS or DVD, so that we could say on the package that all the films are available for hire and projection on 35mm. I don't want it on 16, because 16 wasn't in most cases the original format, and in some cases it would look worse than the VHS/DVD. I'd prefer them to see the films on 35, unless of course they were made on 16. I think that MoMA should continue to do what it has done for so many years. I have no objection to the projection of DVDs. I just want the DVDs to be controlled culturally by the archive, so that the films accurately represent the original. Now, as I say, we have to decide how far we go. I think the *Treasures* is a model DVD. The notes are extremely good, the transfers are good, you don't have situations where you're showing a version of a silent film copied onto sound stock. The DVD is now a suitable form of distribution for archives. It is just simply exerting a level of control, and establishing a Code of Ethics for archive DVD presentations. It's as simple as that. The format is here. It's got to be taken advantage of.

__ML:__ Another example that in a way shook my understanding of the working system and of film presentation, was when I saw the restored version of *The Battle of the Somme* in London, the digitally restored version presented on HDCam. At this event the film was seen in a quality nobody had seen it in possibly since 1917. The picture was free from damage and dirt, and the frameline and title-card typography were stabilized. My first reaction was astonishment as to why I liked it so much, and why it was such an impressive event. I found an easy way out of my dilemma saying, "This is not film anymore: those title cards look like a PowerPoint presentation; nothing moves, you don't have the slightest jitter." But if you go back to historical accounts of what cinema was like then, you find that audiences appreciated things like the three-shutter blade to get rid of all the flickering, and the improvement in projection equipment, and the improvements in technology to make the presentation as perfect as possible, with as little influence of artefacts in the sense of material traces. I suddenly thought, 1917 audiences prob-

ably didn't care which material was projected, as long as it was a good projection. So why should 2007 audiences care?

__DF:__ The audiences don't care, but archives must. I can show you where it can go wrong. For example, look at a Lumière film of people rowing in the harbour, which has been stabilized so effectively that you don't see the rocking of the boat! But no, I mean, I have the same feeling. The quality of digital projection is so good, although it is a slightly different experience – unfortunately, it's very difficult to explain the difference in words. But, you have to say, this often happens. My wife uses films in teaching, and quite often she has the choice of a good 16mm print or a DVD. Invariably she shows the DVD, because it is simpler and more flexible, and often better quality. Her concern is how to give the students the best experience.

__AH:__ It depends on what you want to do. I would never make the argument dependent on what the audiences wanted or felt like, because it's not the museum's job to create a consumer situation. The museum's job, among others, is to make the work and the presentation as transparent as possible, to communicate to visitors the relations between what is onscreen and the processes that brought it about. That's why we shouldn't just substitute one for the other, because then we can't explain it anymore. Only by using the system of film can we explain the whole.

__ML:__ But there's a fine line between transparency, on the one hand, and imposing criteria in a pragmatic fashion. For instance, as you now have the classroom example: if someone at a university was going to screen one of those educational films, to teach a class of cultural history students the impact of historical classroom films, it would be extremely important to set up a 16mm projector, and show it in 16mm, so they can recreate the classroom situation the film was intended for. It's really important to do that. If you can't do it technology-wise, you need to find certain ways, and this is where the museum comes in, because a university probably can't do that. To make transparent all the background is the main problem I have with the Internet Archive, because all the information of the original format and the original intended use, etc., is missing. The pictures are just there.

—AH: As soon as you set up the working system, you suddenly are able to talk about all these elements.

—ML: It's not about the re-enactment of former systems; it is about mediating a certain technological and cultural context.

—AH: That's the main difference to the nostalgic approach. I'm not at all for making audiences believe they are seeing a film "as your grandparents did". If there is too much emphasis on "historical re-enactment", we'll find ourselves in theme park territory soon.

—DF: But there's one thing that we don't do which worries me, and that is use the right-size screen. If you look at a cinema of 1912 or so, and you look at the size of the screen relative to the size of the auditorium, it's very small. And that makes quite a difference to the experience, as does the type of light source used, and the throw. Early screens were also not as reflective. An archive cinema really needs a choice of screens, to represent different periods in film history.

—AH: A real film museum would certainly need more than one space.

—DF: Well, at MOMI in London the cinema had three screens, one behind the other, and you pulled down the screen suitable for your presentation. The textures were different, and the sizes were different, in order to show people what things looked like at a given period in time.

—AH: That's how you can present the various sub-systems. But I think it would be wrong to recreate certain curtains or decorative elements in the room. We should just be able to present to the viewer some basic models of screen experience in relation to the films, which were not only created *for* these specific experiences, but also *by* these experiences.

—DF: Yes, exactly. We want to keep away from nostalgia. Because I think one of the big problems, and I know it is at the National Film Theatre in London, is that it looks like a retirement home. The audience was young when it first started going there, but it's still the same audience, for the most part. There is very little new blood. My sons rarely go to the cinema. They're busy looking at movies on their cell phones or computers. Why go out, when you can see a movie without moving, more cheaply?

—ML: Should museums then devise strategies on how to present film in the age of mobile phones?

—DF: We must engage younger people, because our own future can only exist if there's another generation that's going to be interested in what we have done, and are doing. A lot of things we've been talking about, we talked about when we built the Museum of the Moving Image in London. The whole decision to use 35mm film, and to show visitors the projection process, was part of the idea to explain to people what the experience was. We had to use a continuous projection system, but the film was shown on a screen in a viewing room. The projection was an exhibit in its own right. Again, things like the actors were partly an attempt to try and contextualize exhibits, so that the exhibit was not behind glass, but was something that came to life.

—**ML**: They were not only actors who played a role, they were tour guides and educators.

—**DF**: But the problem was that the actors took about 3 to 4 weeks to train, and yet they were burnt out in 4 months, so we had to train another lot, and eventually we couldn't afford the money to pay them while we were training them. So, again, the system worked against us after a time. It was fine to start with. I liked what you said originally, because you made me think. A lot of the things we were trying to achieve in MOMI were similar to those I would like to see in archival presentations. We didn't quantify our ideas then; they just happened as a result of discussion.

—**ML**: Maybe the question wasn't as pressing when MOMI was designed as it is now. What was the competition at that time, culturally? Television, VHS, never encroached on archival presentations as DVD does. So in this case you had the liberty to create something without having to weigh it up against all those other cultural forms.

—**DF**: But we actually were in the beginnings of the electronic environment, because it was all controlled from videodiscs.

—**ML**: Really?

—**DF**: Yes, all the moving images, except those projected, originated from videodisc. Again, you could see the engineers working in the control room, and ask them questions. The videodisc machines controlled 150 hours of moving images. So we were on the edge of new technology.

—**ML**: In a way I find it so significant that it's closed, and that now the South Bank is this big undecided case.

—**DF**: I'd love to find somebody to fund an experimental archive. You know what I mean – where we could try out ideas without having to worry about the financial implication, and where we could try and put into practice the ideas we are talking about theoretically. I would just like to have the ability to change, represent, and rethink until we got things right.

—**AH**: Where there's no question of failure or success.

—**DF**: No, purely an experiment. If somebody would fund an experimental archive/museum, so that you could try things out, because I feel we are floundering a bit.

—**ML**: A place where you can reverse engineer – to use a digital term – our artefacts back into historical practices. Where you can, on the one hand, historicize, and, on the other hand, work trans-historically in terms of contextualization. But you need certain liberties to do that, and for that you need a strong curatorial agenda. And I think this is why digital is so tempting. It's seems to offer itself exactly to this way of thinking, because it allows for instant change, comparison, and assimilation of certain scenarios.

—**AH**: But it seduces you into using it as a substitution for the thing itself, instead of just using it as an experimental tool.

—**DF**: Well, that's the whole problem. There are so many potential opportunities, and so many issues to solve. It is difficult to know where to start.

Chapter 5

Presentation and Performance

___PCU: I think I'm going to start our discussion head-on, with one of those brutal questions that are part of our ongoing discussions in the museum world. A colleague returned from a conference in Toronto where Sony exhibited their 4K digital projection of *Dr. Strangelove*. The person who I'm talking about is a sophisticated cinephile, and he came to me and said, "Paolo, this projection was fantastic. I couldn't possibly tell the difference, and I think this is it." So here's a typical case of a literate cinephile, basically saying that the whole debate on the alleged superiority of 35mm over digital is now history. In a way, this viewpoint advocates the irrelevance of the medium in relation to the delivery of the cinematic experience. And this fundamentalist, radical viewpoint has come up a number of times. So I thought, why don't we start with this? What is your instinctive reaction to this?

___AH: Well, my reaction is that I somehow felt this would be coming, and I didn't fear it because I always thought that one should not discuss this issue in terms of "does it look better?" There have been a number of attempts at comparison, and the usual line of defence from a certain type of film person reared on celluloid projection was always, "Well, look at the differences in sharpness and colours, look at the blurry effects if there is a certain movement, etc." So it

was always argued wrongly, I think, along the lines of: "Video or digital or whatever doesn't *look as good.*" I always thought that this was a pretty shaky and problematic way to argue for film, because I was sure that what you just described would happen at some point, and sooner or later regular audiences as well as cinephile or cine-literate audiences would say that the image coming from a digital projector looks as good or better, so to speak, than what we know from film. So my argument would never be the question of "better", because you can play the same game with other arts or forms of expression that humanity has developed. There would always be the moment when one certain thing, one certain technology, one certain method of thinking in images or articulating thoughts in a certain medium, could be replaced with a "better-looking" alternative. Talk about this has been going on in the commercial arena of moving-image projection for a decade or so. We're still waiting, but I'm sure that as a matter of course the regular practice of showing and seeing movies will soon be based on digital projection. As long as there is a market, the older, classic films will also be shown that way in the regular venues. *Dr. Strangelove* is a good example, because it's seen as an "enduring" film, and has been regularly re-released in the last 45 years. In

Austria it had at least two or three re-releases, and that sort of re-release will probably be done digitally in 5 years.

I think that the museum argument *vis-à-vis* these situations should never be based on the question of "does it look better in another medium?" The real question is, if we feel the necessity to transmit a certain technology and a certain way of thinking in a specific medium, namely film, to future generations. This is not an issue of "looking better", because many forms of human articulation have been transmitted to future generations even though the perceptual effects that those forms produced were later "improved" by a newer form, according to the logic of "improvement" prevalent at the time. Nevertheless, there was a need, at least among certain constituencies, to transmit the older technology. So the basic issue for me is that museums cannot look at this with the sheer gut feeling of a moviegoer, even if it's a very cine-literate moviegoer, even if it's me myself. If there's a moment when I see *Dr. Strangelove* shown digitally, and I have the gut feeling, "Wow, it's as good or even better than before," this experience will not make the reasons go away why I think people should be able, today, and in 50, and in 500 years, to understand and enjoy the technological and aesthetic processes which, from the late 19th to the late 20th century, added up to a way of thinking that functions very differently than the digital way of thinking does, and that produces very different results. In this line of reasoning, the result – the work, the experience – is inextricably bound with the processes by which it came into being, even if the viewer's consciousness does not make that difference. I still think that uncon-sciously it does make a big difference whether half of what your eyes perceive per second is black or not, as in digital. But that's not the point. The difference is being able to explain and make transparent what this method of thinking and what this type of articulation is really about. I think to do that one needs the film strip, the whole machinery of cinema, the recording machinery, the editing machinery, the projection machinery: all the elements which go into the system of film. So, again, from a museum standpoint the real question is: "What do we need to do to be able to transmit that medium into the future?"

__PCU:__ This raises two key questions. I happen to agree with you on the fact that there clearly is a difference in the kind of perception of the screened photochemical sequence of 24 or whatever frames per second, a point in time when there is black and then another image appears, and the perception of the electronic or digital image. And I'm absolutely convinced that this intervenes at a level that is probably unconscious. I know of people like John Diamond, an American researcher who is doing experiments on the consequences of these two kinds of perception, both visual and aural, on the human body. That's one point. The other point: at the cost of over-simplifying the issue, I'm going to put it in these terms: it's not a matter of saying this is "better", or this is "worse", but this is *different*. It's a *different* kind of experience.

__AH:__ Exactly. Well, it's not only an experience, but also a different method of creation. It's a different method of making certain things happen, and the things that happen become different in the process.

__PCU:__ Yes, a different experience, and a different

method of creating moving images. When it comes to the different experience, the standard answer we get is either "What is this difference?" or "I don't see the difference." And we are actually challenged by people saying to us, "I challenge you either to adequately conceptualize this difference, or even to perceive it at all." Meaning: "If we were not told that this is a strip of polyester film being projected from the projection booth, this difference would not be apparent to us." I, too, maintain that a sophisticated eye could do that, but I'm ready to be told I'm wrong. However, the fact remains that indifference to the diversity is an argument that is used again and again in this context. What is left is the recognition of the historical identity of a certain mode of creating and exhibiting moving images, but even this is easily labelled as fetishism.

—AH: What's interesting is why this accusation of fetishism is not turned against other art forms or other forms of objects, because one could do the same thing, and present digital reproductions of drawings, let's say, and for the general viewer, the difference would not be visible. If we look at the issue of "where's the difference?" only from the point of view of the so-called consumer or the general museum visitor, then we'd run into several areas where this discussion would need to take place. If we don't *see* the difference immediately, where is it? Well, the difference might be in how the work came about, and how this process shaped the result in hundreds of ways.

It's really a question of basic convictions: if you treat these issues as a historical materialist, you can't get around the fact that all phenomena that we encounter in daily life or in culture can and should be derived from material relations. And it becomes quite a high value to understand – and to educate others to understand – these relations, such as the genealogies of where things come from. This extends, of course, to the realm of politics, ideology, discourse. Where do the prevalent notions, myths, beliefs, in a given society come from? What are the material sources of certain discourses? The debate more or less ends if you say, "Well, that's not my world-view." If your world-view is based on the position that what really counts is how things appear to us, and that it is unimportant where they come from, which stages they went through along their historical development, then the discussion we're having is of little use. We could then simply understand a phenomenon by looking at it. We wouldn't need to know what the phenomenon "went through" to become the appearance in front of our eyes and ears.

So in a way, that's where the positions split. For a materialist, it will always be essential to study and engage with certain historical practices, because to him or her nothing is eternal, nothing is out of history. Any historical practice – including present-day practices, of course – is based on certain material relations and technologies, without which they would be a different practice. If a certain type of mechanical system had not been built, certain kinds of images, effects, experiences, and – importantly – a certain way of thinking with these tools, would not have come into existence. The fact that there are now other systems to create similar images, effects, and experiences, if not the same way of thinking, takes nothing away from the importance of knowing about and being able to enjoy this older historical system that persisted for at least 100 years. To understand why the things it created look the way they look.

Maybe this seems like too "detached" a view, which disengages itself from the general viewer's everyday experience, but for me it's part of the ethics of any educational or museum-type institution, to be transparent and to enlighten everybody who is interested in the backgrounds and historical processes that led to a certain phenomenon, or a certain experience. The moment when Person A sees Artwork B on Screen C transmitted by Process D. That constellation, that moment when 500 people are sitting in a Toronto theatre watching Grover Crisp's 4K digital restoration and projection of *Dr. Strangelove*. I think they should simply be able on a basic level to understand the stages that came before, which led to this moment in time, and to this specific experience they are sharing.

__PCU: OK, now I think you have paved the way for a discussion on a very radical cliché, so I'm going to spend the first part of our conversation really addressing these clichés head-on. The overwhelmingly predictable answer – and it's something we have all experienced one way or another – to what you just said is: "Well, yes, but cinema is an art of reproduction. Don't compare an art of reproduction with the original." Invoking the magic name "Walter Benjamin" is supposed to cut all discussion about this – "cut the nonsense, don't compare apples with oranges". And whenever we advocate the materiality of the film experience, the answer we mostly get is either a sort of an ironic smirk or silence, or, again, the allegation that we are attributing too much importance to this element. At which point one is tempted to say, "Look,

East is East, and West is West, and they are never going to talk to each other." But this won't solve the problem.

__AH: No. What I would say, also trying to answer David's question in Chapter 4, is that the Benjamin argument is a very important one, but it actually supports the position I'm taking. That's why it's probably better, as Michael mentioned before, not to compare film with the types of articulation that produce a unique object, but with those historical processes and types of articulation that produce more than "one thing": methods of printing, lithography, etc. I think what Benjamin teaches us, or what the history of the 19th century shows in the development of mass culture, is actually a rising scepticism about the question of the unique object and its aura. I think that's what Benjamin strongly contributed to. He writes about what happens in the history of human thought and culture when works or forms of expression appear, like photography and film, which can be considered to be among the arts, but do not rest on the unique object. What I would answer to the person you just imagined is that there is a big difference between reproducing "internally" in a reproductive medium, according to the logic of this medium, and substituting one reproductive medium for another. Benjamin also talks about reproductions of fine art. He talks about the loss of the aura in terms of the huge proliferation of famous artworks in late 19th-century households, when suddenly you could "own", so to speak, the *Mona Lisa,* or whatever painting, by buying one of the new – first it was black-and-white – reproductions of these paintings, which were also in illustrated magazines, and made consciously as a commodity for the home market. This also goes for drawings and other things, of course. So there is the loss of an aura, but it is very obvious that this "auratic" loss derives not only from the "lost uniqueness" of the original object, but also from the transfer onto another medium.

On a secondary stage, you get new mass media in the 19th century that are inherently reproductive to begin with, like photography or film. And for Benjamin, these new media made the loss of aura even more obvious. But as we know now, they tend to develop their own "auras", not so much in the sense of the single object, but as systems – just as previous reproductive systems had. At any rate, if you get that ironic smirk from people, it's usually because they won't see the difference between the process of Reproduction A, which is the basic ingredient of a reproductive medium, and the process of Reproduction B, which is the transfer of a work or image from one medium – reproductive or not – to another. It seems so obvious to me that in the case of Reproduction A, you really don't lose anything – apart from generational loss, of course – but you actually fulfil the "dream" of the medium by reproducing it, by making positive copies of a negative, and by making a negative of a master positive. You not only stay inside the framework of the medium, but you're making the dream of the medium come true. Whereas if you enter the type of Reproduction B, you dream another medium's dream; and you have to give up some basic characteristics of the first medium in the process. So it's just necessary to clearly separate those two notions of "reproduction".

Benjamin was certainly right in the sense that when reproductive media like photography and film became so prominent, we basically needed to rethink our relationship to artworks and to cultural objects in general. But that has not kept art museums in the 20th and 21st centuries from engaging in a renaissance or continuation of what I'd call possessive 19th-century bourgeois culture, which Benjamin was so critical of. They try to hold on to that unique object, and make the value of their institutions dependent on the value of the unique objects they have. That is why it was necessary for this type of art museum also to find ways of introducing uniqueness, originality, and authenticity into the reproductive media. That's why, as David has written, they found ways of convincing their constituencies that only the vintage print of a photo touched by the hand of the artist can be counted as an original. Of course, there can be later photographic prints made, but the real "auratic" version of a photograph would be the one that was made during the era by the hand of the photographer.

Now, you could try and extend that on to film, and I think it would become really difficult, as David suggested. Mainly because, if we speak about industrial cinema, or film which is not created by one person, the "touch of the artist" is a real problem. If we think of film as a form that often has many authors, and whose actual author is the producer or company which has released the work into the world, whose stamp are we talking about? Which kind of vintage print could be counted as an original one? You can maybe play the game with Kubrick, because we know that Kubrick really tried to be there and to give his personal approval to individual prints. But not even he was able to do that in every single case. And in most cases of industrial cinema it is not possible at all. So there could not be, in that sense, the "vintage print touched by the hand of the artist". And I think this is not at all a bad thing. It's actually a good thing, because it tells us that we're now dealing with art forms and other kinds of cultural production that go against the idea of the unique object.

Obviously, the "auratic" vintage object is so valuable to art museums because they can claim that the "soul" or the breath of the creator is materially attached to it, and can still be felt on that object. That's what I like so much about film museums, in a way. It's true that in some current debates about the art market – which today includes a lot of moving image works – it does become quite complex, but in general the collection of prints in film museums does not follow the discourse and criteria of uniqueness. You usually acquire a print, and in most cases you pay what it costs to make the print, or a certain additional fee for being able to show it. But it's never a discussion of huge values attached to the object or of a vintage print touched by the hand of Louis B. Mayer or Stanley Kubrick. For me this whole discussion brings into focus not only the field of film but the social role of museums in general. Its seems to me that art museums are now behaving more like 19th-century institutions than they did 30 years ago. So it should be possible from that discourse to focus on the strangely old-fashioned and possessive practices that art museums engage in today.

__PCU: What you are saying is that in a film museum situation, a museum acquires a print not because it's unique, but because it represents what the museum would like to exhibit.

__AH: Yes, it represents what that medium does, and did.

__PCU: What we have called the "ironic smirk" has recently taken on a new variation, a more subtle variation, from people giving us the argument: "How are we dealing with the fact that an increasing number of films are being released on 35mm, but the intermediate elements are digital?" We also hear remarks such as this: "Well, you're so opposed to the interference between media, so I guess you wouldn't want to show this print, because it was created with a digital intermediate."

__AH: I don't have a problem with that, because I see that film has never been a fixed process or system. It's a system that underwent various dramatic changes during its existence, and one of the most recent ones is that many film works are being produced with digital *and* analog means. I call them "film works" because the point that defines the work for me is the point when it becomes a public fact. If, for whatever reason, the producers or artists have decided that they want a 35mm print to be the shape in which the work reaches its public, then it's that 35mm film we should be able to represent in the future. If the producers decide to make the film public both in the form of analog and digital projection, we should be able to represent both in the future. And if they believe, as is the case with many documentaries today, and will soon be the case with other works, that digital projection should be the way in which the work reaches its public, then we have to preserve and represent it that way. It's becoming quite obvious what this means for digital preservationists. There are already discussions now about preserving on film certain works that are fully digital – created digitally and made public digitally – just to be on the "safe side", because too little is known about the long-term viability of digital storage. I'm sure, or at least hopeful, that solutions will be found for the long-term preservation of digital works, but let's imagine what might happen in 50 years' time. Maybe the curators of digital-culture museums and archives will have a hard time in correctly representing the digital works. What if they want to show the great Pixar film from 2013 which was made digitally and only shown digitally? Will they have to go back to the polyester negative that was made by the Disney archivist who feared that all the data could get lost? Will they have to make a new scan of that archived 35mm material to be able to show that digital work in its original form?

___PCU: I can assume they will do that, on the basis of what I see as the fundamental issue of the indifference to the medium. They will not have a problem with that.

___AH: No, and maybe they shouldn't. But they should realize that to be able to represent this Pixar film "correctly", they may then have to go back to the film intermediate in order to restore the work's original digital form. Just as today in digital restoration a film is being scanned, then worked on digitally, and then recorded on film. This can be criticized, of course, because we are changing the "genetics" of the work by using digital means in restoration, even if we record it back on film in the end. It's the same discussion as in the example that I tried to give – just vice versa.

___PCU: I think that the fact that we're having this conversation at this point in time – and this point in history is also significant – is that I assume that we are now thinking about how often this photochemical film heritage will be pre-

sented in the digital world. In a world where moving images will be created and distributed digitally, the "product" will either not exist as an artefact, or will present itself in a different form. I will be discussing this later, but just to mention it briefly: what will be the role of the film museum, what will the film museum collect in a world where moving images are exhibited digitally? And will the film museum be allowed to collect at all? Will the film museum be allowed to collect images digitally? I have my doubts.

___AH: Well, I mean, there are two levels on which that question should be answered. The first is: is a film museum or archive professionally even equipped or able to collect and preserve digital work? Because I think from an ethics standpoint that is the first question an institution needs to ask itself. "Can we even do it in a way that's not ridiculous from the start? Do we have the budget, the machinery, the competence, the human resources, the space, and whatever is needed to start collecting those works?" If they are truthful, some institutions would probably have to say, "Well, we are not, or not yet, equipped to do that." On the other hand, I know there are some – not museums as such, but national archives, let's say – who have already had to deal with this question, and are already in the middle of the process of dealing with it – like the Scandinavian archives, for instance. Jon Wengström and Thomas Christensen talked to me a lot about this issue in Bologna last year: "Are we able to?" "What do we need?" "How many people do we need?" "How much money do we need?" "What kinds of machinery do we need?", etc. Because in their case the rights-holders are not the real problem. In most of these countries there is a law that rights-holders, in whatever shape or form the work is, have to give it to the national archives, and the national archives have to be able to preserve it.

But the second layer, the one that you addressed, is the question of an institution like the one I'm responsible for, the Austrian Film Museum, which does not have a legal national brief of that sort. Rather, it is supposed to collect representatively the film heritage of the world. I feel quite similar to you in that I do not see the studios making available copies, digital or on whatever medium, to be collected in the film museums of the world. They will probably say, "The film will always be where we are, and anyone who wants to show it can get it from us" – since it won't be a physical object anymore. It can be loaned: you simply hook into the rights-holder's licensing department, and after payment the stream of data starts to flow. So the museum's dependency on the rights-holders may become far greater than it is now. But to talk about this difficulty means we have cleared the question on the first level. Would we even be able to store and preserve the data of Sony's digital film, if it were available for collection? I'm not sure if that is the case.

What I'm consciously saying – and this is a no-no, or the biggest fear for many film-museum people – is that film at some point soon may be understood as a historical medium that is no longer practiced in contemporary industrial production, and only on a small scale in the world of independent, artisanal creation. I for one have no real problem with the notion that a film museum cares for a medium or for objects which are "historical", which are no longer in widespread use in contemporary cul-

ture. Just as I have no problem visiting a museum of technology and seeing the big locomotives of the 19th century there. I want to see them, and I think we should be able to see them, to understand how transportation developed, how the industrial society of the 19th century developed – and ideally, we should see them in action, of course! In order to understand 20th-century art and mass culture, we should also be able to go to a museum of film, which takes care of this aesthetic system even if it is no longer in use in the contemporary culture of 2030. There are so many important museums and collections that deal with the "past achievements" of humanity – from archaeological museums to the Musée d'Orsay in Paris. It does not make this institution a less interesting place just because it's not engaged with contemporary culture in terms of its collections. It's at least *one* possibility I see for film museums, and I'd have no problem with it if it were to become a reality.

_PCU: This, of course, assumes that – it was easier long ago, now it is not so easy – if you want to have a new 35mm print of Eisenstein's *October,* you could do that: "I think this film is important. I would like to have it for this museum's collection because I think we should have it." If a film of this kind was made in the year 2013, or whenever digital projection becomes the norm, regardless of what we think of the historical importance of the film, this may no longer be the case. Or, if we want to push the argument a little bit further, it may be that 100 years into the widespread distribution of films in digital form – if in the year 2200 someone in the field of moving images wants to show this milestone of a film that was created in the year 2055, this may not necessarily be possible. So what I'm saying is that the very existence of what we call a film museum beyond the analog era is completely open to question.

__AH: At the bottom of all this, we have the question of whether humanity will be able to represent all of this history in the service of the public and not in the service of the rights-holder. This is a level of debate that is not new, because it has been discussed in relation to film for a long time. Again, it takes us back to the political arena, to the question, if governments have by now been able to accept that film production is not only a private economic endeavour in order to make money for those who take part in it, but something that should survive in another realm, that should serve the public beyond the economic needs of the producers. We have discussed that in relation to film, and we are discussing it more and more in relation to digital works, because, as you said, the prints will not be around as much as they used to be in the "film era". So the question is, will the French, Swiss, Swedish, U.S. governments be able to formulate a policy in the service of the public, in the service of history, in the service of being able to study cultures of all eras? Will there be policies which make it a necessity for any producer of moving-image works – and this would include of course the digital works like the digital *October* of 2013 that you mentioned – that these works are deposited and are made available for museums who are responsible for that type of culture, for that type of experience, in order to enable public servants in the cultural arena to show them? In the digital world it's not so much a question of having a print or a replica or whatever in the museum, the policy could also simply try and make sure that – on the basis

of certain rules and regulations – any producer of a work needs to make it available for research, for presentation through museums, and that there are limits to how the rights-holders can stop the public from being able to engage with these works. It's about copyright regulation, about finding a balance between the rights of the producer and the rights of the public, who should be able to engage with these things beyond their commercial characteristics, but also as artefacts and objects of a culture that needs to be studied. So, for that digital *October* from 2013, there should be policies enabling a student in 2028, without being asked to pay a million dollars, to see and work with it. And museums should be able to show it in the way it was originally made public.

__PCU: So this means in practical terms that – to translate this into a scenario – one may say, OK, it is no longer conceivable for the producer to give anything to the museum or the archive. I think there should be a provision that in certain cases or under certain circumstances the copyright owner will not unreasonably deny the film museum the right to publicly exhibit this digital moving image for cultural purposes.

__AH: Exactly. That's more or less what I mean. And there's another aspect implicit in your previous question: When I say I don't mind film museums becoming historical, in the sense that they stop collecting new works – because none are being made any longer – or that they only deal with a past technology, it certainly includes the necessity to have the means, the budget, and the ability to reproduce the basic ingredients of that past system they are caring for. Just as it has happened in the area of restoration in other fields: certain technologies, certain methods of applying colour to a ground, let's say, do not exist anymore as widespread everyday practices; they only exist because museums need to be able to work with them in restoration. So, in that sense, historical film technology, including the raw film materials, needs to survive for the purposes of this museum I've been describing. This will really be a question of the cultural status and the political and social acceptance of the medium as an important form of expression in the history of humankind. In order to transmit the medium to future societies, we need to have the possibility, which also means the money, to reproduce all the basic elements, like the film strip, editing machinery, film projection, etc. Of course, all of these will have to be continued on a much smaller scale than in the commercially defined film system, but on a high level of quality that allows the museological standards to be kept. This is definitely a pressing question, and it depends on the social awareness that film cannot simply be supplanted by digital technology. That's why I think it is so important to discuss these differences and characteristics, in order to better communicate and understand on a political and public level why it makes sense to "invest" in the preservation of this system or medium.

___PCU: From my perspective, I am convinced that the survival of the technology that makes it possible to re-create the analog cinematic experience is simply linked to the demands of the industry, insofar as the industry will feel safe in keeping an analog printing or preservation element, because the industry does not trust any form of long-term digital storage (which seems to be the case, incidentally). That is the best guarantee that these facilities will continue to exist.

___AH: You're probably right.

___PCU: I do not see any other way. In addition to this – and this may seem a kind of grossly pragmatic consideration – but from my vantage point I have seen that even the environmental regulations being imposed on labs for the treatment of photochemical film are becoming so strict that it will become increasingly difficult to put together a lab. Just to give you an example: the main issue for a film lab is that it uses an inordinate amount of water, and this water is being contaminated by chemicals. Even in Hollywood this is becoming a problem. What was until not long ago considered a matter of course for a film lab is closer to becoming a liability. The residuals of a film lab are now becoming a liability for the labs themselves: they have to pay very large amounts of money in order to ensure this contaminated water is properly treated. Now, we're going from the world of ideas to the protection of the environment! But if I put all these things together, I keep thinking, as far as the analog period is concerned, every time I hear that major companies are protecting what they call their "assets" in photochemical form, that's when I am persuaded that film will continue to exist for a while. That's also why I regard *The Digital Dilemma,* the 2007 report from the Academy of Motion Picture Arts and Sciences, as such a revealing document, the most important piece of literature for our field in the current decade.

But now I would like to talk a little bit about the public, as this chapter is about the screen experience. When I get deeper and deeper into these discussions about the qualitative differences between one kind of experience and another, or one mode of production and another, somewhere in a corner of my mind it occurs to me that there is another phenomenon we have to take into account, a phenomenon which derives from the proliferation of what – in the current terminology – is called the "platforms", an increasingly larger variety of formats. Be it on an iPod, on phones, or on YouTube – you get the impression that audiences are caring less and less about the quality of the visual experience. And this perception is taking a variety of forms, ranging from the fact that young people are perfectly happy to see *Pirates of the Caribbean* in a relatively low-resolution format on the monitor of their computer – and they're fine with it – to the fact that the degree of tolerance to what I consider appalling conditions of projection is increasing. People do not complain anymore. Actually they never did much, in a way, but things are getting worse. I have witnessed since I began going to the movies people accepting something that in a museum context would be unacceptable. But this rapidly growing indifference to the quality of the projection is taking amazing proportions. Now if that is the case, if the world of YouTube, iPods, you name it, is increasingly desensitized to quality, or is perhaps developing a notion of quality that is completely different from ours: what is our hope to create enough awareness in public institutions so that the public will care? This is what museums are about. Museums will be the place where you can see things the way you cannot see them anywhere else. But what if people don't care? What if people say, "Why should we spend this money on doing that?" Well, of course, our immediate answer is, the difference will be the quality of presentation. I myself hope people will be able to see films here in the archive which

they won't be able to see elsewhere in this country. But the question is, will it matter?
—AH: Well, I really have no answer – apart from one which, again, many people will probably dislike, because it seems to go against the grain of what film has always been for most people, namely, a mass medium. What I see, and what I actually have no real problem with, is the so-called "élite" – but actually quite normal – perspective of wanting to experience a medium, an artwork, or any kind of historical object, in a truthful, transparent manner which is adequate to the medium in question. When you say "the audience" – very many of whom do not care if they see *Pirates of the Caribbean* on their mobile phone or on their computers – I am thinking of previous moments in time, when formerly limited art or cultural experiences suddenly became widespread in other formats, in other media, in other or "lesser quality" shapes and forms.
—PCU: Are you talking of Dürer, for example? Popular prints derived from great works of art?
—AH: Yes, for instance.
—PCU: They were widespread, let's say, in Europe and America in the 19th century, and they were everywhere – especially in rural areas – and these were the way certain works were known. Is that what you mean?
—AH: Yes, and it happened like you say. Suddenly works became "degraded", not only by reproduction *per se,* but in transferral to other media – just as the showing and watching of a film on a computer, iPod, or mobile phone is a transferral to other media. Of course that's a highly popular process, and it was popular before. When we entered a "society of the image", with photography proliferating in huge ways,

and art proliferating through photography, etc., this did not lead to the obsolescence of the original forms of expression. What it *has* led to, in certain periods at least, is that these original experiences tended to become so-called "élite" practices, for select audiences who developed a more detailed interest in the works than the general population. They were now able to go to the Albertina, or any other museum, and see that Dürer etching, or any other work, in the original medium. This discussion about the "élitism" of the museum is an old one, of course, and the ironic, or, rather, extremely ambivalent thing about the recent history of the museum world is that many bigger institutions, in order to counter the discourse about élitism, and also in alliance with the general mass-marketing of everything, have become part of mass culture.

—PCU: There is a populist trend.

—AH: Exactly. I don't see why society shouldn't have certain types of institution that are only interesting for a limited audience. I don't think that all institutions have to be for all people. That would be a very stupid concept of democracy! Anyway, this populist trend has led many museums to a point where they now act in the service of a mass market, but still cling to the "original", to the idea of uniqueness, and to the aura attached to it. It's really a complex topic, and full of ironies, because if you look at how they generally deal with film and other products of mass culture, they are not at all – or not yet – adhering to the same practices that they would adhere to in terms of the other arts. In a way, film and moving images in general are often being used by "museums of unique objects" to become more attractive. They try to produce a discourse that says, "Well, we're not elitist at all, because we have all these moving images, we work with contemporary media, we have Internet stations, mediatheques, etc. We practice the same modes of communication that the general population practices."

I know this leads away from our discussion a little bit, but it's an interesting phenomenon. I believe – and that's what I mean by "ironic" – that film museums, museums that mainly collect and present reproductive media and mass media, can actually play an avant-garde role here. They can be more ethical than the unique-object museums which are now "opening up", as they call it, to the contemporary media experience. What one has to accept in taking a position like this is that these kinds of institutions will not be "for everyone". But they *will* be for everyone who starts to be interested in a certain culture or art form; they should be very open to that person. I don't think it's our job to make every single citizen of our countries a cinephile, or a student of cinema. That's simply beyond the scope of what museums can do. And it would also be a totalitarian dream, like Microsoft's dream of making every citizen of the world a Windows user. Museums can be a public service, I think, for those who are developing an interest; they can stoke the flames of people who are really looking for something, and who might go on to study the field in depth. I do think some of the new populist art museums border on a totalitarian dream. They behave as if every citizen in our brave new world can now become an art lover, or is already an art lover at heart, and we just have to be "open" enough, and use the current media the best we can, to bring out the art lover in every citizen of the world. That leads to the kind of tourist-populist museum which, for real art students, for people who really care about and engage with the medium or field of their choice, makes it almost impossible to use the institution the way they should be able to use it.

—PCU: Yes, but the decisions in this case are not made by those who work in the museums or archives; the decisions are made by those who give the money to run them. These people are the politicians, the government, the ministries, the donors, the founders, the sponsors, who say, "You deserve to exist if you serve the widest possible audience." You know very well that the pressure is on us, and this pressure is increasing exponentially. I do think we haven't done enough yet in order to educate those who give money to our archives and museums, because we have not yet learned how to speak their language, how to communicate a fairly complex content in a perhaps simplistic but effective way. Every time I deal with a funding agency I realize that the real challenge is to use a language that is simple and clear enough that it can be understood by someone who has absolutely no clue of what we're talking about, but won't be further distorted when it is transmitted from one politician to another.

But aside from this, I want to go back to what you were discussing before. My immediate reaction is that in a world where distribution of moving images will be done differently, I think that even a museum or an archive with the adequate means to exhibit moving images will not be able to have the luxury of behaving like museums of the analog period, because what is being exhibited in the museum is no longer a prerogative of the museum. A predictable

reaction may be: "Why should I go to this museum, if I can see it in qualitative terms which I find acceptable elsewhere?" Which means we will have to find a different answer. Regardless of the uniqueness of the item in the collection, or the uniqueness of the access to the item in the collection, we will have to find different reasons to define its existence, and perhaps we can call this reason curatorship, or interpretation, or whatever. This is about the future.

When it comes to dealing with the past of the moving image, in this sense things are perhaps a little bit clearer to define. To follow up on your comparison, one may say that as much as there is a thing called the Opera, which the majority of people listen to in the form of a broadcast or CD or download, there will be a minority of people who go to the Opera. Or there will be someone who will say, "I'd love to go to the Opera to see *Tristan und Isolde.*" And it will be a special event, and no one will question this. They'll have a perfectly legitimate experience under different economic circumstances, and there will be people listening to the music in different ways, whether or not they're linked to the material. So it will be perfectly fine to see *October* in downloaded form somewhere. While someone else will say, "I'm going to go to this film because I can see this example of cinematic heritage in a certain form in a certain place, provided that I care about watching it in a certain way which will make the difference."

—AH: I fully agree. And I also agree that "live" Opera is a good example of a limited constituency that's actually not that small today. Governments spend more on keeping Opera alive than on other art forms which are seen by many more people. So it seems that Opera has survived. We might like Opera, or we might not, but it's a fact. So our obligation is quite simple. If we believe that film has had a strong enough imprint on human culture for a long enough period of time – which is something I *do* believe – the necessity of keeping it alive should be argued.

__PCU: Now there's another big challenge we'll have to deal with, and in a way this is a combination of all the factors we have been discussing so far. OK, let's say that we are a museum dealing with the history of the cinematic heritage of film in its photochemical form. In which case there are two possibilities: first, we take our admission at face value, and we decide that we are going to give our museological presentation in the same material medium the film was presented in. So we show *October* on 35mm film, we show *Dr. Strangelove* on 35mm film. The second possibility is that we take a hybrid approach, meaning that if we can show a good 35mm film of *October*, we do that, and if we can't, or if there is something that passes as a great digital preservation, we will provide a digital preservation of the film. Either way, things are not going to be so simple.

I would like to address each possibility separately. Let's start with the most obvious problem. If we decide to be the place where the 35mm experience is being promoted, this is going to be increasingly difficult, firstly because museums will be increasingly reluctant to borrow prints, expensive as they will be – even more so if the prints are in the hands of commercial entities – and those who have the print will be reluctant to loan them. It will be a case of the survival of the fittest. If you already have a substantial film collection in your vault, you're likely to increase your chances as a museum. If not, it's going to be tough.

__AH: May I interrupt for a second? Just to say one brief thing. That's exactly why I feel it's urgent to go back to the laboratory, and keep the practice of reproducing prints, because in the scenario that you've described film does become the unique object of the art museum, that precious rarity that "I have and you don't, and I will only loan it to you if you loan me that other precious rarity", and so on, with all the attendant issues that exist in the world of "possessive" museums of unique objects. Since film is, in its essence, a different kind of object, it's also necessary to keep the reproduction technology alive: to make editing tables, labs, prints.

__PCU: I would argue that, with a certain regret, there was a time when it would have been possible to make prints more easily that it is now – and we didn't do it. There never was enough money. But that wasn't the only reason. We didn't do it because we were under the illusion that this so-called print exchange would continue to be easy; we were hiding our heads in the sand, not seeing what was around the corner, the fact that this exchange would become increasingly difficult. And, secondly, we did not take enough into account the fact that making a print would be increasingly hard. So where we are now, or where we are heading now, reminds me of what happened in the fine arts in general. If you normally want to see an original Piero della Francesca you've got to go to different places. And then, once in a lifetime, or once every 20 years, thanks to a major financial investment, there is an exhibition assembling all the so-called movable works of Piero della Francesca, but that's an extraordinary occurrence. Or if you want to see Michelangelo, well, there are certain Michelangelos that cannot be moved, so you have to go there. So I wouldn't be surprised if one day someone will be told, "If you want to have a cinematic experience of film so-and-so, you have to go to this film museum, at this time of year." And this film will be announced 6 months in advance, because it will be an exceptional screening of so-and-so. There will be a time when the film museum will have to say, "I'm sorry, this film has to stay on the premises because we're too afraid of moving this print around."

__AH: Yes, we've talked about this before, and I see the possibility of that happening. In my mind, it's not only not ideal, but it's also against the grain of what the medium is. That's why I would argue for keeping the whole system of film production and reproduction alive, to avoid films becoming that type of unique object. But of course I see the possibility that it may turn out like that.

__PCU: I have the feeling that you're more optimistic than I am about our ability to maintain or create the conditions for the production of photochemical film. What comes to mind is Peter Kubelka's comparing what we were talking about with the fact that, until recently, there was no medieval or Renaissance music performed with original instruments – it seemed to be a lost art. And then there were those who found the way, the people who either had these instruments, or knew how to build these instruments according to the original techniques. So Kubelka says, if it happened for very sophisticated musical instruments, it can happen for film. It is a matter which fills me with hope, of course, but I always feel a tinge of scepticism,

because I keep thinking of the fact that the difference between these two possibilities is that the creation of a manufacturing plant presupposes an industrial system, which has nothing to do with the craftsmanship of making an instrument.

__AH: That's true.

__PCU: So now let's look at the second scenario. I'm thinking about future generations of museums, curators, and archivists, about the place where, in the name of so-called "film culture", a curator will accept a film in the best available format, whether this is photochemical or digital. In this scenario, the curator accepts a compromise. Even in this case the life of this curator is going to be potentially very difficult. Or, if I can push the example to the extreme, let's talk about the curator who says, "I do believe that this is all about a story being told on the screen. I want to show the story being told by Bergman, Murnau, and Antonioni, and I'm going to show this digitally." The curator decides to dismantle a 35mm projection booth and replace it with digital projection, assuming that all the economic conditions to do so are there. This curator can upgrade the projection equipment whenever necessary; but he or she will still have a hard time doing so. I have the feeling that this is because of the nature of this technology; there may not be that many films available for viewing. I'm talking about both individual viewing and collective viewing. Will there be fewer films available in digital projection because of the costs associated with that?

__AH: Well, I think that can only be answered if we look at the major producers and major studios. I have too little knowledge, say, of how many digital masters Sony or any other of the major studios make for their library. I would assume that there are many more films with digital masters at the studios than there are DVDs released of these films. It's a question of what the DVD departments believe there is a market for. So a museum – as is the case now – which would have to deal with the rights-holders and certain places material is loaned from, would then go to Fox, or Columbia, or Canal+, and ask, "Do you have a 35mm print on loan of this film? Or do you have a high-definition digital master of that same film for me to show on my wonderful digital machine?" I'm speaking now as the hybrid curator. The answer to your question is: I don't know. I don't think that on that level it will be complementary. I think there will be a number of films that the rights-holders or archives have on 35; there will be a certain group of films that they also have on digital; and there will probably be a third group – which we are encountering now, for instance, in the field of documentary – where the rights-holders will only have digital versions. So in that sense I would think that the number of available films – always thinking in terms of hybrid – might even increase.

For instance, right now we're preparing a show on the "essay film", which is being curated by Jean-Pierre Gorin, and a number of works from the 1970s and 1980s which were made and shown at that time as 16mm prints are hardly available anymore except on DigiBeta. Places like the National Film Board of Canada offer a DigiBeta of a 16mm film they've produced or co-funded – and it takes us weeks and weeks to find out if some archive or previous distributor still has a 16mm print. So for the hybrid curator the unavailable film suddenly becomes available, if he or she is willing to show the DigiBeta of that 1970s 16mm film.

I'd like to use your scenario with the hybrid curator to divert us from the accusation of purism. For me, what's much more important than sticking 100% to analog for as long as we live is the question of truthfulness and transparency in educational work, and I include museums in this domain. I see the hybrid place that you've started to describe as a museum which has a wonderful cinematic screening space, plus an installation-type space with no seats, like the "black box" of many art museums, plus a mediatheque, or a type of "living room" with a television monitor, for works made in this medium. Instead of the audio-guides that are used in art museums, this museum might have mobile phones or iPods for the visitors, with moving images produced for such a medium. The visitors would be made aware that moving images have undergone a long history, in which at certain points in time new carrier media were introduced. For example, people in the 1950s and 60s started to see films not only in cinemas but also on their television screens at home. In the 1970s and 80s it became possible to record films from television, or buy commercially issued VHS tapes, which you could put into a new machine called the VCR, and watch them at home. And then, 15 years later, a medium called DVD was invented; and so on. What the visitors of this kind of museum could take home is a real "bodily" understanding of the differences and distances between these media, and of how, over the 19th, 20th, and 21st centuries, films came into being, how they mutated, and how they were perceived in various media. They would realize that film history is not out on

DVD in its totality, far from it; that there is a limit to what he or she can select from the VHS or DVD library; that it's an already programmed or preselected collection, just as much as the commercial market is.

This museum would also have a programme of "film performances" – by which I mean screenings – in a cinematic space where, defined by time, the act of showing a film, whether it is a 1-minute, 100-minute, or 300-minute film, is presented like Opera is. Say, on a certain date, at a certain time, *October* by Eisenstein will be presented as a 35mm print, and anyone who's interested in that historical era of cinema experience can see that film at that particular time. But they can also decide to go to the video library, and see *October* in a mutated form by self-selecting a time. This would be a different space, more like the one at home; they could take a break, and then continue with *October* an hour later. This whole experience should make everyone aware of the sociological, architectural, and spatial differences between these various ways in which film has had a life. For me this is the important aspect: this clearness in differentiating between ways in which people *have* seen and *are* seeing things, instead of saying there's one space in which we'll show everything on every available medium.

___PCU: So, let me clarify one point. By drawing this scenario are you implicitly or explicitly excluding the fact that there is a place where the cinema experience is portrayed in different ways? And in this place you do not show, let's say, a DigiBeta version of another film in the same space and on the same screen, even if you tell the audiences, "Sorry, this is a DigiBeta"? Would you prefer not to do this?

___AH: Since it's a dream anyway – well, not a dream, but a certain idea of a place that doesn't really exist – I would like to envisage a second type of public space in that same museum, which would represent the 21st-century experience of watching digital works. A space where the upcoming era of digital cinema can find its place. I'm sure that in a few decades we will have the need to show in a museum-like fashion how it was when digital cinema first became a widespread reality. And since ideally I see the presentation machinery as part of the museum experience, visual contact with the machinery should be possible. In that future hybrid moving-image museum, both the "film space" and the "digital space" would include the option to walk past and see the machinery. This sounds super-didactic, I know, but just for argument's sake: I'd also like to see an Avid editing suite, and a Steenbeck, and have it explained how they work…

___PCU: Now I know this may sound like a digression, but I want to raise this point. I'm reiterating it because of what we're discussing. I have the gut feeling that when it comes to the first 50 years of cinema, the fact that there is much less availability of works in the digital domain than in the analog/electronic domain means something. It is a signal. The fact that studying the first 50 years of cinema is more difficult on DVD than doing it on 35 is something we should pay attention to.

___AH: But maybe that's a good sign, because it means that both the providers of moving images and the audiences increasingly understand that in order to experience silent cinema or even early sound cinema, the place to go is not the DVD monitor, but the cinema. All this hype and success of the "restored version", and of silent films with live music – maybe this development is a sign of an increasing awareness, at least for the earlier part of film history. It may be optimistic, but it supports my feeling that the farther away we get from a certain historical practice, the clearer the distinctions become and the less we need to discuss them, because people easily understand them. It's almost impossible to engage on nearly the same level with a silent film on a TV monitor as opposed to a "cinema performance". As you say, DVD mainly focuses on the latter part of film history, because it looks more similar to our everyday contemporary film-going experience. But as film history becomes "longer and longer", more and more eras will fall into what I'd call the "double public domain", not only in the sense of copyright, but also in the sense that it will be the museums, the public institutions, which will be responsible for keeping it alive. Maybe this is something of a natural development, and therefore it grounds my so-called "optimism".

—PCU: From my perspective I was linking this to our discussion of the work of the programmer. I was thinking this must happen because the economic and technological parameters of creating a DVD are more sophisticated and complex than those necessary to create a VHS, meaning that, for better or for worse, creating an OK or a mediocre VHS from a film with modern equipment was easier than creating a DVD. Or, to put it differently, even the way a DVD is packaged is such that – for instance, Milestone Film & Video cannot create as many DVDs as it could VHS tapes, because of the different economy of scale or the different economic parameters related to the creation of a DVD. And I kind of instinctively translate this

into another arena, which is the programmers' domain. And I truly feel that if this is happening with the creation of DVD as opposed to VHS, is this a signal of something that may happen in the programmers' world as well?

But to go back to the core of the question, by making a comparison with the fine arts – by the way, I do not feel ashamed at all in relying on the tradition of fine arts, and I do not feel any kind of slavery or deference towards fine arts – I would say the predominant trend is to have the exhibition aiming either at completeness, or the "ultimate" exhibition, meaning that it is the curator's dream to have the ultimate Cézanne show. This trend can be subdivided into two trends: those who apply curatorship in the most demanding way, meaning having the guts to select, and saying, "I don't care if we don't have the complete works because the complete works are just too many. But I want you to leave the museum with a clear understanding of what the art of Cézanne is," and those who say, "I'm going to put together the most complete possible assembly of Cézanne works." In the latter case, whatever we think about one Cézanne or another, there are cases where the curator who cannot find the key Cézanne will go for the copy.

—AH: Do you mean that is the case, or is that the future scenario?

—PCU: In the fine arts I've seen a copy of a Rubens, or in another case, I've even seen photographs – of something which would be so important to contextualize, that the curator will even accept showing photographs. It is a minority trend, but I've seen it. So when, in the programmers' world, as far as the moving image is concerned, is it your view that if you think that there is a body of work, and think these 20 works are key, but you cannot find Number 19, even though you know it is available in the form you want – OK, which approach do you take? Do you say you will not show this film if it's not in the form that you want it, because you know that a 35mm print exists, and therefore it's that or nothing? Or if you are reasonably assuming that there is no longer a 35mm print available, it's DigiBeta or nothing, and therefore you're making a conscious decision to show or not to show the DigiBeta. So you have different layers of choices here.

—AH: Let me start with your example of the fine art museum. I have no problem with a fine art museum that does a show of those 20 essential works, of which work Number 19 is not available for whatever reason, even though it exists. And it doesn't matter if it exists, or is a lost work. If the curator decides to represent this work Number 19 as a copy, the question is only if he or she decides to present the copy on the same level of experience and appearance as the other 19 works. The curator can lead the visitor to believe that work Number 19 is there, in the same shape and form as the other 19, by reproducing it "close to perfection"; but he or she can also simply supply a photograph or paper copy of that Cézanne painting – thereby clearly stating that this represents a gap, a space in which the work itself is not available, but that in order to make a certain argument not related to the materiality and the actual presence of that work, the curator still had reasons enough to give the viewer a substitute of that work. It's obvious to a child that it's a paper copy copied on a Xerox machine, or it's a photo. I would find that to be an acceptable solution, because it's

truthful; it does not lie to the visitor. It makes a clear distinction.

Now, transferring that example to film curatorial work, I fear, and I actually think – and that's why our policies at the Austrian Film Museum are the way they are – that if you use the same cinema space which people are used to coming to, and used to seeing works in the original medium, for a 35mm projection of *Vertigo* at 7 p.m., and for a high-quality digital projection of *Psycho* at 9 p.m. – maybe because *Psycho* is not available on film right now – then you've landed on the side of untruthfulness. Sure, the curator could stand in front of the audience and explain the whole thing to them. But still, by presenting the digital facsimile in the same way you've presented the other 19 Hitchcocks, you invite the audience to assume it's the same thing.

—PCU: The policy in our theatre at the NFSA is, for example, that works are shown in the new theatre in their original medium. The current theatre has a very good high-definition digital projector, which is used for the exhibition of digital-born works. And we have a 16mm projector and a 35mm projector, so that in the current standing photochemical films are being shown in their native formats. If it's an experimental film on 16mm, we'll show it on 16mm. As a rule, we do not show a film that was born on 35mm in a 16mm format. The only compromise I have accepted is that there is a proviso insofar as a 35mm print exists. This means that if a given work by…

—AH: Let's take the Nicholas Ray example from the Eastman House [*Born to Be Bad*, 1950]. I see it's now being restored on 35, but we had this discussion 3 years ago, and then it was a film from Nicholas Ray's *œuvre* which only survived as a 16mm print, right?

__PCU: Yes. In that case, in this theatre I'll accept a compromise, in that if the only photochemical version is a 16mm, I am making a curatorial judgement that it is still a cinematic experience of a lesser quality, but I'm willing to go that far.
__AH: Same here.
__PCU: Then there is a smaller theatre, which used to be the only theatre of the archive until recently, and that's the place where I would like to show what you were talking about. If work Number 19 is not available, I would rather show a video version there. Now in the fine arts world, there's a sentence commonly found in a review of an exhibition. Let's say you read a prestigious review in the *New York Times*. This sentence goes something like this: "It is regrettable that the important work so-and-so by artist so-and-so was not included in the exhibition." Sometimes they write this with regret, sometimes they write it with the thought, "How could they do this exhibition, and not show this fundamental work?" As if it were a mistake not to do so. And sometimes they say, "It is regrettable, but we understand why, because it is in the very inaccessible private collection of X, or in this faraway collection, which would have been too difficult."

Now, trying to translate this into film terms, leaving aside the discussion on completeness or incompleteness, I imagine an equivalent sentence like, "Regrettably, this Hitchcock exhibition did not include *Under Capricorn,* which is widely considered a minor film in his *œuvre,* but we think it should have been included because of so-and-so." OK, can we imagine a reviewer of this kind addressing a Hitchcock retrospective in this way? Would such a reviewer say, "You know, I think this film should have been included in the exhibition, at least in the media room?"

__AH: Excuse me for interrupting, but I have experienced that a number of times. A film programme that I or other people have curated, where the idea is not to present a complete monographic body of work – let's say our Western show last year, the second part of which is coming up now – we have critics who write, "Well, the curatorial approach is this or that, it's good and interesting, and they include that group of films because the curator wants to highlight that aspect of the genre, but it is regrettable that the East German socialist Westerns of the 1970s are not included." So that type of argument is not foreign to me in terms of film shows, and up to now it has always referred to the curatorial choice. I have no experience yet of a review saying, "It's regrettable it's not there, because they couldn't get it." I don't know how even the qualified media would react if there were a kind of second space where you make it clear that the curator wanted to select a work, but it was not available, so it was decided to make it available in the media room. It's like making the paper copy of the Cézanne available – for the curator's argument, because it was important to represent that work, in some form. I think viewers in general would accept a separation, because it makes even clearer what the curator stands for. As it is now, if a work is not there, the question as to why it's not there is left open – is it because the curator didn't select it, or because they just didn't find a print? I don't see any negative vibes coming from a future policy of that sort.
__PCU: Another topic I wanted to touch on, which is perhaps closer to your heart. You are known as someone who claims that the difference between a film programmer and a curator is that film programming is a creative act, while

curatorship is an interpretative act. Whether or not this is true, I thought, I never heard of the curator of a Cézanne exhibition describing himself or herself as a "creator". I always heard of people proudly presenting themselves as curators, therefore as interpreters. Now, is there any ground for this difference I've described?

—AH: I don't remember ever having made that distinction, I must say! I would say my use of the word "creative" in relation to curatorial or programming work is included in the word "interpreting". At best, a curator in the fields of art, film, or music is the creator of a certain "contextual experience". A person who, mostly through existing works, but in some cases also through commissioning and being involved in the creation of new works, creates a context for the individual works. To interpret and to contextualize is to produce meaning. In that sense it is something of a creative act. Meaning is not something that's openly visible, and it's not fixed either, so it has to be produced all the time. In that sense I do find curatorial work creative, and I'd say the same about critical work, but I would not use the term "creative" in order to place the critic or curator on the same plane of expression as the artist. I don't think there should be a hierarchy, either; both are important activities, but one should understand the different levels of expression. In general, I don't like it when curators in the contemporary art world sometimes play the role of the artist.

—PCU: Well, I completely agree with that. I think this is also the difference between a good festival and a bad festival. The fact that a certain theme is interpreted in a creative or intelligent way, where interesting connections are being made – these are creative acts, in a more or less accomplished way. I think we both recognize that we live in troubled times in relation to curatorship. We are in trouble. Has classical cinephilia contributed to the problem?

—AH: Good question. Maybe it has. But that's a complex affair. On the one hand, cinephilia has contributed a lot of positive things to the current situation – to the fact that there *are* film museums and archives, and that film is, by and large, seen as something that's worth keeping, and transmitting to the future. The various stages of cinephilia in the West – starting with the Surrealist avant-garde in early 1920s Paris – always had a love of popular cinema, and wrote it up as a culture that was about more than just immediate consumption. There's a spin-off in the early 1930s, with silent cinema receding so quickly from the marketplace, and people like the young Langlois feeling the need to keep and collect it. And then, skipping over the "classical" era of cinephile activity to the present age, there has been a lot of debate since the mid-1990s about a "new cinephilia", which is certainly related to the mutational era we're in, the move from film to digital and to the exploding moving-image cultures we see. Some part of this, I think, also supports the creation and expansion of film heritage and educational institutions.

But there is always another element in cinephilia, which tends to be opposed to archival as well as film studies contexts. This element is very much about the "passion" and "desire" – sometimes short for "greed" – which are seen as inherent to cinema, and which the other disciplines supposedly lack. That has to do with a historical constellation; in the era of "classical" cinephilia – let's say 1946 to 1968 – cinema was still a medium "for everybody", so it could be invested not only with an aesthetic, but also a political or social utopia. This side of cinephilia tends to believe that the "real" engagement with film can never happen in an archival or academic context, so there is a certain element of anti-intellectualism or rather anti-institutionalism to it. I know it quite well, because to a certain degree I even feel it in my own relationship to film culture. Something that this side of cinephilia has rarely or never addressed is the concrete material existence of film, and the effects of how we see films.

Just to give you an example: I recently met Jonathan Rosenbaum in Zagreb. He's very much involved now with subcultural DVD and download communities or clubs in Chicago and elsewhere, where there's a massive exchange of rare films beyond the commercial or copyright-dominated realm. Like Jonathan, I am quite fond of these "mutated" film cultures. For Jonathan, the age of the DVD and the download also means a huge expansion of film-historical and film-philosophical thought and criticism – it solves a lot of problems for him. I can, of course, also see it like that from a certain angle. But what I tried to discuss with him is that it makes our work and our job harder at the same time. Because it contributes to the chimera of film's and film history's "all-over availability". And it doesn't put a lot of focus on the issue of *how* we engage with films. From this perspective, the material history of works and the different stages they went through is often a side-thought – as long as we can "access" the film as "content" in whatever way. So, in essence, I wouldn't go so far as to say cinephilia has contributed to our problem, but it certainly makes our problem harder to solve sometimes.

___PCU: Then the next question is, granted that sometimes there is no point in trying to write history with the "what-ifs": "Is there something in our profession and its past history and programmers and curators that you wish had not happened?" I'm talking about mistakes. Is there a key mistake you think we have made?

___AH: I do think that the definition of curatorial work in film was too long defined by people who are not interested in the concrete material aspects of the medium. In the majority of cases, the film programmer is somebody who is very far removed from the actual collections of existing films, from the archivist, let's say. I think one of the reasons for this is that archives are traditionally seen as not very open, so there has been very little exchange between so-called "freelance" film programmers and archive people. This is where the various definitions of the word "curator" stem from. After I had started to work in a film museum, I quickly realized that many people who call themselves "curators" of film have very little interest in how films exist and survive, how they will be and should be presented, or what the relationship is between the concrete film artefact and its individual screening history. I know there are differing notions of the term "curator" in the Anglo-American world and elsewhere. But at least on the European continent, and at least in my and the following generations, a film programmer or curator is regarded mostly as a freelance person, not essentially connected to any collection. As I see it now, with a few years of museum experience behind me, and certainly informed by this experience, a film curator should be someone who knows about "the" collection, or many collections. He or she should not only have seen a lot of films, and made beautiful "wish-lists" from these viewing experiences, but have a knowledge about and an interest in how films have moved about through the ages, what social use was made of them, where they ended up, which versions there are, and, very importantly, how the film screening itself needs to be "performed".

—PCU: Let me interrupt you here. Really, I need to interject. What alarms me is that even today it is not uncommon to see what we call curators and programmers treating film as an abstract entity, far removed from the importance of the materiality of what they are exhibiting. We are talking about a form of curatorship which sees the archival parameters as a nuisance, something that is configured as an obstacle. So the traditional friction between the programmer and the curator in an archive is increasing instead of decreasing. This friction has always been there. The programmer would like to show something that isn't in the collection, and the curator/archivist will say, "Sorry, this is an archival print which cannot be shown," and the film programmer rolls his or her eyes. This is still very much there. We are talking about programmers who are not really interested in what happens in the projection booth. They will complain if the aspect ratio is wrong, or if the speed is not right. But they are not interested in what makes the speed right or wrong. It's this lack of engagement which I find troublesome today; and it's from the same people who are advocating a more sophisticated programming culture.

—AH: I agree, and that's why I would almost want to ban the term "film programmer", at least in archives. You've made the distinction yourself now, between curator in an archive and film programmer. My definition of a "curator" in an archive or museum is the person who knows about the collection, and knows about these aspects you've just mentioned; the person responsible for interpreting the collection, and making the decisions on what the museum should show. The term "film programmer" is something that I associate more and more with the TV person who decides which film to show at 8:30 on Channel 5, or maybe the person who puts together a festival programme – at least they often call themselves "programmers". The real distinction is that in a film museum, "programmer" and "curator" should not exist as separate entities. In museum terms, the "programme" of a film museum is identical to the exhibitions in art museums. Ideally, in both cases it's the curators who decide what is being exhibited or "programmed".

—PCU: In other words – and maybe you are saying the same thing in a different way – so far, if I could express a hope for the future, I would like to see the end of the distinction within the museum and archival institution between the person who protects the collection and the person who exhibits it.

—AH: Absolutely.

—PCU: The person who exhibits the film should also be its best guardian. And the best guardian of the collection, the person who fiercely protects the material, should also be the person who promotes its proper exhibition. There should no longer be a conflict between these two positions: they should be one and the same.

Chapter 6

Curatorial Values: Two Case Studies

CASE STUDY #1:

CURATING THE DOCUMENTA 12 FILM PROGRAMME

__ML: Alex, I'd like to highlight and discuss one aspect of curatorship Paolo and you have discussed: the art and craft of programming, or, moreover, the curatorial dimension of selecting and combining specific works for a specific presentational context. As a case study I'd like to discuss your contribution of a cinema programme, a season of films, to the *Documenta* art exhibition in 2007. What was your motivation – as a curator in a film museum – to do this? I find the idea intriguing, as the programme to me resembles the crossroads of various disciplines and "cultural spaces": The cinema. The archive. The art gallery. The film festival.

__AH: I think there were three motivations, three reasons why I was not scared to get involved in an endeavour as huge and foreign to me as the *Documenta*: (1) I was invited *as* a Film Museum person, not as an amateur art curator. (2) I was also invited as an educator in a way, so I felt that the "missionary" element that's always been part of my working life would not conflict with the job at hand. (3) I liked the possibilities that you mention – to create something that's a bit outside the regular, everyday appearances of film. It could become something like a zoo where the individual cages are gone for a night – or for 100 days, in this case. Without the "cages" all the animals would roam around freely, and love each other or eat each other, or become a beautiful new species together. Which could also be a very old, almost forgotten species. I wanted to deal with a utopian idea (or ideal), where film is not yet split into the various categories or cages – popular, esoteric, documentary, fantastic, short, feature-length, scientific, artisanal, industrial, experimental, vulgar, whatever. I think I was successful to a certain degree, but not totally, because in the end I must admit that I do read every film through the prism of aesthetic creation. To me, cinema is a place where new perceptual, emotional, intellectual, even physical, experiences are being made, where I can get unique readings and "viewings" and "hearings" of the world. I use this perspective even when looking at and loving a scientific film or a newsreel or George Romero's *Land of the Dead*. Apart from several other connotations, the title of the *Documenta* film programme, *"Zweimal leben / Second Lives"*, is also related to this, to the aesthetic function of cinema – in the old-fashioned (but proven) sense of individual renewal through aesthetic experiences.

__ML: Have you, over the course of the last

decade, followed what has happened to "film" – or moving images – in the art world?

___AH: I have followed this field, and the development of the "filmic" as a celebrated art world phenomenon, more or less continuously since the early 1990s, but with varying degrees of intensity. I co-curated two shows which also fall into this in-between area. In 1998, together with the critic Bert Rebhandl, I *did* accept the role of amateur art curator for an exhibition at the Vienna Künstlerhaus. It was called *Ghost Story – Nachbilder des Kinos* ("The After-image of Film"), and was grouped around three film installations by Stan Douglas. The other works in the show were still images, mostly photography and non-moving installations – except Chris Marker's CD-ROM *Immemory,* on a PC, which marked the end or beginning of the show. There was also a small film programme to go with it, in a cinema that belongs to the same building and the same institution, but even though we thought we had strongly connected these screenings to the exhibition, it somehow felt like an addendum, and not like an intrinsic part of the show. The main reason was that they only allowed us to use the weekend slots at 12 noon and at 11 p.m. for these screenings, with the "main showing times" being reserved for commercial / art-house releases that the Künstlerhaus needed for box-office reasons.

___ML: Which is kind of odd, since it differentiates between an "art show" theatrical screening, and a "cinema screening" – whereas in reality they are indistinguishable! Did this teach you a lesson, in terms of the structural framework in which a film screening needs to be situated within an art event?

___AH: It did. In 2001, I was part of a curatorial team for a multi-disciplinary exhibition / festival called *Du bist die Welt* ("You Are the World"). It was conceived by Hortensia Völckers, and also took place at the Künstlerhaus. In this case, I was more "at home", because I took over the part that took place at the Künstlerhaus cinema – a sort of festival of 40 films, with three shows every day, for a total of 6 weeks. Since the "departments" worked together closely, and also developed the shape and content of the whole event as a group, it was a highly fruitful experience for me. There were individual, "disciplinary" expertise and certain individual responsibilities, and there was also a strong understanding that we were jointly creating a "multiple" time and space experience. I see it as something of a model for such in-between projects. Apart from the film shows in the cinema, the exhibition also included several moving image installations, but it was clear for every visitor – in terms of how viewing time, viewing space, sound and image "bleed", and mode of reception were structured by the works themselves – that there are distinctly different types of "moving image works" with individual habitats. There are installations to roam around in the gallery space, "timelessly" so to speak; there are video works for monitor, where you sit down "to watch television"; and there are "installations for the cinema", which are traditionally called "films". James Benning ironically used this great expression – "installations for the cinema" – when he presented his film *casting a glance* at the Gloria-Kino in Kassel, at *Documenta 12.* As an alternative term for "movie theatre screening" it sounds quite foreign to the movie person, of course; it's an "experimental expression". It looks at the normal film situation through the eyes of an art world "Martian", who has never heard of cinemas and movies before, but who knows what a gallery installation is.

During these years of watching the growth of film or film-like elements in art shows, I came across several great works that I probably would not have seen anywhere else, but I also became more and more sceptical of a certain art-world rhetoric that accompanied this growth, especially when it talks about the "freedom" and "independence" that the visitor of a film installation enjoys *vis-à-vis* the "authoritarian" single-screen, fixed-seat experience of the movie-goer; or the "reflectiveness" that the installation engenders *vis-à-vis* the "illusionary" enthrallment of the cinema. All of this feels like a lukewarm echo or a silly remake of the Expanded Cinema polemics from the 1960s and 70s. At the time, these polemics had a lot going for them against the comparatively "iron-clad" cultural apparatuses of mainstream cinema and conservative museum practice. But today, under the conditions of Post-Fordism, where each citizen and consumer is expected to be an "expanded", shape-shifting, multi-identity, multi-sensory creature, the "new museum", with its expanded, multi-screen experiences, and its "freely roaming", "reflective" visitors, has actually become the epitome of what used to be called the apparatuses of the ruling class – just like the shopping mall. The German theorist Volker Pantenburg is studying the history of film-art world relations in some detail. He recently suggested something that I find really valid: that it will be necessary to develop a critique of the supposedly "liberating" and "reflection-inducing" Black Boxes in museums along similar lines to the

political critique of the supposedly "neutral" White Cube gallery model begun in the 1970s.

ML: So, in a way, a philosophical and political reading such as yours juxtaposes CINEMA as a modernist, radical alternative to the "consumerism" of the art exhibition model – or the theme park, and the shopping mall? Or – this might be a little far-fetched – to the digital exhibition space of an online film database?!

AH: The point is that, both in critical cinema theory and in everyday movie-going experience, the view of the cinema spectator as a prisoner – of the fixed time and place, and of the illusions hurled at him or her – doesn't hold a lot of currency anymore. I would even suggest, a bit crudely maybe, and still recognizing the barely diminished power of blockbuster cinema, that in today's socio-economic and cultural climate the spatially and durationally "inflexible" space of cinema is potentially more inviting to a reflective or critical experience of the world via images than most museum spaces are. From the perspective of current "governmental practices", the cinema is certainly not the hegemonic "ideal space" anymore; it's just not fluid and "expanded" and distracting enough.

ML: Since you've emphasized the collaborative, interdisciplinary dimension of your 2001 programme – when conceiving the *Documenta* programme, did you always have CINEMA shows in mind, or did you toy with the idea of a broader way of trying out other forms of presentation? Did you enter into a debate with Roger Buergel, the curator of *Documenta 12*, over the concept of presenting film within the exhibition?

AH: Not really. When Buergel and Ruth Noack, the co-curator of *Documenta 12*, invited me to contribute a "film presence" to the show, the first thing we agreed on, almost enthusiastically, was to create a separate space for film. Also, it was clear from the start that there would be a much smaller number of moving image installations in the exhibition – compared to *Documenta 11* (2002), for instance. I think it is fair to say that all three of us were clearly aware of the dead-ends that certain exhibition strategies, including film works, had reached at that point. The high popularity of film in art shows today (and of "film in art" shows) stands in an inverse relation to the number of successful presentation models that we see. And I'm not talking about historically oriented Expanded Cinema shows like "Into the Light" at the Whitney Museum, or "X-Screen" at the Vienna MUMOK, or about artists like Anthony McCall, James Coleman, Stan Douglas, Tacita Dean, or Matthew Buckingham, who have developed unique and highly convincing ways of working with film or para-film in the context of installation; they are contributing to film history just as much as to art history. What I'm talking about are the various attempts, mainly curatorial but often also by artists themselves, to turn existing film works into pseudo-installations or into pallid plasma pictures on the wall.

At any rate, since Buergel and Noack also have a strong background in film theory and are regular cinema-goers, the issue of how to display film at *Documenta* was not contentious at all. They also agreed to my proposal that it should be a programme with a historical viewpoint; I think it fit well with their own aims of showing a lot of non-contemporary art in the exhibition halls. In the end about 40% of the film programme was contemporary works,

made during the last decade, and 60% was older works.

At the beginning of our discussions, the actual space for the film programme in Kassel was not decided yet; we just agreed that it would have to be a cinema space. A multiplex cinema located at the centre of town was discussed for a while, but apart from certain ironies or "counter-intuitive" effects this might have had, it proved less than ideal. When I heard about the Gloria-Kino in Kassel, which had originally opened in 1955, the same year as the first *Documenta,* and which had been restored recently, it was clear that this would be the perfect film space. It made sense, then, to limit the programme to what I called the "second half of cinema", starting with films from the early-to-mid 1950s that *could* have shown at *Documenta 1,* and running up to the present day. Several decisive notions of modernity in cinema can be located in the film cultures that came after the immediate post-war years, and this time zone also played well with the "Deleuzian split" in film aesthetics between the "movement image" and the "time image".

—**ML:** An interesting argument, since Deleuze's concept of a correlation between a change in modes of narration (Italian neorealism, for instance) and a post-World War II political and ontological condition, in a way introduces a film-historical argument within the framework of what is largely perceived as a philosophical study.

—**AH:** His two books on cinema have been important to me for a long time. It was an obvious decision to start the series with Rossellini's *Viaggio in Italia* (1954), because of the especially strange and moving way it deals with time and duration, drama and the "undramatic", history and antiquity, death and alienation, celebrity and anonymity, the staged and the unstaged, and so on. It leads towards several "cine-political" genealogies that I wanted the programme to cover. However, it was also important for me to stage two other "beginnings", to oppose the too-narrow viewpoint of narrative *auteur*/art cinema. That's why I included a small-scale but very interesting John Ford picture from 1953, *The Sun Shines Bright,* as a way to bring in commercial studio filmmaking right from the start. And also as a way to link a "receding" film politics with one that's "on the horizon", without playing one against the other in progressivist terms. As a matter of fact, both the Ford and the Rossellini film failed at the box office when they came out in 1953/54, maybe because they were both "too backwards" and too advanced at the same time. The third "beginning" was drawn from the so-called "marginal" traditions of avant-garde, independent, or – as it is called today by museum people – "artists" film. Here, too, with the classical avant-garde of the 1920s and 30s no longer active, and the pre-war documentary tradition having lost its momentum, several new "handmade" approaches to the film medium became visible during the 1950s. In the programme, they were represented by filmmakers such as Helen Levitt, Robert Breer, Roger Tilton, Guy Debord, Peter Kubelka, Bruce Conner, or Vittorio De Seta.

—ML: What's the relationship between your way of programming and the current debate about a "canon" of cinema? This is probably the aspect of "programming as a curatorial discipline" which is most visible in public debates: what are the essential 100 films of all time, or, as your predecessor in the Film Museum, Peter Kubelka, phrased it: "What is film?"

—AH: If we understand the "canon" in its original sense, either in religion or in antiquity – as a real prescription – I don't think we can speak of a film canon at all. There is a later version, of course, the *Bildungskanon,* which – in the German-language world – refers to a 19th- and 20th-century concept of education for the good, cultured citizen. It was historically applied to literature, art, music, but never to film – or only in the sense of using film as a "modern tool" to disseminate knowledge about the older arts. In German educational policies, the film medium as a rich cultural field in itself entered this realm quite slowly, maybe in the 1970s; it has become more visible in education only in the past decade. But the relative disinterest with which the attempt to install a film canon for school-children was met in Germany around the year 2000 tells me that this is not the way to deal with the issue. Not only because cinema is seen as "anarchic" or wild, and is often biographically linked to anti-school activities, but also because the idea of the *Bildungskanon* as such has become a highly endangered species. It has been replaced by something that might be called *Aufmerksamkeitskanon* – the "attention canon", instead of "education canon" – and it operates differently, though not more democratically than its predecessor. The cinema, being a major factor in the rise of mass culture since the early 20th century, has itself contributed to this mutation. Today, we are no longer in thrall of high-minded or arrogantly authoritarian teachers of art or literature (or film), who "know it all" and tell us about the canon, but we are surrounded by Top Tens, best-seller lists, art market "thermometers", TV ratings, and box-office charts which leave little doubt about the "most important" works; they also define who the most important individuals in the various disciplines are. I would think that the "prescriptions" coming from these sources are much more effective today in terms of real canon formation than any old-style school education.

All of which is a way of saying that "canonization" is happening whether we like it or not. It is a larger historical process, consisting of many more or less visible streams that contribute to it. It includes everything from the tiny streams or "micro-contributions" that every critic, teacher, festival or museum programmer, or preservationist makes every single day when choosing to engage with a certain work or artist, to the main streams or "macro-contributions" made by strongly mediatized discourses such as the Academy Awards, box-office charts (and how journalists react to them), or the agendas of television programming. There is also a middle level that's quite influential: the DVD release policies of the major studios or of highly reputed companies like the Criterion Collection; a certain level of film book publishing, especially university presses and coffee-table books; and the current art world, with its liking for re-canonizing or almost "re-making" earlier positions in independent film as art history positions.

For the curator-programmer in a film museum, this means two very obvious things: (a) that you should be acutely aware of all these "streams" and how they change course over the years; and (b) that your own choices are definitely a (political) part of this process – but also that they are *only* a part, meaning that their influence on a wider scale is limited. Nevertheless,

the job at hand is immense, if one thinks of Benjamin's argument that "in every era the attempt must be made anew to wrest tradition away from a conformism that is about to overpower it". (In German: "In jeder Epoche muss versucht werden, die Überlieferung von neuem dem Konformismus abzugewinnen, der im Begriff steht, sie zu überwältigen.") I totally subscribe to this.

There is a dichotomy which we often hear from critics, or from the midst of our own profession – between a "canonical" type of programming and an "anti-canonical" one. I think that's a false dichotomy. First of all, because one person's (or one local film cultural) canon is another person's unknown continent. Are Karl Valentin, Mae West, or Monte Hellman's *Two-Lane Blacktop* (1971) part of *the* film canon? In terms of Viennese film culture I'd say they are – but probably not in Bombay or Norway. The director Willi Forst is canonical in Japan and Austria, but where else?

What I'm trying to say is that it seems as simple-minded to "rebelliously" demand a programming "against the grain", against the canon, as it is to just follow what one perceives as the existing canon. I would rather banally opt for a double-edged strategy of film museum programming that actively acknowledges both demands at the same time: (a) to consider and always re-examine the works and artists which are seen as central on other cultural platforms, such as universities, film literature, journalism, DVD publishing, television, etc. – I think as public institutions we owe it to our constituencies to give a certain representation of what is "generally felt" to be important in film history, even though we should always be prepared to question it. And (b) to constantly bring to the fore little-known or so-called "marginal" positions in filmmaking – and to put them on the same level of visibility and importance as the more "canonical" ones. For me, as a viewer, the most productive and creative programmes or "programming calendars" are the ones that play with the energies of affirmation and subversion/confrontation at the same time. As a viewer, I *do* want to constantly re-visit and re-evaluate the works that are held in high esteem, and I also constantly want to be made aware of all the great things that the consensus-building "machines" in our society have been excluding from view. I think both types of work can only profit if seen in such a kind of "friendly" tension between the "canonical" and the "non-canonical", whatever each might be in the individual instance. It's maybe more a sort of communion than a tension, or maybe both.

I also take a somewhat critical – or conservative – view of the current "anti-canonical" trend in programming, which aims at strengthening "context" at the cost of "text" (the individual work). By "context", I don't mean a grouping of films according to "genre", "film-maker", "studio", "era", "collection", "style", etc. (these are not foreign concepts to cinema, and I think they are valid criteria for making a programme), but the grouping of films according to larger themes or concepts that have a momentary currency in our cultural or social debates. Often, in such shows, the individual strength of a film is of little importance, as long as the "content-connections" to the theme are there. In these cases, the curator-as-philosopher, curator-as-artist, curator-as-cultural theorist often uses films just as illustration for his or her social insight. To me,

that's not curatorship, but misplaced theorizing. I know that such a call for always balancing cultural/thematic considerations with *aesthetic* ones may seem somewhat outmoded today. But at least for a *film* museum curator I think it's the only way to go about it. I think we truly, madly, deeply need this balance in order to make the important works stand out *as works,* for them to be remembered and transmitted into the future as works with their specific histories and qualities, and not just as "representative examples" of this or that socio-cultural constellation.

In a way, this brings me back to the *Documenta* example. To a certain degree, I tried to take into account the four basic ideas that Roger Buergel had proposed early on as his guidelines for thinking about the whole exhibition: "Is modernity our antiquity?", "What is bare life?", "What to do? (Education)", and "Migrating forms". But it quickly turned out that, even though I can fully share the view of the world that these words indicate, I had to completely transform them into film-specific notions, including film's relation to politics, of course – otherwise, the programme would have become a weak form of illustration. Maybe it still is, but I hope that in the process of thinking about, revisiting, and selecting individual films I ended up in a place that's unique to the medium I was dealing with. I guess I did think about the aspect of "the canonical" a lot during the whole work, but hopefully with a twist. Wouldn't it be great if the citizens of Kassel and the citizens of the art world who followed this programme come away with a series of vastly differing film experiences that refuse to coalesce into a canon or "anti-canon", and that can't be subsumed under headings such as "artists film" or "art-house cinema"? I thought that the prevalent concept of film in the art world today, and the prevalent concept of art in the film world today, should both be buried under a barrage of experiences that create the need for new concepts – or create the possibility for some very old concepts to live again.

This is such an impossible thought, of course, if you look at how pre-arranged most utterances of human life seem to be. It's probably even an idiotic thought, to think that one long summer programme in one cinema could change people's minds about what film is, or what film could potentially be.

——ML: I think transforming people's thinking about cinema through the act of presenting a programme is a brave endeavour any way. How can you overcome a passive, probably authoritarian mind-set on the part of the audience, which "endures" or merely accepts your choice of films, the combination of a programme as "content" being provided, and are oblivious to the curatorial thinking preceding every aspect of your exhibition design: the architectural setting, the machinery of cinema, the cultural-historical implications of programming, and so on?

——AH: Especially if it's not your own city, and you can't be there all the time. Which, by the way, is something too rarely discussed when we speak about a curator's job: it's hard or alienating to do it from a distance. That's when curatorship can quickly turn into some sort of dry "programme-making". When we highlight the notion that the curator should be deeply involved with the realities of where the films come from, their material life so far, the archive, the collections, the traditions by which a film has been passed on, etc., we should definitely also highlight the other end of the process – the realities of when and where the film becomes an instance of public life, the screening, the moments before and after, the exact characteristics and qualities of the screening, and the communication with the audience. I think I can say that at *Documenta,* with the immense help of several people, we really tried to take into account all these material realities of where films come from, which prints to show, how to show them in all their different shapes and forms, and to allow them to breathe.

But the fact that I had to be in Vienna most of the time while the show was alive in Kassel was certainly a weak link in the whole chain. I envy Roger Buergel and Ruth Noack the opportunity they had to physically experience and be part of the show every single day; they could really "complete" their curatorial work during those 100 days.

LIST OF PROGRAMMES

1	The Sun Shines Bright 1953, John Ford, 35mm, b/w, 90 min
	Jazz Dance 1954, Roger Tilton, 16mm, b/w, 20 min
	Lights 1966, Marie Menken, 16mm, color, 7 min
2	Viaggio in Italia 1954, Roberto Rossellini, 35mm, b/w, 85 min
3	Sanshô dayû (Sanshô the Bailiff) 1954, Mizoguchi Kenji, 35mm, b/w, 123 min
4	Mosaik im Vertrauen 1955, Peter Kubelka, 35mm, b/w & color, 16 min
	Recreation 1956, Robert Breer, 16mm, color, 2 min
	A Movie 1958, Bruce Conner, 16mm, b/w, 11 min
	Schwechater 1958, Peter Kubelka, 35mm, color, 1 min
	Sur le passage de quelques personnes à travers une assez courte unité de temps 1959, Guy Debord, 35mm, b/w, 20 min
	The Cut-Ups 1961–66, Anthony Balch/William Burroughs/Brion Gysin, 16mm, b/w, 20 min
5	Pyaasa (Thirst) 1957, Guru Dutt, 35mm, b/w, 146 min
6	Vertigo 1958, Alfred Hitchcock, 35mm, color, 128 min
	10 minute break
	La Jetée 1962, Chris Marker, 35mm, b/w, 28 min
	The Spiral Jetty 1970, Robert Smithson, 16mm, color, 35 min
7	Meghe Dhaka Tara (The Cloud-Capped Star) 1960, Ritwik Ghatak, 35mm, b/w, 127 min
8	Psalm III: Night of the Meek 2002, Phil Solomon, 16mm, b/w, 23 min
	Pasažerka (The Passenger) 1961/63, Andrzej Munk, 35mm, b/w, 61 min
	Machorka-Muff 1962, Jean-Marie Straub & Danièle Huillet, 35mm, b/w, 18 min
9	Porto das Caixas 1963, Paulo César Saraceni, 35mm, b/w, 76 min
	Saute ma ville 1968, Chantal Akerman, 35mm, b/w, 13 min
	Der Bräutigam, die Komödiantin und der Zuhälter 1968, Jean-Marie Straub & Danièle Huillet, 35mm, b/w, 23 min
10	Quixote 1965–68, Bruce Baillie, 16mm, color & b/w, 40 min
	Shake! 1967/1989, D. A. Pennebaker, 35mm, color, 19 min
	Camp 1965, Andy Warhol, 16mm, b/w, 67 min
11	Mouchette 1967, Robert Bresson, 35mm, b/w, 81 min
12	In the Street 1944/1952, Helen Levitt, 16mm, b/w, 16 min
	Un giorno in Barbagia 1958, Vittorio De Seta, 35mm, color, 11 min
	Aufsätze 1963, Peter Nestler, 35mm, b/w, 10 min
	High School 1968, Frederick Wiseman, 16mm, b/w, 75 min

13	Invasión 1969, Hugo Santiago, 35mm, b/w, 123 min
14	Gently Down the Stream 1981, Su Friedrich, 16mm, b/w, 14 min (18 fps)
	Wanda 1970, Barbara Loden, 35mm, color, 102 min
15	Touki Bouki 1973, Djibril Diop Mambéty, 35mm, color, 89 min
16	Langsamer Sommer 1974–76, John Cook, 35mm, b/w, 86 min
	The Present 1996, Robert Frank, 35mm, color, 24 min
17	Professione: Reporter 1975, Michelangelo Antonioni, 35mm, color, 125 min
18	In einem Jahr mit 13 Monden 1978, Rainer Werner Fassbinder, 35mm, color, 124 min
19	En rachâchant 1982, Jean-Marie Straub & Danièle Huillet, 35mm, b/w, 7 min
	Poto and Cabengo 1979, Jean-Pierre Gorin, 16mm, color, 76 min
20	Flaming Creatures 1963, Jack Smith, 16mm, b/w, 41 min
	IXE 1980, Lionel Soukaz, 35mm, color, 47 min
21	Reisender Krieger 1981, Christian Schocher, 16mm, b/w, 195 min
22	Les Maîtres fous 1955, Jean Rouch, 35mm, color, 30 min
	Bodybuilding 1966, Ernst Schmidt jr., 16mm, color, 9 min
	Coup de Boule 1987, Romuald Karmakar, 16mm, color, 8 min
	Community of Praise (Director's Cut) 1981, Richard Leacock, 16mm, color, 58 min
23	Himatsuri (Fire Festival) 1985, Yanagimachi Mitsuo, 35mm, color, 120 min
24	Crni film (Black Film) 1971, Želimir Žilnik, 35mm, b/w, 14 min
	Sans toit ni loi 1985, Agnès Varda, 35mm, color, 105 min
25	Khaneh siah ast (The House Is Black) 1963, Forugh Farrokhzad, 35mm, b/w, 20 min
	... Remote ... Remote ... 1973, VALIE EXPORT, 16mm, color, 12 min
	Peggy and Fred in Hell 1985–2006, Leslie Thornton, Video, b/w & color, 95 min
26	Route One/USA 1989, Robert Kramer, 35mm, color, 255 min
27	Semiotic Ghosts 1991, Lisl Ponger, 16mm, color, 17 min
	Leben – BRD 1990, Harun Farocki, 16mm, color, 82 min
28	Dva vremena u jednom prostoru / Two Times In One Space
	1976–84, Ivan Ladislav Galeta, 35mm, b/w, 12 min
	Nouvelle Vague 1990, Jean-Luc Godard, 35mm, color, 89 min
29	Va zendegi edameh darad (And Life Goes On...)
	1992, Abbas Kiarostami, 35mm, color, 91 min
30	Outer Space 1999, Peter Tscherkassky, 35mm, b/w, 10 min
	Irma Vep 1996, Olivier Assayas, 35mm, color, 97 min
31	Velvet Goldmine 1998, Todd Haynes, 35mm, color, 124 min
32	Killer 1998, Darežan Omirbajev, 35mm, color, 80 min
33	eXistenZ 1999, David Cronenberg, 35mm, color, 97 min
	The Act of Seeing With One's Own Eyes 1971, Stan Brakhage, 16mm, color, 32 min
34	Rosetta 1999, Jean-Pierre & Luc Dardenne, 35mm, color, 94 min

35	**Le Baromètre** 2004, Friedl Kubelka, 35mm, b/w, 3 min (18 fps)
	Beau travail 1999, Claire Denis, 35mm, color, 92 min
36	**Zhantai / Platform** 2000, Jia Zhangke, 35mm, color, 154 min
37	**De grote vakantie (The Long Holiday)** 2000, Johan van der Keuken, 35mm, color, 145 min
38	**Halcion** 2007, Dietmar Brehm, 16mm, color, 20 min
	O Fantasma 2000, João Pedro Rodrigues, 35mm, color, 90 min
39	**Film spricht viele Sprachen** 1995, Gustav Deutsch, 35mm, color 1 min
	Dogfar nai mae marn / Mysterious Object at Noon
	2000, Apichatpong Weerasethakul, 35mm, b/w, 83 min
40	**La Libertad** 2001, Lisandro Alonso, 35mm, color, 73 min
	10 minute break
	Ce vieux rêve qui bouge 2001, Alain Guiraudie, 35mm, color, 50 min
41	**3/60 Bäume im Herbst** 1960, Kurt Kren, 16mm, b/w, 5 min
	Id… / I'm going… 1973, Józef Robakowski, 35mm, s/w, 3 min
	Railroad Turnbridge 1975, Richard Serra, 16mm, b/w, 17 min
	Serene Velocity 1971, Ernie Gehr, 16mm, color, 23 min (18 fps)
	37/78 Tree again 1978, Kurt Kren, 16mm, color, 4 min
	15 minute break
	Bliss 1967, Gregory J. Markopoulos, 16mm, color, 6 min
	The Hedge Theater 1986–90/2002, Robert Beavers, 35mm, color, 19 min
	Ming Green 1966, Gregory J. Markopoulos, 16mm, color, 7 min
	A Pitcher of Colored Light 2007, Robert Beavers, 35mm, color, 24 min
42	**L'Esquive** 2003, Abdellatif Kechiche, 35mm, color, 124 min
43	**Okay Bye-Bye** 1998, Rebecca Baron, 16mm, color, 39 min
	S21, la machine de mort Khmère rouge 2003, Rithy Panh, 35mm, color, 105 min
44	**Star Spangled to Death** 2004 (1957–2004), Ken Jacobs, Video, color & b/w, 400 min
45	**Moolaadé** 2004, Ousmane Sembène, 35mm, color, 124 min
46	**Hat Wolff von Amerongen Konkursdelikte begangen?**
	2004, Gerhard Benedikt Friedl, 35mm, color, 73 min
47	**Land of the Dead** 2005, George A. Romero, 35mm, color, 92 min
48	**Mein Stern** 2001, Valeska Grisebach, 35mm, color, 60 min
	10 minute break
	Im Glück (Neger) 2006, Thomas Heise, 35mm, color & b/w, 87 min
49	**Opera Jawa** 2006, Garin Nugroho, 35mm, color, 120 min
50	**Casting a Glance** 2007, James Benning, 16mm, color, 80 min

CASE STUDY #2:
A CHARTER OF CURATORIAL VALUES

___ML: Paolo, I think your "Charter of Curatorial Values" is an extremely valuable and complex document. While the sources are clearly outlined, I wonder how you arrived at the idea of producing such a document. As we understand it, "curatorship" for a film archive hasn't been formalized. What was your reason for coming up with the idea to produce an official document, and what was the process of creating it like?

___PCU: I vividly recall the circumstances leading to this. I'm the new kid on the block at the National Film and Sound Archive of Australia, and having studied this situation at the NFSA, having read a lot of papers about it over the years, I thought, "What is at stake for the NFSA, and its identity as a national, cultural institution?" It struck me that both at the national and international level, the reputation of the NFSA was mainly linked to its technological expertise. The NFSA is the place where, by comparison with other archives, there is something pretty close to state-of-the-art preservation – whoever comes to the NFSA and looks at the laboratory leaves the archive amazed, because what it does, it does extremely well.

So, over the years, the archive has developed a reputation on a technological, or even a technocratic, basis. Interestingly enough, this reputation has either obscured the issue of interpretation of the collection, or it has created the perception that the excellence of the archive only needed to be a technological or technocratic excellence, which for me is only part of the equation. I felt that the second part of the

equation, to give the NFSA the necessary political strength to be regarded as an essential institution, was to demonstrate that the NFSA is not only a place where works are collected and properly preserved and put on shelves and then made available upon request, but also a place where the meaning of these works is explained to the public.

In all this, there was the consideration that access was and is a very big thing. For Australians, quite appropriately, and quite correctly, the specificity and the geography of the country make the role of the NFSA something that is inextricably linked to access; but what I felt was missing, what needed to be added to the formula, was interpretation. For me interpretation is curatorship, and, with my naivety perhaps, I assumed that all it took was to tell staff: "Look, this is a wonderful place. I know the reputation of this place. It has always been a reputation that's linked to technology. Let's add the ingredient of curatorship." It took some time to understand that what I was taking for granted was not being taken for granted by staff or managers, in the sense that "curatorship" was indeed a known word – but how curatorship would apply to the work of the NFSA was something that was not taken for granted at all.

Eventually a question emerged, formulated in more or less explicit terms: "Excuse me, but what is curatorship? You talk about curatorial values, of a curatorship approach, but can you give me a definition of curatorship?" That was a defining moment for me, because it was like the time when I was asked to explain what was obvious for me, as if I did not need to explain it because I never had to explain it to anybody.

Even when I was teaching at the Selznick School of Film Preservation, I never had to explain what curatorship is. Having to explain was a wonderful moment for me, because it made me pause, and realize that to explain curatorship in a logical, succinct, clear way was something I had not done before. And it *was* needed at the time, and in this place, because I was dealing with talented people who never felt that curatorship had to be part of their agenda or their mission.

For me it was like sitting down in front of a blank page, and explaining what was clear to me from the start. As you know, when you have to explain to others what you've always thought was clear to you, it is an extremely challenging process. I decided not to take anything for granted; more specifically, I had to tackle a fundamental question. When I was trying to explain to my staff what I mean by curatorship, and I was uttering words such as "curatorship is about explaining; curatorship is about interpreting; curatorship is about choosing, making selections," they stared at me, and said, "Well, this is precisely what we are doing. Of course we select; of course we interpret; we explain." From my perspective, what the staff of the NFSA was doing was what is commonly defined as archiving. Meaning by that, fundamentally, the process of ensuring that a collection institution gathers a representative body of works, documents these works in an appropriate manner, makes sure that these works are properly preserved, and makes sure these works are properly made accessible.

__ML: So, their principles, the way they already did act professionally, say, for the last two decades, was something that was never formulated in a systematic manner, but was rather born out of need – you can't collect everything; you can't process all your materials. At the same time, you need to be selective, you need to think about significance; you need to think of the future in terms of, what is the cultural significance of a certain item going to be in 20 years' time, etc. Something that was more or less running subcutaneously, but never articulated in a systematic manner, and so it was never formulated as a set of values, but rather like something of individual practice.

__PCU: I would argue that there was nothing defensive about the staff's attitude; moreover, that at the time I arrived, there was an aim to gather, not a selective body of works, but a comprehensive body of works depicting Australia's audiovisual culture. That was a time when, basically, the mission of the archive was to collect Australian audiovisual works, and not foreign audiovisual works. It was actually a time when giving foreign audiovisual works away to other institutions would be the norm. Additionally, the archive was originally an offspring of the National Library. So the staff came from a culture that is a librarian's culture in the noblest sense of the term, because it was a place where the term "film library", or "film librarian", was considered a dignified way to approach the work that was being done.

What was most intriguing to me was the fact that the notion of selection or interpretation was perceived as already being an inherent part of the archive's mission. When I asked the staff of the access branch, "What happens when someone requests a certain work from the collection?", I was told that the access service provides access to the film, videotape, audio-cassette or CD. I then asked, "So are you providing basically access to what the user wants?" Then I discovered that the user was defined at the archive as a "client", which was perceived as being a neutral term. For me it is *not* a neutral term, because it has a strong economic connotation: this is what the client wants, and if the client wants the VHS tape, we give them the VHS tape. This was when I began to suggest, "What if you tell what you call the 'client', you can have the VHS tape, but you can also have the 35mm print, or you can also have the 16mm print?" But, I was told, if this is what the client wants, why should we argue with the client? I thought, Aha! That's where interpretation begins. It is suggesting that, "If you really want to have the VHS tape, that's fine – but do you know that we have a beautiful 35mm print of the film?" That is, in itself, a form of interpretation. In short, I felt compelled to put these thoughts in writing, which is what resulted in the creation of the paper.

This paper fulfilled two important goals at the time. The first, at a political level, was to protect the cultural identity of the NFSA at the time when the NFSA had just been merged with an industry body. It was my way of saying, "Okay, we are now a part of the industry body, but just remember we are playing a cultural role. We must act curatorially." By saying this, I was explicitly pointing to the fact that our activity should not be dependent on economic or financial imperatives, and from this perspective the strategy worked. The second goal was to demonstrate or explain that, without denying at all its past, the archive could be even more than it was then. It was not only a collecting institution, but also an active, cultural agent.

I do recall that when I wrote the paper the single most important challenge I faced was precisely the description of the distinction between "archivist" and "curator", because I was mindful of what the staff was telling me. We have always done interpretation, so they said, and I had to find a way to argue convincingly that while the roles of the archivist and curator are certainly complementary, and they need each other, they cannot be defined in a binary way: You do "A," and I do "B," and there is a straight line in-between. The two roles are linked by a continuum, and at the two extremes of the continuum there are fundamental differences. Both the archivist and the curator may not feel comfortable with them, but these are commonly recognized in our field.

These are the facts: the archivist is mainly the custodian, the organizer, the person who protects, while the curator is the person who explains and interprets. I am well aware that at the very moment I am defining this polarization, I am recognizing that I do expect the curator to be fluent in whatever he / she is dealing with protecting and organizing, as well as being systematic, and obeying certain rules. By the same token, I would like to expect that the way the archivist works is not a timeless abstract entity; it is a system or set of procedures geared towards, or that facilitates, or fosters, interpretation and explanation. It is very much like two people speaking two different languages, two people who expect that the other person will be somehow fluent in his or her language, but will speak a different language. Let's say you speak English, I speak Italian; and I speak a decent English, you speak a decent Italian. We understand each other, but my mother language is

Italian, and your mother language is English – so I expect you to be the authority when it comes to English, and you expect me to be the authority when it comes to Italian.

___ML: Even more, what makes mutual communication possible is that I can trust in you that your Italian is not *gramelot,* meaningless syllables, but that it adheres to the laws of Italian language. So we both know that we have a working system, and a set of rules and values backing our doings; and this is the ground where mutual exchange can take place.

___PCU: This means, in practical terms, that an archivist must expect that the curator will not only know, and be aware of, but also support and endorse the knowledge, the process, the methods implemented by the archivist. By the same token, the archivist will play an active role in helping the curator do his or her job. For example, I would expect the archivist to tell the curator, "Look, have you seen this? This is extraordinary; I think we can do something with it." Conversely, the curator is expected to suggest that by doing cataloguing in a certain way rather than another, his or her research may become easier. It is not a matter of dividing territories; I do not expect any of the two parties to say, "This is none of your business." The two parties should help each other. This is easy in theory. But in practice this is difficult, for two fundamental reasons. First, because, not surprisingly, the archivist is somehow reluctant to accept that there is a need for the existence of a curator: "Why do you need a curator? Am I not enough?" On the other hand, because the curator is so geared towards interpretation and explanation, the curator tends to feel impatient when the archivist says, "Sorry, you cannot do this." If the curator says, "I'd like to organize a number of clips, and I'm going to cut this 35mm print," the archivist has to say, "I'm sorry, you should know better. This is not the way things are done." I freely admit that this is an ongoing tension between the two parties. When I was at the Eastman House, I was working with a very talented curator who had wonderful ideas, but he was feeling so impatient and frustrated with anything that would limit his ability to interpret the collection: "This is a unique and unpreserved print, but such a beautiful film! Let's show it."

Conversely, an archivist taking a strict approach to the collection may oppose the fact that a certain print can be accessed at all. I have always accepted the fact that under certain conditions, a good projectable print that is still not fully preserved could be exhibited under certain exceptional circumstances in the museum. This demonstrates that both archiving and curating are an art. An art means having the gift of finding a balance between a rule and the flexibility inherent in creativity. The archivist will insist on the rule; the curator will insist on the creativity: hence my challenge at the NFSA. I took pains to explain that rules are not dogmas; that while I'm the first to endorse and promote archival values, these archival values should be justified and complemented by curatorial values. It doesn't mean playing with exceptions. These exceptions are not at the arbitrary whim of the curator; they must have a compelling reason. In short, I had to put this into a comprehensible language. And that was at the origin of the creation of the paper.

___ML: Why did you call it "A Charter of Curatorial Values", and not, for instance, "This Is

Curatorship in the NFSA"? I find the choice of words, "Charter of Curatorial *Values*", interesting, but I'd like to hear your opinion.

___PCU: There were a number of reasons for this: I was addressing multiple audiences; I was addressing my own staff; I was addressing an industry body called the Australian Film Commission, and I wanted the AFC to formally, very formally, endorse these principles. I wanted to make sure that it would not be that easy to throw these principles out the window. I needed to give this document the clout of a binding statement, which is why I asked the Commission to formally approve it. That is why if you look at the volume on the NFSA Collection Policy, attached to the Collection Policy there is the "Charter of Curatorial Values". It was a way of saying, "While we are part of an industry body, the AFC formally agrees that these are values to be followed." Here I thought (but you are a better judge than I am on this matter) that what I ended up writing could be of some use beyond the NFSA. I thought, while I'm at it, I can perhaps write something that applies to our field in general. By doing so, I thought I was also suggesting that I was not doing this simply because I had a specific issue at stake within the NFSA. I was making a statement, which should apply, in my view, to the generality of audio-visual collecting institutions. And, in a way, it was also a way of exposing this ongoing gap or dilemma between the archive and the museum, the archivist and the curator. It was only the first step towards what I see as a desirable fusion of the archival and curatorial functions. I don't think this is something that will be achieved in the course of our lifetime. Maybe it will *never* be achieved, and maybe there is even a good reason why this polarity should continue to exist…

___ML: Because it's not only an obstacle, it's productive, too.

___PCU: Yes, because it's productive. I'm not for merging concepts simply because I want to. Who am I to want to merge concepts? And besides, who am I to try to erase hundreds of years of tradition where these two distinct roles have been identified? The best way to formulate the issue was by saying that, on the one hand there is the need to explain a creative work to the outside world, and on the other hand there is the need to protect it. Inevitably, one function is perceived as more outward-looking, and the other one as more inward-looking. Maybe this is something that can be achieved – to demonstrate that an archivist does not have to be inward-looking at all, and that the curator should be mindful of the integrity of the collection within the gates of the institution itself.

A CHARTER OF CURATORIAL VALUES

1. Introduction

In October 2004, with the formulation of a new strategic direction, the National Film and Sound Archive [of Australia] began a process of transformation based on the development of a curatorial structure. This new structure seeks to integrate the existing skills in acquiring, preserving, and making accessible the national audiovisual heritage with an added emphasis on interpretation of the collection based on curatorial expertise and the imperative to further cultivate and promote the ethical standards of audiovisual archiving. This document is an overview of the main cultural principles governing the activity of curators, with special reference to audiovisual collections in the context of the national and international archiving community, and is consistent with international best practice.

The main focus of this paper is the intellectual nature of curatorship and its principal manifestations in the audiovisual world. Among the reference points for the views outlined below are:
· The FIAF Code of Ethics;
· The UNESCO Recommendation on the Preservation of Moving Images (1985);
· The General Guidelines of UNESCO's "Memory of the World" project;
· The codes of ethics and definitions of organizations such as FIAF, IFLA, ICA, ICOM;
· The Code of Ethics of the Australian Society of Archivists and of the Australian Institute for the Conservation of Cultural Material;
· "Time in Our Hands" (Canberra: Department of Arts, Heritage and Environment, 1985);
· Ray Edmondson, "Audiovisual Archiving: Philosophy and Practice" (Paris: UNESCO, 2004).

2. Curatorship is an art, not a science

Modern curatorship is the outcome of centuries of practice in archives and museums, and of the ongoing interaction between history and society: the heritage of the past, the imperatives, values, and trends of the present, the challenges and opportunities provided by an educated forecast of the future. Curatorial values are not the expression of a quantifiable science. They are a system of ideas which find their expression in three areas: the fundamental imperative to preserve cultural artefacts and make them permanently accessible; the expertise necessary to interpret the recent and distant past; the organizational structure necessary to protect and develop the cultural manifestations of history. It is in these areas that the curator exercises his or her role of interpreter of culture: he or she is an intellectual bridge between the past and the future, endowed with the strategic vision necessary to decipher the traces of what has happened, to explain them for the benefit of his or her community, and to anticipate the ways in which his or her present will be understood and judged by those who will come after us. The curator is a messenger who has the authority and the obligation to ensure that the message itself will foster memory and creativity at the same time.

3. The archivist and the curator

While there is no universally accepted definition of "curator" and "archivist", a degree of consensus on the key features of these professions is shared by a number of scholarly and internet sources; among them are the Association des Archivistes Français, www.archivistes.org;
U.S. Department of Labor, *Occupational Outlook Handbook* (2004–05 Edition),
http://www.bls.gov/oco/ocos065.htm;
Isabelle Lachance, "La profession d'archiviste au Québec",
www.ebsi.umontreal.ca/cursus/vol5no1/lachan.htm;

the Fédération Française des Conservateurs-Restaurateurs, www.ffcr-fr.org/ref;

the U.S. Office of Personnel Management, www.pm.gov/fedclass/1015.pdf;

John M.A. Thompson, ed., *Manual of Curatorship: A Guide to Museum Practice* (London: Butterworth, 1986). These sources are used as the basis for the definitions outlined in this section.

Archivists collect, organize, and maintain control over a wide range of information deemed important enough for permanent safekeeping. They maintain records in accordance with accepted standards and practices that ensure the long-term preservation and easy retrieval of the documents. Archivists often specialize in an area of history or technology. Their goal is to ensure that all the works and materials put under the care of the organization are treated according to coherent conservation, preservation, and access standards. From the viewpoint of an archivist, no work or material accepted as part of the collection (whether it is a preservation or access element) deserves a lesser degree of professional care than others; this does not contradict the archivist's prerogative of recommending acquisition and preservation priorities. Fluency in professional practice related to the conservation, preservation, identification, and cataloguing of the works and materials is an essential requirement of an archivist.

Curators formulate and develop the intellectual and cultural policy of archives and museums. They direct the acquisition, preservation, and exhibition of collections, including negotiating and authorizing the purchase, sale, exchange, or loan of collections. They are also responsible for authenticating and evaluating the significance of the works in a collection on the basis of agreed parameters and in compliance with the institution's Collection Policy (for a definition of "significance" of a cultural artefact, see the UNESCO "Memory of the World", www.amw.org.au). Curators oversee and help conduct the institution's research projects and related access and outreach programmes. An increasing part of a curator's duties involves management and administration. Curators must be intellectually and operationally flexible because of their wide variety of duties. Leadership ability and business skills are crucial, while marketing skills are valuable in increasing attendance and potential funding.

4. So what's the difference?

Given the above definitions, isn't there an overlap of desirable skills for curators and archivists? Don't they both collect, preserve, and make accessible a collection? The answer is yes: curators must actively contribute to the development of archival standards, and archivists are expected to make recommendations to the curators in matters pertaining to their expertise. The collaborative nature of the relationship between curators and archivists is key to the life of a collecting institution. The archivist is the custodian of the standards governing the management of a collection; the curator is the collection's spokesperson. These roles are necessarily intertwined, as a curator is expected to embrace archival standards, and an archivist should be aware of, and be able to promote, the cultural significance of the collection. Before deciding upon a given policy, the curator must consult the archivist in relation to its compliance with the best available archival practice. Curators and archivists have distinct and yet complementary roles; from this standpoint, they have equal professional standing in a collecting organization. This balance of power ensures that no curatorial decision is made without proper consideration of the safety and integrity of the collection.

It should also be pointed out that while an archivist can exist and successfully operate in certain contexts without a curator, a curator cannot fulfill his or her obligations to society in the absence of an archivist, or at least of a thorough archival perspective. Even the organizer of a temporary show needs to identify, locate, and retrieve artefacts existing somewhere, be it in a private collection or in the warehouse of another organization. However, the archivist and the curator have also a distinct set of responsibilities which make their dialogue a necessity. To understand this, one must bear in mind that a cultural artefact is not a monolithic entity. It is a complex reality resulting from the interaction between its three key components:

a) the work, as defined by the carrier – when it exists – and its content;

b) the environmental, social, cultural, and industrial context surrounding its creation;

c) the way in which it was and is experienced.

In curatorial terms, a "content" deprived of its context or experience is just a matter of consumption, a commodity (hence the preferred use of the terms "work" or "artefact" in the archival and museum world); a context and an experience of a work scrutinized or recreated on the basis of a distortion or absence of the content and its original medium is at best an incomplete and at worst a misleading way to interpret and explain society, very much like a biography written with no evidence nor witnesses. The archivist collects, preserves, and makes accessible the works – that is, the contents and the identity of their media. The curator interprets the work both in its "media" (or "carrier") and "work" ("content") manifestations. At times, she or he explores and determines the past, present, and possible future context of its presentation, and ensures that the experience is organized in a way that is both consistent with the historical identity of the work and with the opportunity to generate new knowledge from it. Hence the reciprocal bind (at times a creative tension) between the professions of archivist and curator.

5. The permanent access to history

The first imperative of curatorship is to ensure that the traces of history embodied by the works in a collection will not be altered, manipulated, or modified under any circumstance for any reason whatsoever, be it of a political, racial, religious, or economic nature. While new works may be created through the use of one or more existing items in the collections (something which should always be encouraged by curators who believe in the archive or museum as a catalyst of invention), their creation will never entail the alteration, manipulation, or modification of the collection items. In this respect, the archivist and the curator are powerful allies, in that they both are committed (the former from the perspective of the custodian of the artefact, the second from that of its interpreter) to the protection and availability of the work in its original form. A widely shared view among curators in all disciplines – recently echoed by British film director John Boorman apropos Stanley Kubrick's intention to destroy all surviving prints of his first feature film *Fear and Desire* – is that, from an ethical and cultural perspective, when a work becomes part of an archival or museum collection, it no longer belongs to its makers nor to its custodians, but to history and to posterity. Copyright protects the intellectual and financial interests of a creator, but does not give the right to distort history when its material evidence has been consciously put under the care of a collecting organization. An audiovisual artist who is keen to further modify or dismember the original expressions of his or her past work should do so with copies from the original work, or not give the original work to an archive at all.

In the audiovisual world this means two things: first, no destruction, alteration, nor manipulation of the work (even by its author) is allowed if it entails a permanent alteration of the historical record: George Lucas may well recut and put a new soundtrack to his first *Star Wars* movie, but its 1977 version should still exist and be available as such. The second principle, derived from the first, is that no duplication whatsoever of the original work should be made without prior adequate measures to ensure the stability of the collection item. This means, for instance, that a gramophone disc in the collection should not be played before the sound recording has been transferred to another accessible medium, and that a nitrate print should not be run through a projector or telecine equipment before having been transferred to another stable component. Access activities should be implemented only on access materials.

6. Acquisition, preservation, access:
A balance of power

The notion of the equal importance of acquisition, preservation, and access in an audiovisual archive is a pivotal feature of the curatorial vision for the NFSA, as defined in the five-point document distributed in late 2004. According to this vision, none of these concepts taken individually should be developed to the detriment of the others. This could be described as something similar to the balance of power between legislative, executive, and judiciary in a democratic regime: through a complex system of checks and balances, each component of the political system supports the others and ensures that none of them is allowed to exercise absolute power. While some of them (such as the judicial function) are also expected to act in complete independence from the political party or coalition holding power at a given point in time, all of them obey to agreed rules of the democratic process.

The same applies to the curatorial process, in that acquisition must comply to agreed collection policies which include provisions for preservation and access; the preservation process must take into account the nature of the works acquired and the need to make them permanently accessible; the demands for access to the collections will influence the preservation policies, but cannot alter nor compromise their underlying fundamental values.

The curator is the arbiter of this balance, the person who has the responsibility of ensuring that each of the three components of the process finds its best possible expression, individually and as part of a whole. Curatorship is by all means a heavy practical, political, and moral burden, requiring a unique mix of stamina, judgement, strategy, diplomacy, knowledge, and vision. To provide an idea of what this entails, let's now look at some of curatorship's most obvious manifestations, formally articulated in the archives' collection policy documents. At first sight, they look more like protocols and practices; however, curatorial values are so deeply embedded in them that it is important to briefly describe them in this context.

ACQUISITION

Curators are responsible for deciding which works will be acquired for the collection. While they are encouraged and often required to use the experience and expertise of other colleagues on their curatorial staff, and to take into account suggestions coming from other staff members or from outside the archive, they are personally and ultimately accountable for their choices. They will strive to acquire complete works, in their final and/or commercially released versions, primarily in the media in which they were intended to be experienced by their audiences. The curators also have the sole authority to assess the exceptional circumstances under which it may be advisable or necessary to acquire elements other than the complete works (such as rushes, outtakes of moving image works, or unreleased sound recordings), or to acquire works in formats or media other than the original ones, in the event that acquisition of the original works proves to be impossible to achieve. Other than in the special circumstances described above, curators will decline offers to acquire works in non-original formats or media purely for access purposes, unless a corresponding element of the work in its original format is already part of the collection, and they will notify their supervisors of any undue pressure exercised upon them to act in ways contrary to their mandate.

PRESERVATION

The curator's main mission in relation to the preservation process is to ensure that any preservation work held is
a) reversible;
b) avoids further alteration of the original work;
c) is carefully documented in order to allow others to evaluate the choices made and the procedures chosen, and take corrective action if necessary.

Curators are responsible for deciding, in consultation with their supervisors and the staff in charge of the preservation or conservation facilities, the preservation procedures to be implemented towards the collection as a whole or towards some specific components of the collection. Curators are expected to gather advice from staff in charge of preservation and conservation facilities about the costs of preserving, restoring, duplicating, or reconstructing any given work for special purposes, and about the technical implications of their decisions. Curators are also responsible for ensuring that the works in the collections are preserved according to the highest possible technical and intellectual standards available at the time, and that the works will be remain accessible for as long as possible in their original format or media for future generations. No reproduction, transfer, or migration of the original work for preservation or access purposes will be allowed on other formats or media before a work is accessible in its original format or medium, insofar as the original format or medium exists and is available.

ACCESS

Curators are responsible for maintaining permanent accessibility as the ultimate goal of the acquisition and preservation processes. They have overall responsibility for access policy implementation and for coordinating the efforts of other staff, including but not limited to the staff of preservation and technical services. Mindful of the inherent compromise between acquisition, preservation, and access, the curators will:
a) commit to maintain a clear connection between the display of an audiovisual work and the mission statement of the NFSA;
b) ensure that the inclusion of a work in an exhibition or access programme is consistent with the intellectual integrity of the exhibition or access programme itself;
c) provide the widest possible access to the collections through both formal exhibitions and a wide variety of other methods;
d) serve as a resource for teaching, research, scholarship, inspiration, entertainment, or creation of new works;
e) be limited only by good preservation practice, respect for intellectual property rights, and the unique characteristics of each collection.

The NFSA curators have the authority to limit access to works in the collections only in the event that:
a) the material is judged to be too fragile to handle;
b) the material is extremely valuable and rare;
c) the NFSA does not have a preservation master or preservation element of the work;
d) the requestor has demonstrated carelessness or has otherwise put collection material in jeopardy during previous instances;
e) the requestor refuses to comply with archival policies or procedures;
f) there are donor- or depositor-imposed restrictions on access;

g) there is insufficient staff available for adequate supervision of access;

h) there is risk of damage to, or loss of, the work in the collection.

In addition to responding to access requests, a curator must exercise a proactive role in highlighting the significance of undeservedly neglected works in the collection. Archives and museums often have important items that nobody knows anything about, either because they are not yet catalogued, or because their very existence is virtually unknown.

DEACCESSIONING

Deaccessioning works from the National Collection is a grave decision, which must be evaluated with extreme caution. Curators are responsible for determining, subject to final approval from their supervisors, which elements should be deaccessioned, with a clear and well-documented explanation of the reason for their actions.

In general terms, an item may be deaccessioned from the collection for one or more of the following reasons:

a) because the material is decomposed beyond repair, reproduction, and/or exhibition, and no meaningful information or audiovisual experience whatsoever can be obtained from it;

b) because the NFSA already has other elements of a given work in its original medium and format, and has compared the item with other holdings and determined that it is inferior in all respects;

c) because of the excess number of duplicate elements of the work, well beyond the needs of the NFSA for preservation or access purposes;

d) in the case of a work created in a non-analog format, because the carrier in which the digital-born work was created can no longer be used.

DATA MANAGEMENT

The collection, organization, and availability of data – implemented through guidelines informed by international standards – affects all the key functions of an archive. The accuracy and availability of these records is a shared goal, and a responsibility for all people involved in creating and capturing information about the collection. Curators, accessioners, and cataloguers must agree on data entry standards and the criteria for data quality. The management of these standards and criteria lies with the cataloguers and accessioners, while the curator's distinctive strength is in the ongoing provision of the descriptive and contextual data needed to identify and in the assessment of the intellectual and technical nature of an audiovisual work. This relationship between curatorial and cataloguing staff is sometimes taken for granted; however, it is a key ingredient for providing the most adequate data for the needs of the collecting institution.

7. What is an "original" artefact?

As soon as a work becomes part of a National Collection, each of its components is potentially an "original" and should be treated with all the care necessary to ensure its survival for future generations. At first sight, this notion contradicts the well-worn theory of the "film in the age of mechanical reproduction", that is, the notion that an audiovisual work may be reproduced indefinitely, especially in the digital domain. However, recent practice has demonstrated that such a notion has its flaws.

No matter how "common" an audiovisual work is today, if an archive or a museum decides to acquire it for the collection, the curator has the responsibility of determining what the possibilities are of locating another new element of that work, and deciding whether or not it should be used for access purposes. As a rule, the "original" (determined as such by the curator) should never be touched except for the creation of preservation elements; nor should it be assumed that a single access to an "original" does not compromise its overall integrity. It is possible for an archive to be so technologically advanced as to ensure that an original element can occasionally be made accessible under strictly monitored curatorial conditions; however, the curator is personally responsible for making the choice.

Take the (analog) example of Alfred Hitchcock's *Vertigo*, available in a huge number of analog and digital copies. What should an archive do if a copy of this film is part of the collection or may be acquired? The answer depends on the nature of the copy and the curatorial determination of its use. For many years, the Cinémathèque française in Paris had a stunning 35mm print of this title. Convinced that the film was not rare, the film archive's curators projected it on a regular basis in its theatre, and frequently loaned it to other archives, on the assumption that it would be easy to obtain another print in the event that the existing one were damaged or lost. When Robert A. Harris undertook the restoration of the film on behalf of Universal Pictures, it turned out that the original negative of the film was no longer available in its entirety; that very few vintage prints survived; more importantly, that the Cinémathèque française print was the only surviving copy of the film in its original VistaVision format. By the time Harris got hold of that print, it was in such poor condition that it could no longer be projected nor used for the restoration project, and the final result of his work is a film with significant differences from the 1959 version.

A similar instance can be found in Charles Chaplin's classic Keystone, Mutual, and Essanay short comedies. Thousands of copies in all formats were produced since 1915, and film archives never bothered protecting what they had because they thought it would always be possible to acquire new prints. At the time of the first major Chaplin preservation project, it soon became clear that no archive (let alone the Chaplin Estate) had a complete print in good condition for any of these comedies. Had we preserved at least one copy of one of them soon after their first release, we would now possess a set of cultural treasures!

The Chaplin example is indirectly linked with the prehistory of the NFSA. In the 1930s a small Sydney distributor, National Films, acquired a set of duplicate negatives of the Chaplin Mutuals with soundtracks – the versions produced by the Van Beuren Corporation. In the 1970s, Dorothy Tayler, the widow of the owner of National Films – which by then had closed – was disposing of the company's stock in trade, and much of it was offered to the National Library. Ms. Tayler offered to the National Library the Chaplin negatives, but the offer had to be declined because of shortage in storage space. The National Library put Ms. Tayler in touch with the staff of the American Film Institute, who gladly received them. The AFI later claimed that these negatives were the best surviving material on the Chaplin Mutuals. Later, Blackhawk used them as source material for their own releases.

Another example related to recorded sound may further illustrate the point. It was recently discovered that some Edison cylinder recordings can be played back in genuine, if accidental, "stereo". Sometimes two acoustic masters were made of the same performance with the horns placed in different positions, so each has a different orchestral balance. The purpose was simply one of productivity – double the output. The masters had the same serial number with an A or B suffix. Someone has now figured out the real significance of the suffix from a modern viewpoint: the idea of stereo would have been commercially impracticable at the time the recording was made, even if it had actually occurred to anyone. If the original carriers had not been kept, no one would ever have made this discovery by listening to copies.

It should not be assumed a priori that a digitally-created work is immune from this kind of challenge. A *cause célèbre* in this respect was raised by the partial loss of the audiovisual data used in the film *Toy Story* (1995) during the back-up process of the digital masters, but there are other common instances of data degradation and loss of information in the protocols for digital compression. There is an inherent risk in each migration, and the risk is multiplied in the likely event of massive periodical transfers of large amounts of audiovisual data. In essence, curatorial values are independent from the transition from the analog to the digital world.

8. Why should a work be preserved in its original medium?

As the interpreter of history through the audiovisual collection for the benefit of present and future generations, the curator must ensure that the work is experienced in a form as close as possible to the way it was intended to be seen and/or heard at the time of its creation.

This does not exclude at all the notion that the same work may be also made accessible in other media, as long as

a) a choice is always given (insofar as possible) between the experience of the original medium and of a new one;

b) clarity at the intellectual and experience level is provided about the difference between the original presentation of a work and its modern ersatz.

The video game "Pac-Man", one of the earliest ever produced, offers evidence that a transfer of the original electronic "content" to a more modern medium does not guarantee by itself future accessibility to this work, as playing the game requires an apparatus endowed with a specific material and environmental identity which is now very hard to represent, even only a few years since the demise of the game. An author of virtual reality shows was recently invited to exhibit his creations in a German museum. Digital copies of the softwares had been made; however, it soon became clear that it was impossible to activate the programmes without specific accessories such as joysticks, keyboards, or other devices no longer available on the market. These objects were eventually found through contacts with private collectors worldwide. In an archive or museum, a curator is responsible for deciding whether or not to be concerned about their collection and preservation.

9. What deserves preservation?

Archivists and curators have complementary interests in addressing this question. Both from an archival and a curatorial perspective, the answer is clear: as soon as a work is formally put under the responsibility of an archive or a museum, it becomes as important to the collection as any other work. This is not to deny that certain works may be highlighted as "treasures" of a collection; however, from the perspective of the aim to ensure the integrity of the works formally accepted by a collecting body, there are no layers or degrees of citizenship in an archive or museum: insofar as a deliberate decision has been made about their acquisition, a copy of a 2005 "easy listening" music CD is not less important than the earliest recording of a famous Australian soprano. Each deserves to be treated with the same care and according to the same professional standards. While it is true that some works are rarer than others, and that there may not be enough resources to treat all works according to the highest possible standards, these are the standards we should aim at, irrespective of the cultural status of what has been put under our care. Curators and archivists also agree that certain collection items require special precautions, but this by no means contradicts the "democratic" approach to the maintenance and care of a collection.

Where the curator and the archivist part ways is in the set of intellectual and operational decisions about the choices to be made in order to interpret the collection and the acquisition, preservation, and access priorities to be determined accordingly. Given the scope and size of a National Collection, it is very likely that its archivists and curators do not have the technological and financial resources necessary to give adequate exposure to all works at the same time. Moreover, it is in the very nature of curatorial work to exercise the authority and the responsibility necessary to make informed choices within a body of work so vast as to require a hierarchical approach to their treatment. To further pursue the political metaphors, all citizens are deemed to be equal, but some of them are chosen to represent the values of a society for a given period of time.

History is the most selective, powerful, and often unforgiving curator of the cultural heritage, as it determines (through a series of events ranging from cultural trends and economic influences to wars, genocides, and natural catastrophes) what posterity will have an opportunity to experience and what will be bound to disappear forever. The curator doesn't have the same overwhelming power, but he or she has the responsibility to decide what should be preserved first in the historical time frame within which he or she operates. This prerogative should not be taken lightly, and requires a refined sense of judgement, strategy, and opportunity. In giving shape to their vision, curators will give equal weight to a dual set of considerations.

The first is part of a territory shared with the archivist: how soon will the work become inaccessible forever if it is not preserved? In determining the best course of action, both the archivist and the curator will evaluate the collection from a technical standpoint and assess the risk of physical decay of the works in the collection.

The second set of criteria is of cultural nature: given a number of works equally in need of preservation, which ones should be given priority? Choosing work A instead of B does not mean deliberately condemning B to oblivion: it means declaring that:

a) under the present circumstances,

b) given the already existing heritage,

c) in view of a presumed future landscape of the collection and the cultural context surrounding it,

preservation of A must take priority over treatment of B.

This is by all means a value judgement, the expression of a coherent system of thought, and the curator has a heavy burden in applying it in a responsible manner after consulting with the archivist and the preservation technician, whose knowledge of conservation practices is a necessary prerequisite of any informed curatorial decision. This is also what makes the curatorial profession so inherently challenging, as it requires a multiplicity of skills, ranging from historical expertise, to knowledge in technical and legal matters, and the managerial skills such as the ability to take into account conflicting interests and to allocate the efforts and the financial resources in a way that is consistent with the cultural choices he or she has made. It is quite possible, for instance, that the curator may reach the conclusion that a certain collection should be immediately copied into the digital domain because its value is limited to the "content". How to make such a decision without contradicting or betraying the notion of adherence to the medium is only one of the many challenges facing curatorship in the digital world.

10. Preserving everything vs. selecting

The mandate of the National Film and Sound Archive is to acquire, preserve, and make accessible the Australian audiovisual heritage (a discussion on the definition of "audiovisual heritage" may be found in Ray Edmondson, "Audiovisual Archiving", p. 22). Ideally, the NFSA should apply this principle to the entire body of works produced in Australia; in other countries in which Australians who had a creative reputation before they left Australia – or who are temporarily abroad – are featured; and by other audiovisual makers in the Australian territory. The NFSA should also apply its efforts to works exhibited or distributed in Australia that have had a significant influence on the cultural life and development of the Australian people. A curatorial selection of foreign audiovisual works is now part of the NFSA's collecting agenda. In relative terms, the creative audiovisual output in the former category is more modest than in other countries, such as India or the United States. However, the exponential growth of works produced through digital technologies makes it extremely difficult to achieve even the first task, both on a practical and a financial level. Bearing this in mind, curators should never lose sight of their ideal goal. They should not only explore every opportunity to come closer to it: they should also prepare the ground for future curators and help them increase their capacity to fulfill the mission of the NFSA.

In the meantime, curatorial decisions must be made as to what portion of the audiovisual heritage can and should be acquired, preserved, and made accessible in its entirety. Again, this is a matter of assessing the cultural value of the audiovisual works and their potential significance to posterity within the economic resources currently available. The extreme complexity of this task and of the criteria influencing them defines curatorship as an art. Mindful that these criteria evolve over time, curators are expected to have the professional strength to make difficult choices, and be accountable for them. In doing so, they are assisted by a Collection Policy document that is periodically revised in order to ensure its consistency with best archival practice. The Collection Policy is another tool for the achievement of a balance of power within the archive, in that it gives an opportunity to challenge curatorial decisions and to avoid external pressure or interference.

Some indicative yet concrete examples may be of some help in explaining this point. It is fair to assume that a national audiovisual archive should have all the music CDs and all the feature films and television works (with the corresponding scripts) commercially produced in Australia, as they largely determine the cultural reputation of a country and its influence in relation to the economic forces surrounding it. As their number is relatively limited in Australia, this could be seen in theory as a reasonable goal.

Let's also assume that the curators will determine that it is important to acquire, preserve, and make accessible all the short films and television programmes made in Australia, but that completeness cannot be achieved within the means currently available. In such a case, the curators may want to adopt a dual strategy involving:

a) the acquisition of a representative selection of these works, and

b) an effort towards the creation of institutional mechanisms for the negotiated or mandatory deposit of these works.

Finally, let's imagine a third layer of audiovisual works, including all radio programmes and all Internet works produced in Australia, and assume that there is currently no realistic way to acquire them all. In this instance, curators will adopt the same dual strategy, the only difference being that the body of work in question is much larger and the necessary selection process is aimed at acquiring a much smaller percentage of the entire production. This process may be graphically represented by a pyramid in four or more segments: the top segment describes that part of Australian production which the NFSA will commit (under the above hypothesis) to acquire in its entirety every year; the second segment includes that part which can be acquired in a significant percentage; and so forth. At the very bottom of the pyramid there is the galaxy of all audiovisual works produced in the world, from which the curators will pick a limited but meaningful number of rare, unique, or representative items.

EXAMPLE OF CURATORIAL DECISION: ACQUISITIONS

Australian CDs, feature films and scripts
(100% of production)

Australian shorts, television
(50% of production)

Australian radio, internet
(5% of production)

International
(representative works)

Two caveats are in order here. First, the layers in this pyramid are by no means uniform, in that curators should exercise their authority in deciding that a certain cluster of works should be given priority over the others within the same layer (for example, a curator may decide that Indigenous radio programmes should be given a relatively higher priority in relation to all the radio programmes produced in Australia). Second, the layers of this imaginary pyramid are not fixed in time, and curators must be ready to adapt their acquisition priorities to cultural and practical circumstances and events, and be flexible enough to modify their own acquisition, preservation, and access priorities accordingly. The emergence of a new medium, format style, genre, or mode of audiovisual experience is an opportunity and a challenge for curators, as they can begin preserving what society hasn't yet deemed worthy of long-term preservation, although they may not possess the conceptual framework necessary to integrate the new-born works within the audiovisual tradition with which they are familiar. (It is worth remembering that the term "work" should be used here in its most inclusive sense. Ideally, an archive should not just acquire discrete programmes, recordings, or films. It should also be acquiring their context in the same way: for instance, a whole 12-hour or 24-hour slice of the output of television or radio stations on a cyclical basis, so that the context of discrete programmes – the television or radio experience – is captured.)

11. Preserving a work already preserved elsewhere
To further complicate matters, there is the fact that a national audiovisual archive is part of a broader community of sister institutions with similar goals and objectives. While this is of course a positive thing, it does not simplify an archive's work, in that the boundaries between the responsibilities and prerogatives of the members of the archive, museum, and even library community are not clearly defined, and are constantly shifting. In deciding whether or not an audiovisual work in the collection should be fully preserved even if it is already known to be preserved by another institution, the issue of redundancy should be carefully considered.

For many years, prints of films by Satyajit Ray have not been preserved outside India because it was assumed that they had already been protected in their country of origin. This may have been at least partially true; however, a recent incident at a film laboratory destroyed part of the preservation work already done, and archives undertook a desperate search for the few surviving vintage prints. As a result, several Satyajit Ray films available today are the result of a preservation work based on sub-standard elements. The NFSA has recently acquired a 35mm of a film by Alejandro Jodorowsky, the European cut of *Santa Sangre* (1993). This is a very recent film, and yet no major archive in the world holds a copy of this title. A curatorial decision would dictate in this case the redefinition of the NFSA copy as a "master" element, or at least as a print for restricted access.

In curatorial terms, the default option is to treat every unpreserved collection item as a master copy. It is the curator's prerogative, based on his or her knowledge of the preservation history of a given work and the current international context, to decide which kind of audiovisual elements may be moved from the preservation category to the list of works available for access; hence the importance for curators to keep abreast of the activity of their colleagues abroad.

The issue of "redundancy" may also be examined within a nation's own boundaries. Ray Edmondson has pointed out that the NFSA and the Australian War Memorial have, to some extent, duplicate collections of World War II-era Australian newsreels. That's because the NFSA received the Cinesound Movietone library, and the AWM acquired the "official" footage from the then-Department of Information as government war records. The holdings are far from identical – there are many subtle differences – but there is overlap. However, the crucial difference is one of perspective and context. The NFSA preserves them as cinema newsreels, that is, as part of Australia's wider cinema and newsreel culture and history. The Australian War Memorial preserves them as government war records, within a quite different institutional context.

12. Curatorship and ideology

The curators' responsibility is not limited to the development of a collection according to the current intellectual values of a society. They must also represent values endorsed by cultural, political, and religious minorities, or promoted by individuals and groups whose viewpoints are a direct challenge to the predominant trends of the present, or alien to the beliefs of the curators themselves. In operational terms, this means that curators should maintain a clear separation between what "is" and what "should be", thus demonstrating an equal degree of commitment to the acquisition of works generally recognized as significant, as well as works which do not correspond to their views or to the common opinion.

A curator who is not keen to acquire, preserve, or give access to an audiovisual work because he or she is afraid of being identified with the ideology portrayed in it does a disservice to the field and to society. For instance, the German propaganda documentary *Triumph des Willens* (1934) is a great film and the document of an aberrant ideology. Another cinematic example drawn from the Australian context is *The Birth of White Australia* (1928), an important document on the perception of national identity in the early 20th century and an aggressively racist film; while taking both perspectives into account in the contextualized presentation of this work, a curator should not prevent an audience from experiencing it because of the curator's own beliefs. The curator's job as an interpreter does not extend to the right to think on behalf of the audience.

By the same token, the curator is responsible to posterity in that he or she must possess the vision and sense of history necessary to imagine what the audience of a distant and therefore unimaginable future may ask of a collection of national significance. The measure of success of a curator's endeavour is far more than the mere notion of "completeness"; it is the recognition from posterity that he or she has anticipated needs which were not immediately foreseen at the time and in the context of the curator's professional life. Hence the ongoing question curators must constantly ask themselves: is there an aspect of today's culture which is being totally neglected but may become significant, useful, or necessary to the audience of tomorrow?

There are successful artists who have occasionally produced works generally dismissed by contemporary audiences: these are the works the curator should aim at first, because the likelihood that they will be lost is comparatively high. When deciding preservation priorities, curators will pay attention not only to those works, media, and formats which are in greater demand, but also to those which may be deemed to be of significant cultural value in the future and which are not necessarily perceived as such by the current dominant taste. The ideal goal of the curator of a national audiovisual collection is the awareness that no stone has been left unturned to draw an understandable compelling portrait of the society where he or she lives, giving appropriate weight to the mainstream and the independent, to the consensus and the creative marginality, to the canon and its meaningful subversion.

In 1905, the destruction of films, phonograph cylinders, and the printed scores of early operettas was seen not only as inevitable: it was taken for granted, very much as happened with newspapers. Film and popular music were not considered as cultural works, let alone as forms of artistic expression. Those who saved early films from destruction were inadvertently the first curators of the audiovisual world; similarly, those who kept cylinder phonographs after the advent and overwhelming success of the gramophone record made an unconscious curatorial decision: they saved what society deemed unnecessary, thus creating the conditions for their availability to posterity. The same criteria ought to be applied today to more recent media and formats: is there a virtual reality museum? How many institutions preserve the hardware necessary to operate a 1984 video game?

A curator is like a cultural antenna, in that she or he must constantly monitor and participate in the developments of audiovisual creation in order to readily adapt or modify the current acquisition policies. In qualitative terms, the growth of a national audiovisual archive is not a linear process. Its development criteria must be constantly verified against the principles and practices of the audiovisual culture and its modes of production, so that the manifestations and the consequences of changes still undetected by the majority are promptly incorporated into the fabric of the collection policies. In their exploring the opportunities and challenging the limits presented by these policies, curators act like the cultural meteorologists of a collecting institution.

APPENDIX: THE ETHICS OF CURATORIAL PRACTICE

The following is adapted from John M.A. Thompson, ed., Manual of Curatorship: A Guide to Museum Practice (London: Butterworth, 1986), pp. 530–537.

1. Management and Care of Collections

1.1. It is a curator's duty to take all possible steps to ensure that a written acquisition policy is adopted by the governing body of his/her archive. It is therefore his/her duty to recommend revisions of that policy at regular intervals. He/she must ensure that the policy, as formally adopted and revised by the governing body, is implemented, and ensure that his/her colleagues are fully acquainted with it.

1.2 It is a curator's primary responsibility to do all in his/her power to fully protect all items in his/her care against physical deterioration, whether on display, in store, subject to research or conservation procedures, or on loan elsewhere. A curator must apprise his/her supervisor of the recommendations made to him/her by specialists in the field, and enforce all safeguards subsequently adopted.

1.3 All items within a curator's care must be recorded, including the circumstances and conditions of acceptance and such other information as is necessary to complement the object, in an appropriate, secure, and permanent form capable of easy retrieval.

1.4 There must always be a strong presumption against the disposal of specimens to which an archive has assumed formal title. Any form of disposal, whether by donation, exchange, sale, or destruction, requires the exercise of a high order of curatorial judgement, and should be recommended to a curator's supervisor only after full expert and legal advice has been taken.

1.5 A curator may not delegate curatorial functions to persons who lack the appropriate knowledge and skill.

1.6 A curator must never discourage legitimate research into the collections under his/her care by those qualified to perform it.

1.7 All research undertaken in the archive should relate to the institution's collections or objectives.

1.8 A curator has a clear duty to consult professional colleagues outside his/her own institution when his/her expertise and that of his/her immediate colleagues are insufficient to ensure the welfare of items in the collection under his/her care.

2. Accessibility of Data

2.1 It is a curator's responsibility to safeguard the confidentiality of sensitive data contained in the records which he/she maintains. Sensitive data consists of information to which uncontrolled access might put at risk rare, unique, or vulnerable material, and of personal details and statements the disclosure of which could lead to legal action. A curator may disclose such information only to enquirers whose reputations, interests, and intentions he/she has established beyond reasonable doubt to be consistent with the needs of conservation.

3. Personal Activities

3.1 The acquiring, collecting, and owning of objects by a curator for his/her own private collection is not in itself unethical, but it should be discouraged. Serious dangers are implicit when a curator or his/her staff collects for themselves privately objects similar to those which he/she and others collect for his/her archive. In particular, no curator or curatorial staff should compete with their institution either in the acquisition of objects or in any personal collecting activity. Extreme care must be taken to ensure that no conflict of interest arises.

3.2 On no account may a curator solicit a personal gift or bequest from a member of the public.

3.3 Dealing (buying and selling for a profit) in material which is collected by the curator's institution is an unacceptable practice for all curators and their staff.

3.4 A curator must be fully aware that to undertake identification and authentication outside his/her duties for personal gain with the intention of establishing the market value of an object, is fraught with danger. If it is to be done, a curator must declare such intention beforehand to his/her supervisor, and be at pains to observe the highest standards of academic objectivity.

3.5 A curator is not normally qualified to undertake valuations, and must therefore be aware of any implications of using his/her position for direct or indirect personal profit. In the course of his/her duties, a curator will, from time to time, be required to have regard to the financial value of objects. In such circumstances he/she must always pay attention to the possible implications arising from this practice.

3.6 A curator must obtain the written consent of his/her supervisor before undertaking private work from which personal financial gain may accrue. Even when consent has been obtained, such activities should not be allowed to interfere with the discharge of his/her official duties and responsibilities.

4. Responsibilities and Services to the Public

4.1 The acquisition of archive items from members of the public must be conducted with scrupulous fairness to the seller or donor.

4.2 Although circumstances exist wherein a curator may refuse to identify an object, as a general rule he/she is expected to do so when, in the course of his/her employment, he/she is asked by a member of the public. A curator must not withhold significant facts about the object or deliberately mislead the enquirer. If a curator's knowledge of the object is incomplete, this should also be stated.

4.3 In compliance with the UNESCO Convention on the Means of Prohibiting and Preventing the Illicit Import, Export, and Transfer of Ownership of Cultural Property, a curator must not identify, accept on loan, or acquire by any means, an object which he/she has good reason to believe was acquired by its current owner in contravention of the terms of that Convention, or by any other illegal means.

4.4 A curator must not reveal information imparted to him/her in confidence during the course of his/her professional duties (see also 2.1).

4.5 Archive objects on public display, with all forms of accompanying information, should present a clear, accurate, and balanced exposition, and must never deliberately mislead. These principles apply also to books and information published or otherwise disseminated by the archive.

4.6 Material sold in the archive shop should be of a standard and nature relevant to and compatible with the aims and objectives of the archive service.

4.7 The curation of material of ritual significance is a sensitive undertaking, and a curator must be aware of the possible impact of such activity on humanistic feelings or religious beliefs. He/she must therefore take all reasonable steps to avoid giving rise to public outrage or offence in his/her management of such material.

4.8 In cases where his/her professional advice is sought, a curator must ensure that such advice is consistent with archival or museological principles and as far as possible in the best interests of the enquirer.

5. Relationship with Commercial Organizations

5.1 It will often be a legitimate part of a curator's duty to work with commercial organizations, whether they be vendors, suppliers, producers, distributors, exhibitors, auctioneers, or dealers, in respect of possible acquisitions, potential sponsors, or the media (press, radio, television). However, in all such dealings, a curator must never accept from such sources a personal gift in whatever form which might subsequently be interpreted, whether rightly or wrongly, as an inducement to trade with one organization to the exclusion of others. Equally, in the course of his/her duties, should a curator be asked to advise a member of the public on an appropriate commercial organization to be approached, the utmost care must be taken to ensure that no personal prejudice could subsequently be inferred from such advice.

5.2 In the area of industrial sponsorship, there will be an agreed relationship between the archive and the sponsor, and a curator must ensure that the standards and objectives of the archive are not compromised by such a relationship.

5.3 When providing information for the media, a curator must ensure that it is factually accurate and, wherever possible, enhances the reputation of the archive (see also 4.5).

6. Relationship with Professional Colleagues

6.1 A curator's relationship with professional colleagues should always be courteous, both in public and private. Differences of professional opinion should not be expressed in a personal fashion. Particular care must be taken to avoid any dispute coming to public notice so as to bring discredit on the persons concerned and the profession at large.

6.2 When acquisition policies and collecting areas overlap, the curators concerned should draft a mutually satisfactory agreement. This should then be referred to the governing bodies concerned for approval, either as a substantive change or as an appendix to their acquisition policies. Where conflict with other archives over the acquisition of an object is likely, curators must take all possible steps to ensure that the issue is amicably resolved.

6.3 In the course of his/her duties, a curator forms working relationships with numerous other people, both professional and otherwise, within and outside the archive in which he is employed. A curator is expected to conduct these relationships with courtesy and fair-mindedness and to render his/her professional services to others efficiently and at a high standard.

Chapter 7

Archival Control

—DF: Archival control starts with selection and acquisition, subjects seldom considered in depth by film archives. Up till now archives have considered themselves as passive custodians of the film heritage. They acquire everything they can lay their hands on because they don't have the confidence to decide what material the scholar of the future might need.

However, if the archive is to embrace all moving images, and ensure that the most important items in its collection are preserved and made available, it can no longer avoid the issue of selection.

Do you feel that if an archive had a published selection policy and provided justification for each acquisition, that it would find it easier to make the case for preservation and presentation funding, and to change its role from one of passive provider to one of active interventionist? Would curatorial contextualization be more acceptable to its constituency, if it took responsibility for the shape of its collection? And would such a selection policy be in conflict with the archive's responsibility to safeguard and make available its national film heritage?

Do film archives in your opinion need to build their collections differently in the future, and could a change in selection and acquisition policy enhance their status in the cultural hierarchy? Would a proactive approach to selection and acquisition help archives in their struggle to get films accepted as cultural artefacts?

—PCU: This is a battle that must be fought on multiple fronts. The first is the film archive's own philosophical heritage. Not so long ago, the mantra of film archives was "preserve everything". At face value, this aspirational claim was justified by at least two assumptions: first, that so much had been lost already, and it was time to recognize that every moving image is of potential value from a historical, technological, cultural, or aesthetic perspective; second, that the number of films produced worldwide was huge but finite, and that a collective effort on an international basis could achieve the goal of collecting every single film.

The first principle surfaced relatively late, when the inadequacy of the *auteurist* model of film archiving became evident to those who were not content with a history of cinema written on the basis of the surviving "masterpieces". The second principle could be interpreted as a way of advocating the legitimacy of the film archive as a cultural institution. This kind of statement implicitly related the film archive to the book repository: if there's a National Library collecting all books, why not do the same with films? So, the more films were collected, the better. A film archive with 600,000 films would therefore be more "relevant" than the archive with only a couple of thousand titles.

However, I see a third *raison d'être* for this phenomenon. By saying "let's preserve everything", you don't have to choose. Consciously or not, the curator surrenders the responsibility of selection to an undefined "posterity", thus avoiding the risk of being judged by future generations. The dangers and shortcomings of this approach are now becoming evident at a time when it is no longer possible to define the boundaries of the moving image heritage. The number of moving images produced is theoretically "finite", but we all know that it should be treated as infinite, given that no moving image archivist is even considering the possibility that everything can be collected and preserved.

Now we're in a double bind: a new generation of curators feels the urgent need to define selection criteria, but has little or no tradition to rely upon; and by telling funding agencies that certain moving images will be deliberately excluded from the archive (at a time when moving images are a commodity in huge demand), funding bodies may begin to question the legitimacy of the archive itself. It's a bit like saying that if an archive wants the right to exist, it must become a repository of as much "content" as possible. Which is precisely the opposite of what we call curatorship.

This is to say that it is absolutely essential for a moving image archive to publicly declare its methods of acquisition with a Collection Policy; but collection policies are not enough without the ability to explain, promote, and advocate – the ability to persuade that they make sense. I guess this calls into question the traditional distinction between "archive" and "museum". Some are saying that such a distinction is no longer useful. I don't have an answer to this, but it would be foolish to keep thinking that the archive is the place where selection is not necessary. The absence of a stringent collection policy in most moving image archives is, in my opinion, an indicator of the fact that the film curator is still reluctant to say "no". It is still easier to say so in a so-called "museum", but even the authority of the museum curator is now challenged by those who are blaming past generations for not having properly collected what they are now interested in: home movies; pornography; sponsored films. Film curators have not yet learned how to adequately formulate and defend their choices. Collection Policies often exist only in their heads, thus giving them a good excuse to accept indefensible acquisitions for opportunistic reasons.

—DF: I think your historic rationale for the "collect everything" philosophy is spot-on. There is still some justification for collecting everything for the period 1895 to, say, 1915, or perhaps a little later. Even if archives acquire all extant material, it is unlikely that in any major film producing country, they will succeed in saving more than 50% of production. It is difficult to write an interpretive cultural and social history of the American silent cinema in the 1910s, for instance, if one only has access to between 10% and 20% of output. The recent Mitchell and Kenyon discovery in the UK shows how wrong you can be in assessing the relative importance of a specific producer.

However, pressure from funding agencies influenced by those who recycle film commercially and the reluctance of curators to make selections and stand firmly behind them are the most serious issues. We do have technical opportunities today that we did not have even 10 years ago. We don't have to treat all the items in our collections in the same way. A curator can now say items that best illustrate the creative achievements of national film-makers will be given "A" status, and be preserved and made accessible in the form in which they were first seen by the public; items that contribute to an understanding of national history and culture have "B" status, and are preserved in their original format, but are made accessible in an archivally acceptable digital form; and items that are part of our national cinema heritage but not essential to an understanding of national creative achievement or to the interpretation of the nation's history or social development would be in the "C" category, and would be preserved in an archivally acceptable digital form and made available in a lower-resolution digital form.

In this way, all material acquired could be safeguarded and made accessible. Selections that were to end up in the third category could be acquired in digital form even if they had been produced on celluloid, and would not therefore become part of the backlog.

One of the pressures on curators to acquire everything is the desire of programmers to concentrate on complete retrospectives. Selection and acquisition and archival programming should be in the hands of the same person – the curator. This would strengthen the curator's role within the archive and eliminate a source of conflict. Likewise, the curator should have a role in what is made accessible, and in what form, and in the provision of archival material for reuse. Today, those who make films or television programmes that reuse film tend to search archival collections using cataloguing information. If curators handled such enquiries and used their knowledge of the collection to direct users towards material that was for the most part in the "A", or more likely the "B", category, this should enhance the archive's curatorial role in the commercial world.

I see the curators, supported by the archivists, as the core of a film archive. Selection and acquisition decisions, programming decisions, and reuse and access decisions would then be integrated, and the archive would appear externally more coherent and responsible.

Such ideas may seem simplistic, and certainly need to be further developed. However, a museum keeps much of its material in the basement, out of the public eye, and concentrates on contextualizing specific elements of its collections. It plays an active role in interpretation, not a passive one like most film archives. There must be something to learn from their approach.

7.1 COLLECTING

—DF: To start with, a series of questions: Do you feel there should be a relationship between the film collection policy and the collection policy for film-related materials? And should the latter be related to the concept of the National Collection? In other words – should the related materials tie in with the film collection, or is there justification for the related materials to have a broader sphere than the film collection? Do the same rules apply to all materials?

—PCU: At face value the answer would be easy – I can think of a lot of material in our Documentation department [at the National Film and Sound Archive of Australia] that is not directly related to our film and sound collection. An example would be the records of a production company from the silent era where we don't have the films, as 95% of the actual films have been lost.

But then, and that's something I've realized in recent times, it is clear that the curator of the documents and artefacts collection is faced with a major problem: the issue of relevance. Every kind of documentation is potentially useful for a researcher. What if we were offered all the financial documents of a company, all the costumes for a given film? The amount of documentation that could be collected causes a problem for the archive in terms of the capacity to process all this material.

__DF: The question is: how far do you go? For example, the manuals for film projectors, which were not manufactured in Australia, but in use there. Do you keep those as a reference? I'm trying to find the cut-off point. If you have a policy, for film preservation purposes, to collect the national heritage, what is your similar policy for film-related materials?

__PCU: I agree with you that there is no clear cut-off point, or a line which we can easily draw. Yesterday, in a conversation I was having with a colleague, he was making reference to the fact that some private collectors collect video product catalogues. We're talking about brochures which you often find in a newspaper, something institutions don't think about collecting. If you think about what is relevant and what is not, you really have to imagine what a researcher a hundred years from now will be looking for. Today we're grateful because we have the production records for the Biograph Company. But the reasons why this is relevant to us would

probably have been unpredictable a hundred years ago.

But then there's another issue I find equally important, and that is the actual relationship between the national collection *per se* and the related collection. My impression is that in terms of actual use of the collection, there is very little connection between the use of the moving image and recorded sound collection and the use of the documents. The number of people making use of this collection is minimal, almost insignificant, compared to the number of those who use the moving images and recorded sound collections. As we always have to think in managerial terms – we have to deal with storage space, the costs of cataloguing, accessioning, conservation – the truth of the matter is that there is a wild disproportion between the effort we put into gathering the documentation and the actual use that is made of it. Now from an archival perspective, this should not be an argument. The decision of an archive to collect any documentation should not be dictated by what is our current perception of the use that is being made of it. But when you have to answer a governmental authority or a board, in the absence of a clear-cut criterion the acquisition of documentation is an argument that's even harder to defend.

__DF: Two small follow-ups. One could think of a situation where you collect documentation not directly related to, say, Australia, but not put money into preservation – you just see that it is properly handled and stored. Or you could say that you only collect documentation relating to films of other countries if that material is not available in any published form in your own country…

__PCU: I think you have clarified a point that was unclear to me. If you're talking about material related to foreign production, this argument holds very well. I would make a curatorial assessment of the cultural and historical interest of the material, and it's a matter of keeping it without necessarily undertaking a proper preservation plan. That is OK. But: my impression is that the same issue applies to the national collection itself. Again, if we take a broad view of what constitutes a document, and go back to the example of the producer who offers an entire set of costumes for a film: we both know the challenge of preserving and making accessible this kind of collection. My argument would be that even if I were offered an entire set of costumes I would not necessarily acquire all of them, only some of them. My impression is that having all these costumes would not add significantly to the understanding of the works themselves, or the industry surrounding it. But at the moment I say this I know that I'm making myself vulnerable for someone to say "No, no, Paolo, you could gather important information by looking at that material from which these costumes were made."

__DF: I agree. I see a real problem, and the reason I'm concentrating a bit on this is that I don't think the question of material relating to film collections has adequately been covered in our policies, and I don't think there's a structured approach to it. For instance, if you live in a country like Belgium, it may be that all the researchers coming into your library are coming to look at material related to the American or the French cinema! And so, therefore, should you have collections of related material which are the ones most likely to be used by your clientele, or the ones which are most closely related to your own collections?

__PCU: When you say that archives are not paying enough attention to the acquisition policy of that kind of material, I completely agree with you, and I would go even further by saying that the experience I had is that archives are taking these materials a bit indiscriminately. Curators tend not to take the risk of refusing something, because they are afraid that someone in the future may blame them. So they take the "one never knows" approach.

7.2 DOCUMENTATION

__DF: Let's move on to the documentation associated with the actual physical preservation of the film. Should the documentation associated with the preservation of a film be kept in the can with the film itself? Or should this information be included in the archive's online database?

__PCU: In the world where we live one would naturally lean toward the second. These days I'm often presented with media asset management programs that promise miracles about their capacity to record information about the preservation processes on an online database. I'm told "everything is possible and can be done." But then I have a number of doubts, and a number of objections. The obvious one is that the longevity of any media asset management system is either extremely short or it has not been tested, and the migration of the information from one media asset management system to another is always fraught with problems.

We are told that this will no longer be an issue, and that it will become easier. But even then, as we are talking about the preservation of analog works, I instinctively see an advantage in keeping the documentation together with the film itself. But this raises a number of questions. Archives base their storage strategies on the concept of separation, not of joining materials. As much as you want the negatives separated from the positives, or the masters from the viewing prints, you consider it safe to keep related documentation separate.

But that's not the end of the story, because: what do we mean by "documentation"? There was a time, and maybe there still is, when archives were keeping the perforated strip related to the grading in the lab. And this has become a huge problem as you know, as archives have no clear policy on how to handle these rolls. But what do you mean by "documentation" – how a film was preserved? I have read articles and essays about the need to document the preservation process, but my impression is that they make things so complicated. They assume that an archive would have the time to precisely collect the information about preservation, in a way which is clearly not applicable to archives that preserve a large amount of films. It is almost as if we had to write an essay on the preservation of every single work. But: where are the staff who are able, or have the time, to do this? Where are the resources? And, given the fact that we both know that there are no such resources – would it be preferable to establish a minimum criterion of documentation that should be kept, either with a preserved work, or in a database? And then, even if that were agreed upon, do you think that archives would have the stamina to automatically follow this procedure?

___DF: The reason that I think this question is an important issue is because, if you want to find out where the best copy of a film is preserved in the world, all archives need to record preservation information in the same way, and use the same standards of assessment.

___PCU: Yes.

___DF: And how they themselves preserved it – did they use wet gate, what stock did they use? Was it done in 1965, or was it done in 1998? It seems that there is a certain amount of information that can probably be turned into a list of 12 questions. That would make such a huge difference, internationally. When you're looking for the best copy of a particular film in archives, and if you had readily available the information about not only where a film came from – which we know is a sensitive issue – but about what has happened to that film while it was in the archive.

___PCU: But look at what is actually happening today. Whenever an archive or a production company is planning to restore a given film, there is a common procedure of gathering the information that people already have, and from that the organizers of the restoration project already have established a shortlist, such as, "Long versions are extant in archives A, B, C, and we have no information on length in archives D and E, so we contact these archives." Through a process of trial and error, they come up with what they consider reliable information.

___DF: But that's only Stage One. I'm concerned with other kinds of information. For instance, was a silent film printed onto sound stock, and therefore cropped? It could well be that the copy came from the original negative, but if it was printed on sound stock it's virtually useless. I'm concerned with a stage beyond the completeness of the content; what physically has happened to the copy. Knowledge most of the time is pretty good on completeness – through scripts, censorship files, etc. – but I think where we have really failed is to document the physical nature of the material.

___PCU: To play the devil's advocate – there's an example which shows the limitations of what we currently have. If you look at the current state of the database called *Treasures from the Film Archives*, it's basically a checklist of silent film titles with a list of archives which hold materials. In some cases the archives provide information about whether or not the material is available on 35mm, 16mm, or video. There's hardly any indication even of the length of the films. So if it is so difficult to create and maintain such a simple database with so few criteria, and it's not even updated, aren't we being a bit unrealistic to think that what we are suggesting can be achieved?

___DF: We're talking about behaving more like museums. Museums have incredible information available about their collections. We are, at present, not well organized enough to be museums! I actually believe that if we could follow museum practices more closely we would have greater status in the archival community.

___PCU: I agree. Sometimes we do call ourselves museums, and that wishful thinking is plainly arrogant. We're just not doing it.

The trouble is, we're still in a phase where we literally have been amassing thousands and thousands of works in a relatively short period of time. Seventy years is still nothing compared to what museums in other disciplines have done. I do not believe that the fine art museums are acquiring works on a similar basis. In sheer quantitative terms they acquire very little. So maybe, when there's no longer a mass of analog works

to acquire, then we'll begin working more analytically.

___ML: Do the two of you think that it would be feasible at this point in time, when film slowly begins to vanish as a medium of collection, to put a radical stop at collecting materials in some institutions, and introduce a period of say 5–7 years where the focus is not so much on collecting new materials and acquiring new types of materials, more digital works, but rather fall back and concentrate on managing, identifying the existing collections?

___PCU: Realistically, I don't think that archives will fully stop collecting, and I think this will become especially true at the time when production of motion picture film will come to an end. Actually, I foresee that that will be the time when the acquisition of works on analog media will become a more specialized enterprise. After the big wave of disposal of analog materials by production companies will stop, I think this will become a market. What we have been trying to avoid for a long time is to keep the concept of "market value", which is typical of the fine arts community, out of the picture in our field, but the days are numbered. I think the gates will have to be open. That's my view.

___DF: I think there are two collections. There is the retrospective collection, which is what Paolo was talking about. As we move more into the digital environment there will certainly be an increase in the amount of material available. This may be the last chance to acquire traditional formats. So you certainly wouldn't want to stop that now. As far as acquiring digital-born material is concerned, the second collection, I don't think – unless an institution is going to establish a policy whereby it stops collecting altogether material that didn't originate on film; of course that is a possibility, and there may be a few institutions in the world that choose that route – it would be difficult to stop receiving digital-born materials and continue to get the support of funding sources. So, my answer is that it isn't a practical route. Obviously, I would love to think there was some way to increase concentration on assessing the needs of the remaining film material, because one always gets inundated with day-to-day problems, and doesn't have an opportunity to undertake long-term planning, but I don't think this is feasible.

__PCU: When you asked your question, I was assuming you were referring to acquisition of analog artefacts. I have a strong feeling that many archives today are trying to delay the choice of whether or not they want to engage with the digital arena. They are hesitating because they are afraid of losing funding; they are afraid of losing profile and importance – but the time will come when they will be forced to decide. It will be almost a Darwinian process. Some institutions will realize that they just cannot cope with the digital works, and they will have to reconsider their identity. It is possible that some of them will collapse, because they are expected to do what they are unable to do. Once this selection process is completed, there will be a number of decisions dealing with both worlds, and a number of decisions dealing with one world only, the analog or the digital, but in both cases there will still be acquisition strategies. The question is: Can you make a deliberate decision to acquire only a specific kind of moving image material? To me this is the key, the pivotal point of the realization that a choice will be forced upon collecting institutions.

__DF: I think if I were faced with that choice, I would assume that you could not refuse to collect digital materials, but I would want to establish a new department within the archive, or within the parent organization, if applicable, so that you could hopefully find new ongoing resources specifically to cope with the digital-born material, so there wasn't competition between the film-based collection and the digital-born collection. I think in the end I would have to collect digital-born material, but hopefully I would be able to separate the digital-born collection in funding terms from the collection of film material.

__PCU: II do think there will also be a greater degree of clarity, for good or bad reasons, about collection policy in another sense – the sense of the choice between the collection of these tricky meshes of "national patrimony" vs. "international patrimony". This is a question that institutions are already asking themselves. I did hear that the Cinémathèque Suisse is now currently thinking about this issue: should they concentrate more on the acquisition, preservation of, and access to the national Swiss heritage, or should they continue to have an international focus? This is beyond the point of seeing world cinema as part of the national patrimony. Here we are talking about a sort of reductionist definition of national production.

__ML: Given the case that the world divides between, let's say, archives, who focus on collecting and documenting materials relating to their national patrimony, and museums, responsible for the proper documentation, contextualization, and interpretation of the world cinema heritage. Is this binary opposition on an institutional level something that is to be desired?

DF: I don't want the situation to arise. I still believe that even if you are responsible for collecting national production it is vitally important for the survival of the organization that it also has a role in actively disseminating and contextualizing world cinema for its national constituency.

PCU: Or to put it this way: whether or not the gap between the so-called "archive" and the "museum" will widen, the archive will still be faced with the responsibility of not just being a content provider, but an additional interpreter. This is still a chance that the archive has, and I think the reason is a negative one – the fact that we are leaning towards a world where moving images will be available from a variety of sources. The archive will no longer be the only place where you can find moving images. If that's the case, the only *raison d'être* for the archive as a national collecting institution, or an institution of national reputation, will be its ability to provide the added value of interpretation. Even if the so-called "archive" says, look, there is a museum doing interpretation, let us just concentrate on collecting, this will not be enough to guarantee the survival of the archive.

DF: I don't like this concept of separation between archive and museum.

PCU: I don't like it, either. But to challenge it at the present time seems an uphill battle, to put it mildly.

DF: I simply see the way in which one thinks about this in the future is that you have to subsume some of the methodology of museums in disseminating collections to the public within an archival organization, which is also responsible for collecting a national patrimony. It's not about archives and museums as separate entities

– it's about a new organization that incorporates both philosophies.

PCU: This is the crux of the debate, the question we keep arriving at: is this divide going to become more radical, or not? If I look at the current *Zeitgeist,* the impression is that this division will be sharper than before, because of the demands being put on the archives. Again, you just provide content; let someone else interpret it.

DF: But that's a disaster, in my opinion, because the resources are going to be tied to access in future. Access will have to include "celebrity" material, material which has worldwide recognition. It will be more difficult for the archive to safeguard its national production if it's not at the same time involved in dissemination of world cinema and patrimony. If museums and archives separate, I think the archive will actually disappear, and the museum will take on some but not all of the archive functions.

ML: But an archive function for a very limited number of works, what you call the…

PCU: …the Canon.

ML: Today museums are concentrating on producing event after event after event. They have to survive in the current landscape of events in all mediums, on the level of education, on the level of arts. They need to establish every single one of their special shows as something unique, as treasures rediscovered. They are agenda-setters.

PCU: The "wild card" in this forecast game we are trying to play, is the question of the availability of the work for the museum. What puts the museum perhaps in the weaker position is that, by and large, the museum – in the way we mean the word today – does not have a collection as large as the collection of the archive. A museum with only, say, 12,000 or 15,000 titles, cannot hope to survive alone without some form of relationship with fellow museums and with archival institutions.

__DF: Why are we talking about all these separate organizations? To me, I want to graft museum functions onto an archive. Archives already have both the national collections and materials important in the dissemination of world cinema. In the past, archives have not been prepared to select parts of their collections, to contextualize and make them available by projection, on DVD, through books, articles, etc. I want the archive to become a new, broader-based organization, which incorporates museum functions. If you give access functions to another organization, whether it be a museum or not, the archive is going to suffer. Archives are not going to be able to fulfill their responsibilities for the safeguarding of national collections.

__PCU: So, here we are really looking at a hypothesis of a new genetic code for the archival institution, an evolution of the structure, identity, rationale of the archival institution, the archival institution becoming more than it is now. If I may use another example drawn from my own experience, these are precisely the two phases of the activity I've seen so far at the NSFA: first, the archive being pushed as being a simple provider, then reacting to this push with an attempt to establish a museum-like curatorial function within the archive, so that the archive advocates its role in society by saying "we also want to interpret and to act and to think in museum terms". Right now, we are going against the current. That is clear. It all depends on how strong the archives will be to pursue this, and

how much they will be aware of the importance of this strategy for their future.

__DF: Archives have to have much stronger leadership, because they will have to make much more difficult choices in the exercise of their responsibilities. It will be a difficult balance in future. The only way to get money for preservation in the future is by not promoting the word "preservation". Instead, we will need to promote the word "access" – but incorporate preservation within access, rather than the other way around. We have got to get rid of the passivity of the past, and have a more active policy, which is controlled within the archive. It must balance the need to safeguard the national collection, the need to disseminate the national collection, and the need to enable our own nationals to understand the important elements of world cinema. If they can't appreciate the latter, then they are not going to be able to understand the importance of the national production and put it into context.

__ML: Another provocative question: should an organization adhere to a certain quota in their programming of films from their own collections, to be able to borrow copies from a FIAF archive? The point being that in the situation now, you can hardly imagine a film museum not having its own collection, but just being something like an art gallery that lives for the most part on loans of works in whatever form. These institutions are most likely to go digital in the near future, just to increase the number of films they can programme. So, if you were the policy-maker, in a sense, would you recommend a quota of this sort to be part of the international community of film museums?

__PCU: Look, if I were a policy-maker, what I

would aim for would be the enrichment of the collection, an ongoing enrichment of the collection to the point that much of the so-called "film exhibition activities" are not dependent upon other collections. I would go as far as doing what the Art Gallery of Queensland in Brisbane is doing on a small scale, which is acquiring films together with the rights to exhibit the films on the premises of the archive. Having said this, I would say that very few institutions would be able to afford such an ambitious policy. Off the top of my head, I can only really think of a couple of institutions, worldwide, that could aim at this.

___DF: What I would like to do is to reorganize the international organization of film archives. They should not be centered in one organization, like FIAF, but in regional groups. Within each regional environment there should be a stock of first-class prints of films of international importance, which are available to institutions that meet a set of criteria, both in terms of preservation and access. Then FIAF becomes a coordinator on an international level with organizations like UNESCO or with multinational projects to safeguard moving images. FIAF would not organize annual congresses; it would be a body that helps regional groups to establish strong archives within each region.

___PCU: I think there are precedents; there is a model for this. It is my understanding that the so-called "Nordic Archive Group" is doing this to some extent. They are acquiring prints with the agreement that these prints can be used for exhibitions among the group. It is a positive model, which also fosters a greater care for the physical treatment of the artefact because it is in the name of the common good.

___DF: The only way we have a chance of retaining the opportunity to project films would be through a system of regional centres, because, as Paolo said, there's no possibility of an individual archive having a collection of first-quality prints large enough for it to be able to adequately disseminate the history of cinema to its own audience. We do need to reorganize ourselves internationally if we are to be able to retain the ability to project a range of film in our own theatres.

___PCU: Insofar as this matters to us, the projection of the physical print. I don't know if this is germane to this chapter specifically, but I'm also getting increasingly curious. I'd like to have a crystal ball, and see to what extent more titles will become available in digital form for public exhibition or not. I begin to suspect that – I think I pointed this out in another conversation – this may not be the case. The availability of analog prints will necessarily decrease, because prints become more precious. There will not be a corresponding increase in digital…

___DF: Not if DVD is used for public projection, because the younger generation is happy to see new films in a much smaller, personal, environment. However there won't be an audience for a retrospective of older films on DVD.

___PCU: I'm still convinced that the optimists are underestimating the fact that creating a digital version of a film classic is very expensive, and we cannot expect to be able to create large numbers of good-quality digital projection titles, enough to guarantee that there will be diversity, variety, and scope in programme activities.

___DF: I would like to see the archive movement getting to a situation where its contextualization of films would be of interest to the copyright owner, so that in return he/she would give free access to 35mm prints. I would like to see archives dealing with the copyright owner on an equal basis because the archives were able to offer something that the industry couldn't, particularly for the distribution of films via DVD. In return, archives would get the freedom to use on their own premises films belonging to that copyright owner, and, where possible, access either to prints or to the negatives in order to make prints for reference.

7.3 ACCESS/SERVICES

—DF: Should an archive service all requests from television producers for clips, or should it have a published policy indicating the sort of material it will provide and the sort of programmes it will support? And should the producer of a serious TV programme have direct access to a curator, or should he/she work through a reference librarian? Should an archive provide access to all users, or should we be concerned about those to whom we provide materials?

—PCU: Let's assume that an archive has legal control over what it can provide. We're not talking about a television producer asking for access to their own materials. There's little we can do there.

And, well, of course we both know that we cannot service everybody. We are implementing formal or informal procedures to generate a form of spontaneous "natural selection". We're not doing this to make life difficult for the producers or the researchers, but we want to know how serious the researcher is in relation to a certain search. However, this is not a science. And there is an issue of democracy; not making the producer feel that a sort of censorship is being exercised. But, for example: would you deny a producer permission to use a 1915 shot of a battlefield to depict a 1917 battlefield, as it is not authentic? The producer will respond, "Who cares? Nobody's going to notice," or, "This is my business, not yours."

—DF: But are you in most cases going to know what the producer is going to do? Again, I'm thinking about the reputation of archives. Should an archive ask for a copy of the script, and insist on the deposit of the final programme before transmission? Obviously, it is rather hard to see the programme in advance, and demand changes; but in order to find out how our materials are being used, it is important that the script and the programme are deposited in the archive. You can then say, "In your last programme you used materials in an unacceptable way. Sorry, as the guardians of the national heritage we can't permit this. We're representing the creators of a work, and we must insist that it is used in a way that the creators would have found acceptable."

—PCU: Assuming that the archive has the resources to do so, this would be a desirable solution. With the proviso that promises can be breached.

—DF: Yes, of course that's true, but at least it enables you to ask more questions. And you can supply the materials with a watermark, and only release the unmarked actual footage for transmission when they show you a final cut.

—PCU: This at least gives us an opportunity to engage in a dialogue, to explain – "educate" may be a bit too strong – to the producer why the archive exists. However, we know that producers are rather impatient, and with the development of digital technology requests are becoming more urgent, more detailed, more frequent. Every time an archive says, we're unable to provide something in a certain manner, or format, this reflects negatively on the reputation of the archive. The reputation of the archive does not decrease if a curator asks all kinds of questions about the way the material is going to be used; it does decrease, however, if the archive does not provide materials fast enough, in the right format, in the easiest condition for the producer.

—ML: To expand on David's argument: are archives only guardians of materials they provide for money, or are they also guardians of a proper contextualization of those images?

—PCU: My instinctive reaction to this is that this is a lost cause. The sheer amount of new works produced making use of archival material is such that I truly do not see how the archive could exercise any detailed, significant control over the way images are being used. This is already happening today. There are even some basic proofs that producers are willing to use – and they have this permissible argument of pressure – arguments such as this: *You're there. You're supposed to make the works available. The new work is none of your business, and if you do not provide the material, I will protest with your authority, because you are hampering, you're obstructing access to the collections.* Of course, there are things that can be done; some institutions have been more successful than others. My second point is that art history, and the history of the media in general, is also the result of deliberate, ruthless transformation and manipulation of the original, into something else. We can all think of works that make creative use of a manipulation or a distortion of the materials, like taking a photograph of Marilyn Monroe and turning it into an Andy Warhol work.

—ML: A deliberate falsification of the source.

—PCU: Yes. Sometimes I feel that trying to prevent creators from turning original works into something else is not only a useless way of obstructing the development of art, but it actually goes against what we are for, which is creativity. Here I am talking in terms of aesthetics, in terms of creation, in terms of moving images as art. This argument could be extended to the use of moving images in general. I have often argued that the moving image as an art form has something to do with the constant biological transformation of one entity to another, and that's what makes me think, why try to keep the dam from breaking, when this is how things are meant to be? The archive could still maintain the responsibility of being the guardian of the integrity of a work, meaning: "I can give you a copy of this work, and you can manipulate it any way you want – but don't ask me to alter the original, because I'm not going to do that."

—DF: There is, I think, another issue here. The demand for the use of archival material is going to grow exponentially, and it will be necessary to establish policies to determine who has access to archive master material and the services of a curator. To some users I am afraid one is going to have to say, "Well, you are going to have to get that material from an existing access copy or DVD." Otherwise, I don't see how we can cope. I actually believe it's in the interest of the archive movement that material is used creatively, but I don't think we can cope with all of the requests that are going to arise unless we have a graduated structure that decides how much an archive assists a user and who in the archive spends their time doing so. I do think we have to engage with that in order to protect ourselves. I can see a future where we are going to be completely flooded with access requests of one sort or the other, whether they are from a commercial user, from people making DVDs, or from individual researchers. We have a finite amount of time and staff knowledge that can be put towards these requests. Unless we have some way of limiting access, we're never going to be able to contextualize the parts of our own collection we as archivists feel are important; ones that will only ever come to public attention if we have the time to contextualize them by producing material both for projection and possibly DVD release, etc. I share your views, and I don't want to restrict access. I do, however, want to make certain that specialist time within archives is allocated according to some principles, so that we get the best value for staff time.

__PCU: And all this, taking into account the reality that support to the archives in the foreseeable future will be linked to the authorities, with the pressure to demonstrate that archives are useful because they are being used. That is the keyword today: the more you provide access for the public good, the more your existence will be justified. It is a matter of turning this pressure, this imperative, into something that can be fulfilled according to certain principles. It is acting strategically. If access is what you want, I'll give you what you want, but I will be inserting certain criteria, rules, parameters, which will also fulfill the long-term good of the collection.

__DF: There is a new problem facing archives at the moment. In the past we were very happy to make materials available, but now archives are putting so much work into the presentation of DVDs that they are worried that the DVDs are going to be copied. They are starting to take the same position as the copyright owner, a position they themselves have fought in the past. For instance, the NFPF has faced this problem with some of its *Treasures* sets. In the past we would all have been delighted if someone had made films from the archive available more widely. Now, in order to protect our own future, we might have to start copyrighting contextualized work that we've done.

__ML: Within a very short time, you will have to have a legal department to take control of this whole issue. I am always glad if copies on either UbuWeb or YouTube at least turn up ripped from authorized sources. I would at least prefer to have a film pirated from an archival DVD, instead of being taped from television at the wrong speed with added music to it, an abridged version, whatever.

__DF: I don't see archives ever making a profit out of anything, but if you rely on a certain level of income to continue to produce, to contextualize, your collection and make it available, then you do need some sort of protection for your product.

__ML: This includes two steps. If I follow your train of thought it's not, to put it bluntly, a good idea for an archive or a museum to sub-license part of their collections or broader parts of their collections to footage vendors. For instance, some archives might give the rights of exploitation of their materials to third parties, like Getty Images, ITN, whatever. This is a growing business; you see more and more mergers, companies who buy exploitation rights, and submasters for a limited use, and then re-license. This looks like a good solution, as the archive doesn't have the resources to actively sell their footage and make a profit or contextualize it for re-use. But in this world, where you want commercial access to be something that is in a way *curated,* this is fatal, isn't it?

___DF: Yes, I would be very worried if archives were entering into that sort of arrangement, rather than dealing directly with individual enquiries, either from TV producers or DVD producers. I would want to be certain that they would represent the archive's contextualization correctly.

___ML: I don't think national archives are doing it yet, but I think that the possibility is lurking on the horizon. At one point in this scenario, an organization is also going to address traditional archives. Not only private collectors and distributors. I can imagine a situation in the coming years where such an agency might knock on the door and say, "We'll handle it for you. You'll get a share of the profit; you don't need to take care of all the digitization, the Web-access databasing..."

___PCU: This is already happening with photography. The reason why this danger is concrete is that a commercial company may say, look, because we are a commercial company we are not bound by the same kind of limitations and parameters that the archive is bound to follow.

___DF: Yes, that is true, but the more material from archives that is available for use in any way a commercial organization chooses, the more difficult it will be for archives to justify their existence, except on the basis of quality or on their ability to contextualize. I want to see a partnership developing between archives and commercial organizations, to develop media for public consumption, to develop DVDs, and also, as a result of that partnership, ensure that archives can continue to show 35mm prints on their own premises. If we start entering into arrangements like that, I think we're maintaining bargaining power with the industry. We need that relationship in order to continue to meet our terms of reference and to secure our future.

___ML: Another follow-up question to this: should archives not only choose to whom they license materials, and under what conditions, but also actively stimulate the creation of works of art that in a way communicate to the public the whole idea of the cinema heritage, and also the archive's practices? Of course, at the Austrian Film Museum we ask fees for material use in commercial production. But if a film-maker like Gustav Deutsch comes to the archive, and says he wants to review a large body of footage, and he's going to use it in an experimental film, we would possibly waive charges. Archives become active sponsors of films. The point is, these policies in a way demonstrate our ability to enable the creation of new works.

___DF: It's a very tricky situation. There are film-makers who quite genuinely are unable to afford archival rates because what they are producing is not popular fare. In some cases the archive wants to be associated with such productions, but you've got to compromise between the need to earn income to support other archival activities and free support of worthwhile projects. In every case I would like to find a quid pro quo. Even if you were supporting an experimental film-maker who had no ability to pay, I would want something in return, even if it were an annual lecture, or material for one's archive, because I believe the film-maker will then value our services. Otherwise, you'll never be able to defend yourself against critics who say, "You gave that service to so-and-so, and we're making an experimental film too, but it just happens to be for a wider audience." I think there should never be a case when you don't get some quid pro quo.

—ML: You need to actively draw a line, because whenever we give someone the right to use materials but don't charge for material use, the next time somebody applies for funding for an experimental film, and they have the cost of using materials in their budgets, funding agencies are going to ignore it.

—DF: Every time material is made available, that means there is more material in the marketplace, more material out there, and less need for filmmakers to come back to the archive. Your power in the marketplace is being reduced. That's why there always needs to be some quid pro quo. In dealing with a commercial company, it might be more important to get the company to waive the copyright charges for anything you're showing in your theatre, rather than have them pay a fee. I would, of course, recommend that nothing should be done for nothing.

There is limited specialized knowledge in archives, because it is only built up after being in the job for a long time. Going to Eastman House and getting an MA doesn't give you knowledge about a specific collection. People who have considerable knowledge need to spend their time wisely. One needs rules and regulations about who you give time to and how much time you devote. If you don't have them, I can see the archive floundering, and never having the opportunity to originate its own programmes and to contextualize parts of its own collection which it feels are important and under-utilized. Otherwise, the archive will always be passively responding to third parties. That is what still often happens at the moment, and has been happening for a long time. It's one of the reasons why the identity of an archive is often far lower than the identity of an art museum.

—ML: If I were a documentary producer, and looking for materials traditionally, I would hire a researcher, even a freelance researcher working between the archives and production companies. This is a dying craft. On the other hand, commercial archives provide an upfront database, where you can enter the right keywords and get the right footage without your having any proper knowledge.

—DF: But, you see, that is stock-shot supply; that is not the archives' business. To me, if somebody said, "I want a shot of a train going through a tunnel," my view is that the request does not need a curator's knowledge, and has nothing to do with the archive's role. I would just turn them away. If they wanted a shot of a train going through a specific tunnel at a specific time, in a film where the train's role is significant to the presentation of the story, that's a different matter. This is why I want there to be rules and regulations about who you supply and what you supply. Otherwise, I can see one supplying stock shots, and using valuable archive time and knowledge to do this, which I think is wrong.

—ML: Absolutely; I agree. If a film-maker calls and says, "I'm working on a documentary on a writer in Vienna in the 1910s; I'm looking for material that not only conveys the traditional stock shots of Vienna, but I want to convey a certain anxiety before the war, I want to convey the mentality of urban Central Europe, etc.,"

I say, "You are right up my alley, because I've got beautiful material that speaks for itself."

—DF: That is justifiable, particularly if the film is being made about someone of national importance, because you want that person to be represented in the most accurate way possible.

—ML: And if archives offer this added value, which differentiates them from stock-footage libraries, should proper credit for the archive individual or the curatorial unit who has provided services, be mandatory in the film's credits?

—DF: That again is very important, but I don't think it's then necessary to say that the film-maker should not pay for that material. If someone says their grant does not contain funds for the purchase of archival extracts, the archive should write to the grant-giving body and say, "You have not included anything in the film-maker's budget for this purpose." Firstly, you need to educate these bodies. Secondly, it may be that you have to ask, if it's a very large project, for a special grant in order to supply the film-maker's needs. I think it's a very difficult area. I think too many things happen in archives because of uncontrollable pressure. I think there has to be stronger management, which says, "Well, in this period we have to do the following things. We must not spend more time than X on such-and-such. We must not spend more time than Y on such-and-such. If we cannot do what we want to do within the time schedule, you'll have to wait until we can allocate time for your project, and if there are other people ahead of you, you'll have to wait until their needs are satisfied." It's a very tough job to resist both a commercial enterprise and one that has access to influential people who can put pressure on you. In some ways it might be necessary to make it

known how you intend to allocate your time, so that you've got a document to fall back on; have the principle agreed by a board of trustees, or whatever government agency you feel would be prepared to support you.

—PCU: This is what occupies most of my time, aside from dealing with financial issues. Converting what is presented as a simple access request into something that could be fairly interesting. Otherwise, sometimes I begin to feel like I'm an access machine, a jukebox of moving images and recorded sounds. This is also important in relation to the staff, because if you let this one go, the staff begin to feel that they are working in an audiovisual archival factory, where there's a sort of detachment from the meaning of the object. I proposed to my staff that when they receive a request for, say, a digital copy of a simple shot, I told them, from now on, would you please propose that the same work could be made accessible on 35mm instead of digital. Their first reaction was, "Why? If digital is what they want, why do we want to make things more complicated? This is what they're asking for." We have to propose other ways of using the material – at least make the gesture, that this not necessarily the best way to look at a certain work. Don't say, "The faster the better. We have a digital version available, and here it is, and I can go to the next client." Archives are increasingly using the word "client", and it's a term I don't like.

—DF: I agree. One thing we used to do at the NFA was always insist that the minimum unit of film we duplicated was one reel, whether it was 1,000 or 2,000 feet. If somebody wanted an extract from a 35mm film, we would print a 35mm positive, or negative and positive from that material, and the user had to pay for the total cost. They would leave the 35mm material we printed for them with us. We would only supply to them the footage for which they had cleared copyright. In other words, if they wanted an extract from a 1,000-foot reel, we would print the 1,000-foot positive, or negative and positive, and then we would make, say, a DigiBeta copy with a timecode. And we would retain the 35mm material. That way we would be gradually building up 35mm material which could be used for other archival purposes. We couldn't do it for a whole feature film; but we did say the material printed had to be from leader to leader. There were a lot of people who hated this policy. They complained to our governing board, and we said, "No. This is our policy. We are a film archive; we are responsible for looking after our film collection; we will not do anything that endangers that collection."

—PCU: But here you're talking about material that is being created specifically for those purposes of access. What if the archive had already created a digital version of a given reel?

—DF: That's fine, because if we have an access copy already, that means the archive has preserved the film, and has it available in 35mm form. But if we don't, then the only way of getting access to it is by printing the whole reel. That might leave you with an odd reel of 35mm, but it's still leaving you with more 35mm material.

—PCU: Let me go back to what I was saying before. I have been both dealing with and operating within archives where any service provided, whether it's from an outside party or another part of the archive, is provided to someone called the "client". For example, I asked, "Can I have a VHS tape of this?" I was told, "Yes, okay,

you have to fill out an internal client request." And I said, "Client?" And the answer was, "Well, for practical purposes, as far as the lab is concerned, you're a client." I was trying to look for an alternative word to define this, one that would not make me feel I'm dealing with a stock-footage factory.

—DF: It is important that there is a work order for anything you do. I use the term "work order" intentionally. The only way users understand how time is spent, is if time is accounted for. For instance, you have a work order, which shows that one part of the organization is undertaking work that needs to be accounted for on behalf of another part. It's valuable to say, "OK, that took us X hours. Was it worth it? Was it a good use of our time, for us to spend 4 hours making a copy, or repairing a film, or doing something for a particular occasion? Is there an alternative way we could have met that particular demand within the terms of reference of the archive, without tying up our staff to that extent?" So, I do agree with an internal work order system, but I wouldn't use the word "client". I'm really just concerned to see how time is being used, and whether that's the best way of using it.

—ML: Now, as television makes it into HD, the format is going to be widescreen 16:9. How should archives react to demands where you know that materials from your collection are most likely going to be reformatted, others are going to be manipulated in a programme, and you do not have control over the proper speed of, say, silent documentary material? Should an archive make its materials available under the proviso that it must be an authorized transfer supervised by the archive? So you can make recommendations as to the materials' form in terms of speed, colour, and screen format. Is this feasible?

—PCU: I think we're going back to something we've been discussing before: it's a matter of the critical mass of the request for access, which makes it impossible to monitor individually every single use of material. Some archives can create the access elements themselves. In this case we, one archive, would create the access according to our standards, what we want. If the person requesting access wants to have the images speeded up, or slowed down, we would say, "This is not the way we are providing it." Implicitly, I would have to say, "If you slow it down or speed it up, this is not something we are going to do." Instead of saying, "You have to respect the speed or certain colour or grading in order to have access," which I don't think is possible, the best thing we can do is to do what we can to monitor how the images are being used. And if they don't respect that, the next time they come to us requesting access to the material, we can find an argument to refuse access, saying that it's because you did something that we found to be so inherently wrong, that we do not want to be associated with it.

—DF: That's one thing. The other side of it is education. I mean, there was a time when television showed silent films at the wrong speed, usually 25 frames a second.

—PCU: They still do.

—DF: They still do sometimes, but an awful lot has changed. It's a much better situation than it used to be, and I think this is partly because archives have educated the users. Now the users themselves are happy to show silent films at the right speed, because their peer group will criticize them if they don't.

—PCU: Well, it depends. I have been dealing with users who would deliberately speed up the so-called "natural" speed of a given image in order to convey the impression that it's historical footage. They think you have to have people that are walking too fast. That means it's history. If it moved naturally, they think it would look like a modern reconstructed image. In a way it is surreal. It is interesting in terms of the psychology of perception.

—DF: I think your concern over HD-TV is a very interesting one, because, to me, ensuring the aspect ratio of the original is correct; it is just as important as ensuring the speed of the original is correct. If you are going to change the aspect ratio significantly, which I believe you do with HD-TV, you are seriously altering the original intention. I'm not sure there's any solution to presenting historical images on HD-TV, except in the aspect ratio they were originally presented in, possibly with pillarboxing.

—ML: My next question comes from a very practical implication. I was providing research services for a documentary, and I found beautiful footage from the early 1910s, and then I even offered to go to the lab with the director to supervise test runs into HD. The first thing the telecine operator started doing was to reframe the image to 16:9, and the next thing was that the director said, "Please transfer to B&W, because we want to get the same sepia tint for all archival footage so it looks 'historical'." This is hard to accept if you're a curator. If you're a stock shot librarian, it's not a problem at all; your clients can do whatever they wish.

—DF: You have the right to say to the director, "Yes, you're the director of the film, but I'm the director of the archive, and I have my responsibilities. And if you ignore my advice, we will not be able to help you in the future."

___PCU: Yes, but then, you know what's going to happen next: the producer will go to the board of trustees, the minister, or some other authority, and say, "Your institution is preventing me from doing my job."

___ML: "You're using taxpayers' money, and you're not allowing access."

___DF: Even if you might not win, you must have the opportunity to say it, and to explain to your governing board why you've done it. In other words, actually, the refusal to help, even if in the end you have to give in, gives you that opportunity to educate. I think that if you just don't challenge this kind of thing, you don't get a chance to educate.

___PCU: That's why you absolutely need a collection policy, because if you do it only on a personal basis, people will simply wait until you leave the institution, and will find someone else who will be easier to handle. If this becomes ingrained in the collection policy, so that there's an official document, officially endorsed by your governing body, you can say, "Hey, it's in the collection policy." It's harder to manipulate things if there is an official document. You can use it as a shield.

___DF: Particularly if that official document is presented to your board of governors, if you have one, so they've had a chance to look at it and comment on it, and it has therefore an official standing; I think that's even better.

___ML: The next thing that comes up is the question of credits. What form of credit should archives insist on if their materials are re-used or exhibited elsewhere?

___PCU: I'll take a view that perhaps does not correspond to David's. My impression is that it makes no difference. I look at credits, and what I normally see is a scrolling credit at the end with a list of institutions providing footage. Assuming that these titles scroll slowly enough to actually be legible – look around to see how many people are actually left in the theatre, reading them. And only a miniscule percentage of this miniscule minority pays attention to this specific piece of information. This doesn't mean we shouldn't ask for credit anymore, to remind the producer that we care about our reputation. But it is more about the relation between us and the producer than about us and the public.

___DF: Well the reason why I probably disagree is that a more important thing is the relationship with your funding agency. If you can show how many programmes you've serviced, it's easier to justify the size of your grant. I don't see it from the point of view of the public, but it is important to show that you provided services to important people whose work reaches a larger public, as well as your wider constituency. The reason Frantz Schmitt insisted on having "Bois d'Arcy" in the corner of the screen when his archive's material was transmitted on television was because television often removes credits that have been agreed to in the past.

___PCU: My feeling why Frantz Schmitt was going too far, is that by superimposing the name of the institution on the moving image itself, it was becoming part of the artefact itself. But his over-reaction was a reaction to a legitimate concern.

We had at the National Film and Sound Archive of Australia a discussion about watermarks – where to put the logo, what it should look like – and I discovered a few things. First, I learned that most TV stations would refuse to buy footage that is watermarked. Secondly, even if they accept this footage, it is easy for them to erase the watermark. I've seen plenty of footage recently where there's a little cloud in the corner of the screen.

__DF: I want to talk about the more general idea of how you credit archives. Obviously, one of the things we both agree with is, if anyone shows a film, that there not only should be a credit to the archive, but something about the history of that particular print. What do we really need to do to ensure that the people know that we have high standards, and that we are committed to looking after the interests of the film's creators?

__PCU: OK, I see it – we're talking more in museum terms now. We're going beyond just the name of the institution. I see a number of festival catalogues where information about format, colour technique, the format of origin, is documented, information to indicate that the archive is not just providing "a movie", but is providing something that is being carefully preserved, selected, treated, and interpreted.

__DF: I want the viewer at a festival, the public, to become more aware of the presence of archives, to hear about the particular history of a print – where it comes from, has it been restored. I want them to have a certain consciousness. In the end people who are enthusiastic for cinema will start asking these questions. It would help us to be treated more like a museum if there were more interest in the work we're doing.

The difficult situation is when you help copyright owners to restore a film for a DVD release – they always tend to underplay the contribution of the archive. Hollywood continues to say "we don't need the archives," although the archives' involvement in terms of material, documentation, or restoration, has led to a much better product. I don't know how to ensure greater understanding within the industry of the importance of archives.

__PCU: And, most importantly: how can the archive make sure its contribution is acknowledged, reflected in what people see? In this case it is not enough to have a mention in a festival catalogue, or a brief introduction before the screening of a restored film. Here we're talking about the widespread dissemination of a work. Yesterday I was looking at a Peter Fonda film, *The Hired Hand,* and at the end of the film there were credits recognizing the role of archives. OK, they're end credits. But even this is rare! It is not just about the active contribution to a certain restoration, but the fact that an archive has been protecting the original elements of a given work for decades. Look – the *Mona Lisa* has been at the Louvre for so many years. If a painting is exhibited elsewhere, the museum takes credit: "This is from the Hermitage." It actually adds value to the exhibition of a work. But this is still not happening with film.

7.4 LOAN POLICIES

__DF: This naturally moves us on to loan policies. Not many archives nowadays are concerned about lending films to other archives, but there are cases where other organizations, like film festivals, can look after materials as well as archives. I'm torn between being restrictive, or encouraging anyone who presents the films in the right manner – on celluloid, in a dark room, with an audience.

_PCU: Well, am I wrong in my impression that in the past 10 years or so there has finally been some sign of a gradual shift in the overall perception of the importance of this issue? I'm not asking a rhetorical question, as I do remember very well a time when colleagues – not just festival directors or archive managers – would complain about the restrictions of lending from an archive. Probably only 5 years ago, at the Pordenone festival, I could hear fellow archivists saying, "Well, we made these 35mm prints because we want them actually to be screened. If they get damaged we'll strike a new print."

Now, with the digital avalanche about to overwhelm us, it's becoming more difficult and costly to replace prints. The opportunity to show a 35mm print is becoming a privilege. But for some people it is a burden; they think, "God bless the moment when we'll be able to show films as digital files, because there'll no longer be a decline in print quality."

_DF: I'm torn. Because on the one hand I want to protect 35mm reference prints, as it is getting difficult to replace them. On the other hand, I'm aware that there are less and less people able to see a film as it should be shown, and one should be encouraging archives and festivals to present film in the way it was intended to be shown, to audiences of people who would appreciate seeing it that way.

_PCU: There is another crisis, in relation to the expertise of the projectionist. We are not doing enough to grow a generation of archivally trained projectionists. Or, to put it differently: the number of projectionists I see who are less and less competent in the projection of film is growing at an alarming rate.

One thing I forgot to say: we should be able to argue that even if there was still the opportunity to replace a 35mm print in case of damage, this should not be used as a justification to mistreat the existing print (the "who cares?" approach). Now the tide is turning, but it's not turning for the right reasons. I'm beginning to notice two things in relation to digital projection, which we already discussed. First: the non-availability of important titles: "Sorry, the 35mm print is unavailable, and there's too little demand to produce a digital master for a digital cinema release." Second: as a consequence of this I'm beginning to suspect that in the medium-term future the number of works available for museum exhibition, whether analog or digital, may actually decrease! Look at the debate surrounding the destruction of thousands of viewing prints in the June 2008 fire at Universal Studios, and the question of whether or not positive film copies can be easily replaced.

_ML: The two of you have agreed that one should, by all means, try to provide proper film copies to be screened at festivals or partner institutions. If this was not possible, or if there was the decision on the part of the other institution to say, "Do it digitally," should an archive provide "authorized digital facsimiles" to, say, a festival that will properly contextualize everything, but says, "We do screen digitally"? Should an archive provide this service, or would you refuse?

_PCU: The practical approach I have taken, insofar as this was possible, was to establish a sort of minimum guaranteed condition, meaning that for any given work that is made accessible to a festival or another venue, there has to be the option of showing the film in its proper form, which means, in practical terms, it's our ability to say, "You want this film on DigiBeta. I want you to be aware that we have a 35mm element. We would prefer that you show it on 35mm." The festival may say, "No, we have turned to the digital way, and all we are interested in is a DigiBeta." As long as there is a choice – because according to our collection policy, we do not make accessible work in digital form if it is not already preserved in its proper form – I'm okay. For us it's also a necessity, because I currently operate in a country where, because of its nature, there are many, many venues which cannot possibly afford it.

___ML: And there are probably venues who cannot handle archival copies properly, too.

___PCU: There are, because we live in an imperfect world. This raises some interesting cases. I recall the case of the classic Australian film, *The Sentimental Bloke*. Before the restoration there had been standard 16mm prints of the film in what we no longer consider the best available version, a shorter version. And we're having venues saying, "We would like to show the 16mm. We are perfectly happy with that because it's a shorter film, and our kids don't have a long attention span." We are faced with this dilemma: they are requesting a lesser version, knowing that there is a better one. It's in cinematic form, it corresponds to what we knew about the film in the 1970s or 80s, but it's not perfect. Ultimately, my answer was, "It is in the collection; it is technically a viewing print." They are aware that they have a choice that they can also show it in a longer version, but that's what they want.

___DF: I totally agree with your policy. I think the question is whether or not an archive, if it can offer a film in 35mm, needs to be involved with the enquiry if the only thing requested is a

DVD. The chances are that a DVD is available for commercial purchase from the copyright owner or the archive itself, so I don't know why they should be bothering you.

___PCU: But my hypothesis is based on something that they can only find at the archive.

___DF: I think in most cases, unless the DVD was only available from the archive, the issue to me is, "Well, you've come to the wrong place. What we have here is a 35mm. There is a DVD out on the marketplace, which may well have been put out by the archive, because there are cases where the DVD is a satisfactory form of making a film available. If you want a DVD, go to the appropriate shop and buy it, pay the rights to show that DVD." There will be a few cases where the DVD is only available from the archive, but for the most part I think we want to avoid any activity which isn't in line with our policy, simply because of the time it takes. I think, in some ways, the more widely available a DVD is will help us, because we don't have to service requests from people who we will never persuade to follow the basic archival projection practices. On the other hand, I would also like to see the reverse: if a festival is prepared to follow archival practices, I'd like to give them some sort of recognition, some sort of credit to put at the head of their programme, that this is an archivally approved venue, like the Queen has a coat of arms which she allows suppliers to display if they have provided satisfactory service. I would like to reverse the current trend, and actually reward people who do follow archival practices.

___PCU: This may be tangential to our conversation, but as I'm thinking about the future of the Pordenone Silent Film Festival, one of the possible futures may be a festival whose reputation is linked to the fact that this is the place where you can still see 35mm prints, in a world that makes works available in other formats. The way in which the films are shown becomes the formula of the festival itself, meaning, "We could show you this on DigiBeta, but we prefer to show it on 35mm, with all the implications this has."

___ML: You could also imagine the opposite, a totally fictitious scenario: a major donor approaches the Giornate and says, "We will not only install the latest in 4K projection, but we will also subsidize a certain part of your digitization, partially funding the digital restoration of films to be screened in 4K at this very special venue."

___PCU: This is where I must draw a line in the sand. I will say, and I will keep saying, that as long as it will be possible to produce a proper restoration in its original medium, I do not intend to make a work available exclusively in digital form without having done proper analog preservation. When this approach will no longer be possible, well, I'll deal with that. But that's not a good enough reason for me to give up now. There are times when you have to keep fighting against all odds.

___DF: There's no doubt that one of the reasons I, as an archivist, would always support the Giornate would be because I know the films will be projected correctly in an acceptable environment, and appreciated. Also, the people who would see them are people who would likely be able to add to our knowledge of the films. The Festival works on two levels: one, it's showing films correctly; two, it's showing them to a group of people who are going to be able to

provide a new interpretation, because they have had the chance to see the films in association with other relevant titles. Looking at it from an archive point of view, it's often quite a burden to support the Giornate if there happens to be a group of films that come from your archive. We have always co-operated with the Giornate, because the way in which they handle the material has always been in line with our policy. I never remember a case where we had a problem with the Festival, or received our films back damaged.

___ML: Paolo – since I know that this is a topic of huge importance for your organization, the NFSA: what about the relationship between the archive and another cultural entity, film societies? What I mean is that traditionally film societies were giving a certain exposure, disseminating the works preserved by archives to a broader public. Now, imagine a scenario where film societies are going to abolish film projection, due to its being more expensive than digital projection, or for technical reasons, and film archives and museums do not disseminate works in digital yet, or are reluctant to lend their film copies to film societies, or to non-FIAF bodies generally. What do you think the outcome of this process will be? Will archives work more and more towards a point where they become obsolete for a wider public or regional audiences, or, on the other hand, to put it in drastic terms, are film societies going to die?

___PCU: This is an issue that has become clearer to me only by coming to a country [Australia] where film societies play a very important role in the development of film culture, more so than in other countries where I have worked. I had to come here to finally realize what was at stake. Let me go back to the days when I was working in Europe, and I saw film societies in action. A time, and it was quite a long time, when film societies were relying on the availability of film prints from distributors. Film societies did not interact much with archives. They were getting their prints from commercial distributors, who kept their prints in stock. Archives were not as accessible then as they are today. All the film societies really needed from an archive were some classics, and the archive knew that these were in constant demand, and maybe the archive would make them available. But even the commercial distributor knew that, so the commercial distributor would have a copy of *Alexander Nevsky,* or a copy of *Casablanca,* because it was known that these prints would be in relatively frequent demand. It was only in more recent years, when the film distribution network changed so dramatically, that film societies began knocking at the door of archives. I should also add that only very few archives are endowed with some form of lending service or circulating library.

Then there is the widespread recognition that these lending services and circulating libraries gradually fell into a state of crisis, largely due to the fact that these prints were deemed to be increasingly substandard, and the archives did not have the funds to keep these collections fresh. The copies would deteriorate, and eventually the film archives themselves felt that there were better prints of the same films somewhere else. Why should I get a poor 16mm print from a certain lending service or circulating library, when I already know that there is a good 35mm print? That was the point, I think, when the dilemma in the archives between preserving and making

accessible exploded. It became clear that the archives could not continue to think of preservation by ignoring the demand in the outside world. And here I'm still talking about a pre-digital, pre-videotape, pre-DVD era. It was a time when, if you wanted to see a rare film, you had to go either to a private collector or, if you wanted a better print, an archive.

Film societies have traditionally been attached, for a number of historical reasons, to the format of 16mm. I myself learned a lot from 16mm. I can say that a good part of my own film culture comes from the 16mm experience, and I've seen great things on 16mm.

Today, film societies are increasingly faced with an insurmountable dilemma. 16mm is quickly dying; in many places it is already dead. In some countries, such as the United States, 16mm is relegated to a fringe of collectors, aficionados, nostalgic lovers of that format with all its virtues. I do recognize that there is a specific feeling to a 16mm print that no other format will give you. I would even say that it's very different from 35mm, and not just because of the difference in the size of the frame; you have a certain flavour that is typical of 16mm.

With apologies again for dwelling on personal experiences, I now live in a country where there are still very many film societies, and they are still very active, though facing a structural crisis themselves. And they are still very attached to 16mm, for a variety of reasons: because they find a value in 16mm itself, because there is still not enough material in other formats, and because they are unable to show films in 35mm. I'm asked, "Hey, now that you're in charge of this wonderful lending collection of 17,000 titles, what are you going to do with it?" And I go,

"Well, you know that 16mm is fading away." "Yes, but 16mm is good, isn't it?" "Yes, it is, but it's becoming increasingly difficult to find prints on 16mm, and I would like to push for a better quality of projection." Again, naïve as I was, I thought, let's encourage the creation of more venues where 35mm can be shown. But we're talking about Australia, a place where, aside from half a dozen big cities, we're talking about very small communities, where there is no chance in the world that there will be a 35mm venue. These are places where a decent DVD projection would be seen as perfectly appropriate.

So, explicitly or not, I'm asked, "What are you going to do? Are you going to acquire more 16mm prints? And if you can't, can you acquire DVDs?" My immediate answer is, "I'm not representing Blockbuster Video. You can't ask me as a national collecting institution to deny what is our fundamental mission, which is to promote the film experience in its own right." But as I was uttering these words, I was realizing that I was contradicting their reality, the fact that there are places where it's DVD or nothing. The best compromise I could find was to say that, as long as the archive can present a film in its proper format, I will also provide an alternative option for access. So I tell my access staff, they can offer a 35mm print, or a DVD, and when they receive a request for a film, "Can we have a DVD of so and so?", I expect the staff to say, "Yes, we have the DVD, but wouldn't you like to show a 35mm print?" – in the hope that some of these film societies will say, "Darn, let's make an effort to show the film properly." I had to go through this intermediate stage. It is far from being a perfect option, because some film societies say,

"Well, what if we don't get a 35mm print? We're still interested in the film." All I can say is, you can find these DVDs everywhere, at a very modest cost. What complicates the equation here is that the lending service is made up of prints for which copyright has been cleared, meaning that we have been authorized to supply these prints for public, non-commercial, non-theatrical exhibitions. If you get a film from Blockbuster Video, you can watch it privately, but you cannot show it in a film society. Now, I went for a compromise when it comes to Australian cinema: I basically commit as much as possible to make sure that certain films are available in a variety of formats. Only about 20 films are produced in Australia per year, and I'd like to have a 35mm print, a 16mm print, insofar as I can obtain it, and a DVD.

—**ML:** From the distributor who deposits or donates the work to the archive?

—**PCU:** We may end up buying the DVD for that matter, but we still license the work so that it can be shown by film societies. When it comes to non-Australian films, I have to say, "Look, I'm keen to get a copy of this foreign film. Once I have a 35mm of good quality, I may also do my best to get a DVD or a 16mm if that's available, but I cannot commit to a systematic acquisition process of foreign films in a variety of formats." This is not a perfect arrangement, seen from the perspective of the film societies; they find themselves in a dilemma. With all due respect to them, film societies do not know what to ask for. They know that 16mm is fading; they know that DVD is not what they would like, but they ask for it anyway; while they very much like 35mm. Here again, one has to see the cultural environment of Australia to understand that there are film societies which live through the exhibition of DVDs. In the meantime these film societies are in a state of crisis. The people who grew up with the 16mm experience are retiring; or people no longer have the energy to run an association. Meanwhile, there are people who never had a 16mm experience, or who don't particularly care. They don't feel the same need to have the communal experience of the traditional film societies – they are perfectly happy to see the film in their own home with a DVD player.

I think film societies, as important as they are, are only a litmus test for what is going to happen to film festivals; this is something that I've been arguing for quite some time. Sooner or later film festivals will be facing, and are already beginning to face, the same kind of dilemma. Prints will become more difficult to obtain. Some films will no longer be available on 35mm. Their choice will be between DigiBeta or DVD or nothing, and the archives are largely responsible for this. What is happening in some archives today, maybe slowly, but quite distinctively, is that when a given print of an important film becomes worn out, they are deciding it is no longer worth it to strike another 35mm print. Their attitude is: cinema is going to die anyway, so why bother? Instead of creating another 35mm print of *True Heart Susie,* let's make a digital version of the film, and distribute that.

As we stand now, this means that we are creating an illusion that gradually the entire holdings of an archive or museum will eventually be available in digital form, while we know this is not the case. This is why I find Kristin Thompson's article "The Celestial Multiplex" [reprinted in Chapter 8] so important, and so

compelling. There won't be a global cinematheque where you have the obscure or incomplete work that was available in a standard viewing print in digital form. The harsh truth is that the dream of an entirely digitized, projection-quality collection of "analog" films in moving image archives reflects an astonishing form of wishful thinking; I do not see this happening in the foreseeable future.

7.5 TRAINING AND CONTINUOUS EDUCATION

__DF: Let's move on to "training". Do you think that the current MA courses in film archiving adequately provide the training for your ideal of curatorship?

__PCU: Not enough. Some courses are more hands-on; some courses are actually lessons on the Internet. In general, I think that a much greater emphasis should be given to curatorship. The reason why I think there hasn't been enough yet is due to the increased emphasis on the realities of the archival world, to the practical side of what actually happens in the life of a film museum or film archive, after years of theorization that has little or nothing to do with the practicalities of an institution.

I think that the realities of the work of a film museum/archive should be measured against the criteria of what constitutes curatorship. I'm not saying there should be one more class, one more lecture, on "curatorship". I think that we would need at least two things. First, curatorship should be discussed at every level in any curriculum. I cannot think of any topic in an MA course on film archiving where the notion of curatorship cannot be brought in. Even if you teach someone how to rewind a film, you can apply curatorship to that, too: in the act of rewinding a film, in what you're doing, the things you pay attention to, are an act of curatorship. We need to educate students that every aspect of work in an archive can be seen through a curatorial perspective. The second thing that should be done is mainly our responsibility, and probably the reason for this book. Curators, like archivists, have not done enough to describe what they do, and to talk about their job. I think there should be a growth in literature about curatorship. When Edith Kramer asked me for suggestions for literature on curatorship, I ended up recommending literature mainly from other disciplines!

—DF: I would add one other thing. We have now quite a number of MA courses, and we are only giving training to people coming into the profession. I think now at least one major course needs to concentrate on people who have been in the profession for 5 to 10 years or more; an advanced course, which discusses the bigger, more theoretical issues involved in film archiving, and gives a chance to the people who've had the experience of working in an archive to explore further their feelings, ideas, and thoughts.

—PCU: Yes, under one condition, though – it should not be an advanced course that could be taken by people who have not previously worked in the realities of an archive's or museum's operations.

—DF: Yes, the idea is that you have to be employed a number of years in order to attend, because I think it is very important at one point to sit back and think about what you are doing. Your day-to-day work is so hectic, and you're taking decisions instinctively. In most cases your decision is probably right, but you're not really thinking about *why* you're taking that decision.

So you can never pass knowledge on to anybody else!

—PCU: It's like in a laboratory, when somebody does grading for so long that it has become second nature. And when they retire, that knowledge is not passed on. That's the reason we should write about it. And not only should we write about it, but find a forum of sufficient scope and depth to make sure that a new generation has curatorship embedded in their professional profile, and not only added as a sort of afterthought.

—ML: Your idea of continuing education for professionals is intriguing. Do you have any idea at which level, in which governing body, this form of education should be established? Would you formulate this as a plea to an individual institution or regional bodies, or is that something that can be formally introduced by FIAF? That you offer certification of venues, training courses for professionals, and act accordingly in the loan scheme of your individual institution, stipulating something like, "We will only license institutions that take part in continuing education in the field, and you have an approved venue and approved staff."

—DF: I'd like to see the existing established film schools also include update, refresher-type courses. I would also like to see archives, particularly when they have the sort of premises that the Library of Congress has, actually instigating small courses in different fields, so that people can keep up to date with current viewpoints and issues. It should be a mixture of our own institutions, possibly a regional archival body, and the existing film school programme.

—PCU: There has been, for some time now, a discussion about so-called "accreditation", places where things are taught in a certain way, so that if you have attended a certain course, or done something, you are accredited. I have mixed feelings about this, because this can easily become a power tool, and power is not something I am interested in for its own sake. I also have mixed feelings for another reason, and that is that I think that our only choice is to adopt a pervasive strategy in disseminating the principles of curatorship. Meaning that I don't believe there should be one place were curatorship is being taught properly, so if you don't attend that specific course, then you are not a real curator. What I mean by "pervasive strategy" is this: disseminate the principles everywhere – universities, archives, museums, festivals, even in our dialogue with commercial entities. You should cover the entire territory at every level, including within the institution. We as managers have a responsibility to explain.

—DF: I'm undecided about your view of professionalization, because to a certain extent, if you do have to get qualifications, it enables the organization, when making appointments to choose a person who is appropriate. On the other hand, I don't want it to be a basis for promotion within the institution, because promotion within the institution should in the end be judged on a number of different abilities, and not on the receipt of a particular qualification. When you employ people in an archive, they need an accepted qualification if they are to have a chance to proceed to a managerial position in the future. It's a protection against having to employ people who you feel are not suitable for the position. It's a tricky situation. After someone's in the institution, I don't want there to be a reason why they cannot be promoted over time.

I think what Paolo said earlier was very, very important. I believe that everybody has to be part of the curatorial team, because if there are gaps in knowledge, skilled work can be negated because someone in the chain doesn't understand the importance of handling material in a certain way. I think it's incredibly important that everybody is made aware that they are a key part of the team.

—ML: And not reacting on pressure, because this would just duplicate the model of external pressure in your own institution. You need to internalize those principles so you can become active within your institution. If I go to our van driver and say, "You should not smoke in the van," it is like being told that you should not smoke in a restaurant. This is not going to make any difference. But if I can properly explain to him why his role is essential, that he also is a guardian of the film prints, and he actively helps in preserving film for future generations, it's an entirely different approach.

—DF: One of the things one has to put in the terms of reference of a middle manager is that they do spend some time explaining to their staff why they make a particular decision. It shouldn't just be a piece of paper headed "Collection Policy"; it's an explanation that occurs whenever policy is breached. That's the moment to go back and say, "Look, why I'm not happy with what happened is not only because it was against collection policy, but because it shows you don't understand what the point of that policy is."

—ML: So, in a way, one natural conclusion from this is that archives also have to perceive themselves as educators, and move far more actively into higher education. For instance, we cannot sustain a situation where archives complain about media studies and film studies classes not understanding about the realities of the medium.

—PCU: Academia is not the only arena. We should not forget that there is also a clear need for truly specialized technical schools, where the principles of curatorship are clearly embedded in the actual work of those who are employed in moving image laboratories. As they stand today, the so-called "technical courses" are more the expression of wishful thinking than of a solid and carefully structured approach to lab work. Like curatorship, laboratory work is not something one can master in a matter of weeks.

The fact that academia now thinks that terms like "archiving" and "curatorship" should be part of the language is in itself a good thing. There's still a long way to go, because sometimes we feel that students really get only a very superficial notion of archives. But 15 years ago there wasn't even that, so there has been some progress – as long as we do not see any single aspect of our constituency as the only focus of our attempts.

THEATRICAL PROJECTION IN THE TRANSITIONAL PERIOD: FIVE SCENARIOS
Paolo Cherchi Usai

In 1991, the Executive Committee of the International Federation of Film Archives suggested that a new commission should be formed within FIAF, alongside the already existing Technical Commission and the Commission for Cataloguing and Documentation. The name of this new commission had not been decided yet, but there seemed to be a consensus about what the commission was supposed to do – discuss the issues surrounding the question of the *availability* of the moving image heritage, of how the archives' collections could or should be presented to the public. I was relatively new to FIAF then, and when I saw how much debate there had been at the general assemblies of FIAF in the previous years about this topic, I thought this was part of a normal decision-making process. Deep inside, I thought that of course there should be such a commission, and that the reason why there was so much discussion around the table was the fact that most film archives were still shrouded in an aura of mystery, and that not all of them were so keen to open their doors. In short, I thought that the creation of such a commission was a good sign, the indication of a new era in what was then called the "archival movement".

In fact, it *was* a good sign, the beginning of a kind of *glasnost* in the relationship between the archives and their audiences. This commission now exists, and it has produced an excellent manual for archival projection [*The Advanced Projection Manual*], which is bound to become an essential reference point for all those who want to present the archives' collections in a proper cultural context. What I could *not* imagine then, back in 1991, was the fact that there would be so much discussion about what this commission should be called. I was invited to join a working group within FIAF, with the goal

of drafting the terms of reference of the commission, its work plan, its strategy, *and* its official name. A good deal of diplomatic effort was needed in order to reach an agreement on the current name of the commission, the Commission for Programming and Access.

Back then, I had no clue as to what all this fuss was about. Maybe I still don't have a clue, but what I understood then was that the word "access" was loaded with a whole set of meanings, which were perceived by film archives as a threat. There was indeed something "commercial" about that term, and cultural institutions were smelling trouble in the very fact that such a word would be introduced into the vocabulary of moving image archives. In retrospect, I think they were absolutely right – there *was* trouble. However, what they could not predict was the fact that the word "access" was bound to become the key word in the politics of audiovisual archives, the word that would determine much of what has happened to our institutions during the past 15 years. Today, nobody questions the name of the Commission for Programming and Access, but even if they did, the word "access" is there, and it's there to stay for the foreseeable future. We have come to the point where the identity and independence of moving image and recorded sound archives are being confronted by the imperatives of the commercial world. In principle, everyone agrees that national collecting institutions should be independent from commercial imperatives. In practice, the commercial world *is* already within our gates, and it has been within our gates for quite some time. This is no longer a matter of whether or not we want to deal with it; it is a matter of *how* we can we deal with it, without betraying our cultural mission.

In the world where we live, pronouncing the word "access" means invoking another word, "digital". In fact, "access" and "digital" are one and the same word in the recorded sound community, where analog is no longer considered a suitable tool for access to the collections; analog is no longer an option for preservation in the recorded sound area. In the domain of the moving image the debate is still going on, but it's only a matter of time. The future has a name: we all know it's called "digital". But the word "digital" is embedded with a whole array of philosophical, ethical, and strategic questions. How will "digital" change the way we look at film in a museum? And how are we going to explain the history of projection in the Digital Age?

I would like to offer four different scenarios, four different visions of the future. I don't know if they are the most precise scenarios, but I think they represent a good spectrum of the most plausible options. I will present them in a simplified form, and assume two things. First, let's imagine that we already live in a world where all new films are distributed and projected digitally; there is no more 35mm being projected in movie theatres. Second, you work in a film archive with a collection of 35mm or 16mm films representing the first hundred years of cinema, and a collection of digital-born works. So, the question is: what would you do in this situation?

Here's **Scenario Number 1**. You continue to project your 35mm or 16mm film collection in your theatre. If the film was meant to be released on 35mm, you project it as such; if it was meant to be distributed digitally, it is screened with a digital projector. Can you afford taking this course of action? Yes, but you must also take some precautions, and you must do it now. You must acquire and preserve as many good 35mm prints as possible, as long as you can do lab work on 35mm; you must treat your prints with the greatest possible care, because you know you won't be able to replace them when film stock will no longer be manufactured and all film labs will be closed. In short, you must treat film as a museum object. (By the way, I have heard colleagues saying that film archives can join their efforts and operate a specialized manufacturing plant with the help of a major corporate company. I don't believe it will happen. Archives can't even agree on the definition of the term "preservation", and they can't put together a global database of archival holdings. Go figure a whole factory!)

Anyway, let's go back to our scenario of a film archive as the last place on earth where film is being shown on film. The great advantage of this model is that your archive becomes the place where the cinema experience is promoted as a cultural phenomenon, and not as a commodity. You never, ever use the word "content": that's suitable for tuna fish in a tin can; in an archive or a museum, you use the term "artwork", or "artefact". Now, together with this advantage comes a great disadvantage: because the rest of the world has gone digital, and you're still showing analog, your archive may be regarded as a wax museum of cinema, a cinephile mausoleum with little or no connection with the real world. And what you do is no longer regarded as museum work; you become folklore.

Let's now look at **Scenario Number 2**. Because the world has gone digital, you go digital as well, and stop projecting 35mm film. However, because you work in a film archive, you also undertake a mission: you want to make sure that your digital projection remains as close as possible to the original cinema experience, and you want to explain what the difference is all about. You will try to convince your audience that digital projection is not "better" or "worse" than 35mm; it is just a completely different mode of perceiving moving images. Of course you don't throw away your film collection, but you use it exclusively for the purpose of creating digital versions. By doing so, you will also find a convincing way to explain that what you're doing does not contradict good museum practice; and if you can't be convincing, then you will stop talking about the ethics of film preservation or about museography, because now you're doing something completely different, and your place should no longer be called a museum.

It's worth considering the pros and cons of this approach. There is one great advantage, and that is functionality. You can now show your films to a much larger number of festivals, conferences, and special events, as long as they have the necessary equipment. The major disadvantage is that you need much more money, and you must explain to your trustees that digital conservation – whatever that means – will cost the museum ten times more than the conservation of the original artefacts. The other major disadvantage is that your museum is no longer unique. To watch a film in a museum, in a commercial cinema, or at home becomes pretty much the same thing, because the experience you are offering can be easily reproduced outside the museum. It's true that you can still interpret the collection better than in a commercial cinema, because you are a curator; but then you're just another film society, and that's not unique, either. And sooner or later film societies will also be regarded as folklore. So there you are.

Now comes **Scenario Number 3.** You give up projection completely. Instead of doing film programming, on 35mm or digitally, you have decided to go for a completely different business plan, based on the notion of "access on demand", and you embrace Internet distribution or any another mass device aimed at a broader, client-based dissemination of your collection. It's a radical choice, but it's something you may find attractive for at least two reasons: first, your audience is no longer 100 or 200 people at a time, but the entire planet; second, you no longer have to worry about the box office, you don't have to show just the same old classics of cinema or the usual retrospectives – instead, you show whatever is in your collection, and whatever is being requested. Audiences are presumably happy, because they can now see whatever they like, whenever they want it, and at a much lower price. (A lower price for them; but not for you, not for the archive.) Now that you can see cinema on your iPod or on your portable phone, you enjoy Bergman, Kiarostami, and Bresson while you're on the bus.

All this sounds appealing indeed, but there are a number of problems you'll have to deal with. Let's say that the copyright-holders have given you permission to digitize your entire collection (and I find this unlikely); let's say that you have all the money to do so (and I also find this very unlikely); finally, let's say that there's a secure way to make sure that nobody will illegally copy your collection (I don't believe that, either). Even so, what is your interest as a film museum in treating your collections as a supermarket, where there's no difference between a very expensive restoration and a mediocre print struck 50 years ago, or between a masterpiece of cinema and, say, a documentary on the manufacture of flannel? You may say it's all right for you to become a supermarket, but if that's the case, how are you going to survive after your shelves are empty, and all your films are no longer in demand? There may be some organizations such as the Library of Congress that can probably deal with that, because they are huge and because they are actually meant to function as libraries, but how about the rest of us? If your films can be found on your website, or somewhere else, is your institution really necessary any longer? And if sooner or later you're going to treat all films as equals, what's your interest in showcasing one of your best restorations in a film festival?

Finally, **Scenario Number 4.** There's something you like about all the three previous options, and you have decided to adopt them all. Your archive will do some traditional projection, some digital projection, some wider dissemination of the collection via the Internet. At face value, this looks like an ideal solution, right? You can now explain the meaning of the difference between alternative modes of visual perception, and show that a film is not just about storytelling (so-called "content"), but is also a cultural and technological phenomenon with a specific place in history. So this looks like a win-win situation. However, where are you going to find the money to do all this? And even if you had all the money in the world, you have another problem. To achieve this kind of curatorial multi-tasking, you must engage with your audience in three different ways, and maybe more. You must achieve excellence in everything: traditional projection, digital projection, access on demand; if you don't do so, sooner or later someone will begin making comparisons, and tell you what's "better" or "worse", and, for example, come to the conclusion that digital is actually "better" than the original cinema experience.

I have a little anecdote for you about this point. Earlier this year [2006], at the annual meeting of the International Federation of Film Archives, a panelist screened a sequence from Dreyer's *The Passion of Joan of Arc* in digital 2K, and then projected the same excerpt on 35mm. The digital projection had been rehearsed for several days, and was perfectly calibrated; the 35mm was awful – it had the wrong aspect ratio, it was dark, it was fuzzy. Shortly after the presentation, a colleague with many years of experience came to me and said, "Paolo, I'm converted to digital. I feel as if I had seen *Joan of Arc* for the first time in my life. I even wonder, how could people appreciate the film until now?" There we are: the damage is done. Next time your organization asks to cut your budget, you'll be told to stop being a purist, and simply go for what looks better.

As I said before, I have oversimplified a much more complex situation. And I haven't even mentioned the possibility of **Scenario Number 5**, something so dramatic that even curators and archivists don't dare discuss it in public, a scenario that could put an end to all film archives and museums as we know them today. To describe this *Dr. Strangelove* situation, let's return to the early premise of my story. All new films are being distributed digitally, right? It doesn't matter if this will happen in 5, 10, 20, or 50 years; we know it will happen. Now, if I were a film producer or distributor with absolute control over the digital access to my product, and you came to me with the request to include my film in your collection, why in the world should I say yes? I don't need you any more. In the age of 35mm prints, you could try to convince me with the excuse of preservation on behalf of posterity, and I probably would have listened to you, because I would have saved storage costs by allowing you to have my films. Of course, you would take all the responsibility for the maintenance of my films; you would pay for their preservation; you would be liable if something goes wrong – and I could have had access to my films any time I want. But now, in the Digital Age, I am the owner of the server, I own the hard drive, I control the satellite distribution of my film – whatever: I am in control, and I don't need film archives. And you have nothing left to preserve! Except, perhaps, thousands of old analog prints which nobody wants to look at, because they're available digitally anyway. Besides, you don't own the rights, and I can always demand that you give me access to the prints any time I want to go ahead and do a new remastering. In a situation like this, your film archive would become like a warehouse. Now, you may say that there are museums which are full of, let's say, ancient Greek statues; these warehouses are called museums, and we may rename our institution "The Museum of the Analog Experience". But while there are many people who very much want to see the art of ancient Greece and the original statues, I have some doubt of our ability to make people equally interested in photochemical cinema, when they can see what they want without having to come to a museum. Unless, of course, we accept the burden of being the curators of a wax museum – yet again a folklore phenomenon.

Chapter 8

Content, Platforms, and the User

___PCU: It seems hard to engage with anybody on the issue of moving image preservation without using the terms "platform" and "content". It is true that each historical period has its fetish words, but these two seem to be unusually loaded with ideology. Let's start by examining why they have become so popular in the current jargon.

___ML: Well, in computing, "platform" refers to an architecture (a "framework", in computer terms) on which an application, i.e., software, can be run. The popularity of the term in my opinion not only derives from its familiarity for contemporary users (who are probably more computer-literate than media-literate), but from the fact that it supports the idea that film is something which exists regardless of its carrier, as information that can be transmitted in a variety of media (platforms). In other words: pure content – that which is contained, and supposedly can be extracted (liberated) from the confines of its carrier to persevere as information.

The assumption that one can separate the content from its (fault-ridden) carrier is of course ideological. Digitization is by principle a *reduction* in complexity. Digitization reduces various phenomena to a common denominator (a number of discrete values of a finite set). The German philosopher Claus Pias has called the

digital "an instrument of methodical oblivion". Its forms are logical, not historical. The inconsistency of the analog world, the continuous quantity that is the density of silver crystals activated by light and sound waves becomes, by a process of formalization, a logical order of data which can be controlled.

___PCU: Dear Michael: I admit I find this definition intriguing, but very un-conversational. I am wondering if something could be done to put the reader more at ease here.

___ML: Well, this sounds rather drier than it is. What I find fascinating is the implication this idea has for our everyday perception. While *entropy* is inherent to analog states, it is done away with by the digital concept of total reversibility. Nothing is historical anymore, since data doesn't age, decompose, gradually change. But isn't the fact of moribundity, of gradual loss, that all things do perish, an integral part of the human experience, and of human articulation through art?

To use an analogy from cinema: according to Alain Resnais and Chris Marker (and Roland Barthes, probably), "Statues also die" [*Les Statues meurent aussi*]. Digital information on the other hand doesn't expire, it becomes obsolete in the instant its platform does. This implication is important: since it's no longer a matter of tolerating the gradual permutation of a given artefact (this is where the need for interpretation stems from), but of prevention of complete loss, all energy is directed towards building new platforms.

Here "platform" becomes even more problematic, if you consider another definition of the term: "A platform is a set of principles supported by an organization in order to appeal to the public, to draw attention toward itself." Thus the platform's ultimate ratio is self-referentiality – the platform always references itself, since "content", by the nature of the digital paradigm, is arbitrary.

Now if we look at discussions – for example, those on the AMIA-L [AMIA-Listserv, an e-mail discussion list] – one gets the impression that the need to transfer film collections to digital is a natural law. One can debate whether JPEG 2000 is a better format than uncompressed video, whether hard disks should be striped as RAID-0 or RAID-5, or whether gold-coated optical discs will lose data slower than cyan-dye coated discs. Only rarely does somebody dare – I refer to the well-known fairytale – to spoil the party by stating, "But he has nothing on!" The premise of a separation of carrier and content – which is a logical conclusion of the digital world-view – appears as neutral, as the natural course of things, largely immune to challenge. All becomes absorbed in the discussions on how to improve platforms, a debate which is ignorant of the fact that film has existed as a medium – that is, a cultural technique intrinsically linked to the photochemical, analog moving image – even before, and parallel to, the idea of the Digital.

Thus, what used to be at the outset a quest for an improved accessibility of artefacts, becomes even further separated from the original object: a film archive doesn't take care of films anymore, it manages digital data. What used to be the archaeology of a cultural form of expression, the specific knowledge about a specific cultural object, becomes a matter of maintaining a digital infrastructure, no different from any other field of IT work. Which of course has its benefits for administrators, politicians, and service industries alike. Specific requirements, unaccountable knowledge that is highly challenging to formalization (i.e., the tacit knowledge inherent in the best practices handed down by three generations of archivists and curators), can be reduced in complexity, formalized, and broken down to the common denominator of hard- and soft-ware engineering.

Well, so much for ideology. We can of course further discuss the dangers inherent in this debate, which in my opinion – and judging from your initial question, in your opinion too – is not a debate, but rather a veil drawn before our eyes to prevent us from asking the most basic philosophical questions. But as I myself do come from the field of digital production, one should probably also talk about the potentials and utopian aspects digital has for our profession and audiences. What do you think?

—PCU: I'm intrigued by your definition, but I can't resist the temptation of bringing the discussion straight back to earth – that is, to the current reality of archival and museum practice. Broadly speaking, the archival community engaged in the preservation of the moving image can be divided into two categories: there are those who have learned their craft in the "analog" archive, and therefore think in "analog" terms, treating "platform" and "content" as if they belonged to a foreign and vaguely hostile idiom; and there is a small but rapidly growing minority of those who have entered this world from a "digital" perspective, with different degrees of faith in the new gospel. This minority will soon become the majority, and lead the game. What both "factions" have in common is a more or less explicit attitude of antagonism towards each other. So the "digital" archivist tells the "analog" colleague that things will never be the same, and that the other had better adapt to the new reality, or shut up; conversely, the "analog" practitioner treats his or her counterpart as a sort of new, ruthless barbarian who needs to be educated. The former is persuaded that time is on his or her side, as the "analog" generation will eventually disappear; the latter believes that education is the only way to counteract the digital dogma, in the hope that the barbarian will sooner or later become civilized.

Clearly, we won't get very far this way. Hence two parallel needs: for the "digital" Young Turk, to develop a language which can be understood and shared with the "analog" tradition; for the besieged "analog" archivist, to seek a consensus on what the goal is that both parties are trying to achieve. This seems to indicate the need for some kind of joint statement of intent, a terminology encompassing both worlds. One wonders, however, whether or not this is possible at all. East is East, West is West? "Platform" and "content" have the distinct disadvantage of representing the language of only one interlocutor. —ML: I certainly do agree on that. It's the rhetoric of these terms, the "tone" a term such as "platform" or "content" sets, that automatically does away with all the "analog" archivist stands for. I'm afraid this language is not even one interlocutor's original language, but rather the jargon of the information industries and

management trickling down and finding its way into a debate almost inconspicuously. For "them" it does present a clear advantage to level the debate down to topics of digital data management. It sells machines and services, and normalizes complex and diverse challenges down to something every electronic repository experiences. So probably one needs to do away with these terms radically to arrive at a joint statement of intent. For that, in my opinion, we need to return to the underlying question, which is twofold: (1) Why do we even discuss an alternative to traditional means of film preservation and presentation? (2) Can digital technologies augment our experience and our understanding of film?

Just to try and get a shot at this complex relationship, I'd like to proceed in a rather simple fashion, by outlining a scenario.

1. The public of the 21st century demands access to cultural heritage, and film (as well as film archives and museums) is an obstacle to general access to moving images. 2. Film demands specialized venues and a trained élite to be performed for a public, while in digital form moving images are available freely at the audience's discretion.

The analog archivist shakes his/her head, and argues along the lines of "you can't separate content from carrier", which the digital evangelist regards as élitist thinking on behalf of an endangered monopoly on moving images. Wasn't cinema once hailed as the true democratic medium that does away with all notions of the aura? And isn't it some sort of perversion to reintroduce a medium that has obliterated the boundaries between high culture and low culture into the museum?! The analog archivist – or curator – embraces his/her new position as a besieged minority, and pulls his/her last card: long-term preservation. And decides that this battle (and suddenly it has become a war) will be won in the year 2050, when the collections will most probably have outlived any HDD data. The digital archivist-curator couldn't care less – he can count on digital preservation technologies developing progressively, and on the public's support for the person who makes heritage available instead of hiding it in a vault.

The crux obviously is that in the current cultural climate "digital" is perceived as inclusive, while "analog" is perceived as exclusive (which smacks of élitism). I do not consider the Young Turk to be any less enthusiastic or serious than his analog predecessor. He is more or less forced into an antagonism with the "old ways", because he feels his initiative grossly misappreciated by the "establishment" of the analog archival community.

At the same time, the siege mentality the analog community finds itself stuck with averts any potential to connote "film" – its exclusiveness, the unique status of the artefact, the specialized knowledge associated with film preservation and presentation – positively. He perceives "access" again as something threatening one has to endure.

So he arrives at the following pragmatic conclusion: 1. There is no alternative to film in regard to long-term preservation, but no one listens to this sermon anyway. So let's play along and make film preservation a pre-condition to digitization in applying for funds. 2. Since it is a necessary evil to allow digital access, we should make available parts of our collections to satisfy popular demand.

I am generalizing, but this scenario's outcome is fatal. Analog archives and museums do yield to reason without really considering the potentials of the new technologies. To appear "active", they adapt without conviction to a given situation. The result is half-hearted (and over-funded) digitization projects, indiscriminate licensing of films for DVD publications, and archive theatres and museums doing digital projection or displays "because no one cares anyway", and because it's the path of least resistance. This is what makes me angry the most – it discredits what we believe in, and only pays lip-service to a technology we haven't even tried to understand.

___PCU: You are right in introducing the "preservation" variable into the mix, as I believe this is part of what divides the two factions. In my experience, their (implicit) mutual distrust comes from a fundamental disagreement on the goals and objectives of preservation through digital means. From an "analog" perspective, there is no credible permanence in digital preservation; and yet, if an "analog" curator says that digital data are not forever, the digital counterpart will react by saying that this is plainly untrue, and will do so with the tone of someone who has either been the victim of an injustice, or treats the other as someone who just doesn't understand what's going on. I am always suspicious of a discipline where too much time is wasted in seeking definitions, and we both know how much has been said and written about definitions in our field, but the risk is worth taking. Granted that the general public (and public administrators) don't differentiate between "digitization" and "digital preservation" – do you see a benefit in trying to define the latter? I'm not being ironic.

__ML: Well it might be beneficial for the debate to imagine what *true* digital preservation could be, as earnestly and radically as possible. If you do support digital preservation, you must not shy at the implications this has for your object.

Let's imagine a scenario. An organization decides to preserve their collection in a digital format, true enough in resolution to at least provide for the opportunity to record back onto film, for a decent projection print if necessary. What are the benefits compared to traditional (passive and active) preservation? There are none, really – you lose the original qualities of the artefact, its material characteristics, without substantial gain. Even if you don't care about those qualities, archaeologists of the future will most certainly regret your decisions.

But: imagine an archivist who really "thinks digital". To this person the potential of digital is in the equivalent of *information* – the hierarchical order of data is not predetermined by the physical characteristics of the (analog) object, but by a result of programming, a process of re-ordering levels of knowledge by a user accessing the (digital) object. When an artefact becomes digital data its "text" contents – image, sound – become level with contextual data: production history, version history, historical presentation and reception, contemporary references, past significance, and relations to any other object in a collection. In other words: only a radical interleaving of *audiovisual contents* and *metadata* will truly resemble a "digital preservation". This is something entirely different from an analog preservation, which is measured by its degree of verisimilitude to the artefact: not a simulacrum, but a (digital) *simulation*. Why not explore Digital to its full extent, and preserve our holdings

as *hypertext?* If we decide to abolish the idea of preserving the artefact and analog facsimiles we should also do away with the analog scholarly concept of *textus* and *apparatus:* in digital all contents are equally representable. This is a radical move, for we do not preserve *films* anymore, but we do preserve our present cultural understanding of their content. Every digital file, when it's retrieved from an LTO tape or a hard disk in 20 years' time, is itself an artefact: an object that speaks of a culture's position towards its heritage.

Does this sound like Science Fiction to you? Or is this position – on the contrary – quite consistent with historical practices of analog preservation, such as the wholesale destruction of nitrate originals, the duplication on inferior stock or smaller gauges? Are these practices modes of tradition that do not just represent the "original", but rather reflect historical values towards the act of preserving one's audiovisual heritage?

But, in fact, the above scenario might just be a rhetorical exercise. Or do you know of any archive-museum really considering such radical action, or even implementing it?

Anyway – let me share a very pedestrian observation I've made over the last years, that is shared by quite a number of our colleagues. Archives in their preservation strategies have always been very careful to choose technologies that have been thoroughly tested and proven to be sustainable. They've learned their lesson from the "shock" of discovering that even safety film will decompose. So the general consensus is that you use technologies that have a proven track record, in which the archive has expertise, and the knowledge of which it can hand down to the next generation of archivists; finally, technologies which are foolproof in terms of future access to archival holdings.

With all the talk about digital preservation this equation has radically changed. Archives are pressured to make grave decisions within a short time frame – governments and funding agencies won't wait 10–15 years for you to come up with a digitization strategy; they usually expect it during their term of office. Those decisions are about technologies which have no track record that goes back to more than 5–7 years; moreover, the only proven factor with digital technologies is the fact that they become obsolete over a relatively short period of time. Last but not least, the implementation of a digital workflow puts responsibilities largely into the hands of IT departments and providers of proprietary technologies; control over fundamental processes is taken out of the hands of the archive.

This is a massive contradiction of archival practices and philosophies of the past. I'm not arguing that these issues cannot be debated, or that this conflict cannot be solved, but at the present pace archives and museums are clearly at a disadvantage.

~

__PCU: I think it's fair to say that we live in a society where History has lost so much of its place in our system of values that newer generations see it as being fundamentally irrelevant. In this respect, the obliteration of history inherent in digital technology is a perfect mirror of our times.

Faced with the fact that their collections are just too big, some archives are trying to find an acceptable compromise that respects the notion of preservation in the original format and preservation of analog works through digital means. So that, for example, a collection is divided into two broad categories: works which have to be preserved in their original format before being made available on any other so-called platform, and works which, by their nature, are not deemed necessarily to require preservation in analog form before being made available. A typical case in point is, let's say, a collection of early television works which were produced on 16mm and are available at the archive on 16mm. So the physical element is 16mm, but we all know that the way these works were meant to be seen was not on the big screen, it was on television. Therefore it is decided that it is OK to go straight to electronic preservation, while maintaining the notion of keeping the original element in 16mm, but without going through the internegative access print. Now, this is a decision archives are making out of necessity, because they know that they will never have the resources to preserve everything on film. But there is a potential danger in this line of thinking; it is a line of thinking that can be dangerously expanded. If we say the creator of this moving image really did not care how the moving image is curated, so it's OK to make it available in another form, it may be possible that someone extends this to other works which weren't meant to be seen that way. Is there a way to prevent this from happening?
__ML: I'm not entirely sure myself. But what you do is, you basically make a decision. Has the medium as a certain *techne* – the Greek word – been an important part of the work's creation, or has it always been only about content? And you have to go back and ask yourself as a researcher and as a curator: am I mainly interested

in the content of this, or is it also the material that adds another layer of meaning, and stimulates another layer of interpretation? And I think we're not only in danger of having parts of our collection put into question, but the dominance of "content" over materiality basically already applies to almost everything. An exception is experimental cinema, where you have a single artist creating a work, and where you can argue, for example, that a film was hand-painted, that it's a unique artefact. But with every other aspect of a collection there's this separation of content and medium, where you run the danger of not really being able to argue this separation. What happens is that digital technology promises you that – while you cannot fully represent the material qualities of a work – you gain the power of annotation. You can *annotate* all those qualities. You can provide even more contextual information within your digital representation. So this is one of the most dangerous deadlocks. If I imagine a scenario where a technology provider says, "You don't need to be too sad about what you lose in material aspects, because I can offer you a digital preservation package where you can interleave all the metadata with the audiovisual content of the work, so you could either reconstruct it in the future, or can have the work you want to preserve live on in the Information Age."

—PCU: You mean to be able to go back to the original medium if you want to?

—ML: If the technology is available in, say, 50 to 80 years' time, it is possible.

—PCU: I do see that's also where curatorship can play an important role in the archive of the future, because we cannot rule out the idea that something that was deliberately made for com-

pletely practical reasons, such as a medical film, may be seen as having outstanding aesthetic values. It becomes something else for us culturally, and it will make someone say, "This is so beautiful." It is beautiful for reasons that probably go beyond the intentions of the author, who created the film for completely pragmatic reasons, and all of a sudden it takes on a cultural resonance, which makes me feel I need to present this differently.

—ML: Yes. But what we ask for if we say archives should behave more like museums is a contextualization of works. And that the material aspect of the work is part of its context. But if you show a medical film for cultural use in the museum space, you turn it into something it has never been before. You effectively de-contextualize it and then re-contextualize it, probably even *misinterpret* it. On the other hand, it would be perfectly arguable to say classroom films have always used 16mm film, and not for aesthetic purposes, but because it was the technology that was available for non-theatrical use, and nowadays digital technology has the same status. So isn't the proper presentation and also the proper preservation for something which has always been destined for non-theatrical access digital? So here we are again, in the same difficult situation.

You see, I think what is one of the key philosophical components of the whole discussion is whether we are talking about the actual film as it has been handed down and produced, or are we talking about an idea of cinema? For instance, Dziga Vertov. I have one theory in working through Vertov's writings, sketches, and films, which is that the greatest obstacle to his idea of *cinema* is *film* – the limitations of the film medium. I could argue perfectly in a wholly theoretical setting that Dziga Vertov, if television had been available, if digital technology had been available, to capture images, for the montage of images, and the distribution of images, this would have been his preferred medium. What we have done for the last 40 years is to worship those fragmentary copies of his work as essential cinema.

But now I'm in an in-between position. What do I do as a curator? Do I follow the route to, in a way, reverse-engineer from the artefact an idea of Dziga Vertov's cinema, a virtual work, or do I work with what is left? And I think much of the discussion is about whether we are talking about the actual historicity of things in our archives, in our vaults. Is film history constantly rewritten by its presentation, by making it available? Is it the historicity of the actual artefacts and of the actual process of handing down films, or is it something virtual, an idea of cinema?

__PCU: Do you think society cares about the historicity of the moving image?

__ML: I think society would care, if we put more emphasis on the historicity of images. In a way digital technology could help us to do that, but it's also a great obstacle, because if you have the possibility of seamlessly presenting something that has been assembled from various sources, the more you're able to clean it up and reintroduce the idea of the pre-existing *Gestalt,* the less people are going to appreciate the historicity.

__PCU: Yes, but don't you get the feeling that you are perceived as a member of an extremely restricted category of people, who seem to care about something that culture generally does not value? Don't you feel that you are being surrounded by an environment that says you are toying with an idea that is of no importance to today's culture? This whole notion of debating and arguing and questioning the way we are making available the works of the past is seen as something that is irrelevant. If someone would say, "What is the big deal? Why are you struggling with this?"

__ML: I mean, you can always take examples from other arts. For instance, if you compare yourself to an archaeologist or a historian, then the importance of the historicity of the artefact becomes quite obvious. My favourite example – and we already talked about it – is the British Museum and their exhibition on Polynesian art. You have the artefact as it was, a snapshot of something fixed in time, preserved so it doesn't decompose further. Next to the artefact you have a caption that explains the process it has gone through, and next to it you have a simulation of what it possibly looked like. This is important for traditional human artefacts like cutlery, pottery, whatever. In film, there's no notion of this. The "perfect" restoration is something that is seamless and where you cannot differentiate the various levels, where the gaps are bridged. But, on the other hand, there's an almost fetishistic notion about the analog as something that is closer to a material reality that we are beginning to lose in this world of instant communication and simulation. And you have film-makers like Tarantino and Rodriguez digitally emulating [in *Grindhouse,* 2007], for instance, the process of film decay that has been done away with in digital production.

Another example: DVD technology features something called "seamless branching". From a film you can have, say, Version A, the theatrical version, and you can have Version B, the "Director's Cut," which includes additional shots. So the disc contains one movie file (version A) and a series of video fragments (version B). In navigation you can seamlessly bridge the gap, so that in playback, if you choose the Director's Cut, you move from segment A into segment B, and back into segment A seamlessly. Seamlessness is what it's all about – because on a material level everything is equal, data. I always wondered if an archival electronic publication should not be a presentation "with seams", where you can educate via metadata, via text inserts, via a feature that explains the way something analog has been transferred into the digital realm, and educate people, because in a way navigation can reflect a process of thinking. You can make tangible the historian's thinking. You can have versions, and then you suddenly see where they lock together. Here's a gap. What do we do with it? Make it visible, or bridge it?

__PCU: I think by saying what you've just said you're introducing another interesting item for discussion, and that is the notion of fragments. I think we know that what makes our field peculiar in the context of the other arts is this general devaluation of the fragment. The fact is that, while it is perfectly OK to appreciate a fragment of a Roman sculpture, the fragment of a film, however beautiful, will never receive the same degree of attention. So Question Number One is, do you think a time will come when, with the end of the analog world, the value of the analog fragment will resurface? We'll be able to say, "Look, we have found 30 seconds of Charlie Chaplin doing..." Will this happen? And then Question Number Two is: we have not explored yet, because we are not at that stage, to what

extent the term "fragment" may apply to a digital work. Will there be a digital fragment? Will there be a time when we say, "Look, we've found an uncorrupted digital fragment of this digital work." What will be the curatorial implications of the treatment of the digital fragment?

__ML: I have the feeling the first answer will be Yes. But I don't know if it's going to be the kind of appreciation *we* appreciate. Most likely it will be some kind of folkloristic notion of the fragment – more an aesthetic appreciation, instead of something that is going to provoke thinking. An oddity, or old-fashioned in a romantic way. And I'm not sure that we want to follow that route, because I think it has already been done in the sense that I can completely imagine people going to a silent film festival to see all those shaky, incomplete things, as opposed to the mainstream of stable, perfect, identical pictures. But I think the fragment can also be very important in terms of context, and in terms of, for instance, writing history. The digital revolution in a way also changes our perception, since it very much encourages a notion of history that presents some kind of false completeness of things. In a way, it reintroduces the great narrative into culture. So fragments can also be presented as something that refuses the notion of a hegemonic closed narrative and an abstract, objective viewpoint. The analog fragment points to an *incompleteness*. Presenting the fragment properly, and comparing it to various simulations of completeness, can be essential to us as educators and as historians.

I'm not sure about the second question, as artefacts in the analog sense don't exist in the digital realm. If a file is corrupted, it is unusable.

With film you can find information in even half a frame. There is no such thing as a fragmentary file.

___PCU: Can you imagine contributing a curatorial value to a corrupted digital file?

___ML: It can be used. Art does this regularly. You can take corrupted files and try to play them back or retrieve some kind of visual information out of them. You can generate whole new aesthetic effects. For instance, you can take a text document and turn it into Unicode, and then redo it as poetry. You can feed an image into sound processing software, and turn the image into sound. Since it's not analogous representation anymore, but information that can be reconfigured, also in a fragmentary form, you get aesthetic effects out of it. It's like this early example from cybernetics, where you can take a whole digital set like the alphabet, and if you permutate it enough you'll always get a sentence which makes some kind of semantic sense. Be it your original intention or not. I mean, this is possibly a chance for new art forms to emerge. But in terms of preservation and in terms of a certain fidelity to one's original content or original material, this is a disaster.

___PCU: Speaking of fragments, let's have a case study. Let's take the case of Eisenstein's *Qué Viva México!* One of the most fascinating documents about the film, aside from the many versions surviving of the film, is Jay Leyda's study of *Qué Viva México!* as this kind of monster work lasting several hours, where a number of available shots of the same scene are made available together. I still find that an extraordinary document of a certain kind of historical approach to curatorship. How a scholar tried to explain a film by creating what may be seen as basically a new work. When Leyda did this, obviously he did not have digital technology at his disposal. How would you imagine a digital version of *Qué Viva México!*?

___ML: I think I'd imagine it very much along the lines of what Enno Patalas and Anna Bohn did with *Metropolis*. The thing that separates digital reworkings of that kind from analog reworkings is that somebody who is not knowledgeable about the history of *Qué Viva México!* could probably mistake Leyda's work for the Eisenstein film. One could easily mistake this for an authorized version, or a true approximation of what it was. The more you move into digital technology, the more you can move in other directions. On the one hand, you can make it as seamless as imaginable. You can have something that to a general audience is completely indistinguishable from something Eisenstein might have done. But, on the other hand, you have so many more possibilities of annotation, of making "metadata" a visible and legible part of the audiovisual experience, since your presentation can simultaneously present text and apparatus. But the question is, which direction is general audiovisual culture moving in, and which directions do we want to move in?

Archives must consider the danger that with digital tools our choices become indistinguishable from the contradictions which are in the material. On the one hand, we need to be very aware of that, and some colleagues already are, but, on the other hand, I think we should try to understand the possibilities of something like historical critical editions of films, or the possibilities of making transparent our decisions within our presentations, to make them an intrinsic part of them. And for that we need to understand the possibilities of digital tools, and we need to actively produce them on our own. Do you know what I mean?

—PCU: Yes. As you were talking, two other examples came into mind, but these are both examples of curatorship as a work of fiction. The first example comes from what was witnessed at the 2007 Tokyo Congress of the International Federation of Film Archives, where what was being promoted as the discovery of a 3-D Méliès film was presented in the official programme. Here's what the programme booklet says: "The clips planned to show will include the very first (and even to film experts totally unknown) 3-D films by Méliès and Lumière as examples of the traditional 2-strip system with two projectors." We all know that Méliès never made 3-D films, but the very existence of two prints of the same film, shot with two parallel cameras, has made someone concoct the dream of a work of fiction and then smuggle it in as History itself. What I find astonishing in this case is that a deliberate falsification of History is being presented here as not only authentic (that is, History itself), but as hitherto unknown to the community of specialists, and presented to a forum of specialists, at an event for the members of an institution one of whose primary missions is the protection of the creative work from any form of undue alteration or manipulation. Fascinating, isn't it? Do you see this process of corruption of the artwork as a by-product of this sense of freedom that the curator has to reinvent history?

—ML: I think if it leads to falsification and a deliberate deception of the audience, there is absolutely a danger present. But I think that a certain fictional element, the idea that *this* could have also been *that,* is part of curatorial thinking.

—PCU: Why is this operation not being presented as the creation of a new work of art? It would be simpler to say, "Look, because I've found two different elements of the same Méliès film from two different cameras, I'm playing with it, and I'm creating a new work of fiction." Why present this as history?

—ML: This is the difference which is so crucial, because digital technologies blur – very creatively – the border between the analog object you are researching and preserving, and the simulation. If, for instance, a curator goes back and says, we've got these two different versions, and it's now possible using digital technology to reconstruct the *atelier* where the film was shot, this would be the proper answer. This would be a very interesting presentation: not whether Méliès actually made a 3-D film, but that we can now see what the *atelier* was like. I was at a presentation two weeks ago at the Technical University in Vienna, where they demonstrated a technology able to generate a 3-D simulation of a film set from an A and B negative of a shot, as the two cameras give them an angle of almost 180°, and the computer can calculate proximity data from the objects in the shot. So we can use the range of where we can move a virtual camera along this set, and reconstruct a shot that was never made. This is interesting material. If, for instance, you want to analyse film-making processes the way Godard and Fritz Lang did it in *The Dinosaur and the Baby* (1967), where they discuss their strategies of *mise-en-scène*. If you want to visualize these processes, I think it's perfectly feasible to do that with the technology available, and it's perfectly in line with curatorial thinking, but you should never confuse this with your original object. This is just falsification of original sources. It's not far removed from excising people from films.

—PCU: Then what do you do when alteration of history becomes your only plausible choice in order to present film heritage? Here is my second example: The first Pordenone Silent Film Festival, back in 1982, was about Max Linder. I was recently discussing the idea of going back to re-assess his work. We realized that Maud Linder had been working on Max Linder's films for a number of years with clear ideas of what the intentions of her father were, and as a result many films have been modified in order to build up what she perceived as his intentions. These versions represent another interpretation of Max Linder. How would you handle this? Would you just wait until an opportunity to find a sort of authenticity arose again, or do you cope with the fact that there is a set of operations being implemented on a historical artefact?

—ML: But most of us have seen films which are actually reconstructions, and which don't address this. There's no excuse, if you move into the digital realm and say you are going to make those Max Linder films available digitally, not to reflect the process, with the means provided by digital technology. I think every edition presenting something as a "restored" or "reconstructed" version should make use of the opportunity to present the original materials, and at least one case study of a deliberate choice of source materials. Another example, which I've been discussing at this year's Pordenone festival, is *Paris qui dort*. The print was a reconstruction of the form the film originally had when it was released. We know that René Clair later went back to the film and cut it down considerably to excise all the mistakes he had made. I talked to a colleague, who said he was extremely annoyed about the version presented because the artist had decided to excise all this stuff. There is an authorized version of the film available, and, on the other hand, you have all those annoying mistakes in there. You see a Paris supposedly put to sleep, where there are people moving in the background. A digital version nowadays would be a compromise. You'd leave in all those shots, but you'd get rid of all the people and all the mistakes in the picture. So what do you do with that? Now, your answer can be twofold: you can either say this is completely offhand – you can't do that. You know that with every shot that has been tampered with, you must give your audience the opportunity to have an additional layer of presentation that tells what has been done with it, which can lead to contextual materials. If you follow this route, what you will have in a digital edition, be it a CD-ROM, a Web presentation, or a DVD, is not the film; it's something entirely different.

—PCU: In the digital world, this possibility has created a number of conundrums for archives and museums, which go even deeper into the fabric of what we consider as the integrity of the film experience or of the film as an event. We are told that thanks to digital technology you can, so to speak, "preserve" a film and make it viewable by bypassing the stage of the intermediate negative. Even if the outcome is a print, it is a print that theoretically did not come from a negative. So you see an image whose quality could not possibly have been achieved with analog means. This in a way is a paradoxical fulfilment of what they call the "model image", which goes from the camera negative directly to the retina of the eye. And you wonder: is this a desirable outcome, or does it simply respond to the modern notion of "the sharper, the better"?

—ML: I think it's both.

—PCU: Should this be seen as something of value from a curatorial standpoint?

—ML: I think it is definitely of value, but it is a value where we must make decisions on whether it is of value to us. It is of value not only in picture quality, but also in this whole notion of digital culture, and the bigger economic and telecommunications culture, where nothing is fixed, everything is in constant flux, and can be reconfigured at any point. Not only do you have an image sharpness that could not have been achieved in the traditional ways of the medium, but you also do not have the master negative – you have something that is more like a virtual film, which can be put out in new editions. I mean, it's not that easy, and it's not that cheap – but basically, a version you make a print from, then you can go back, alter something, correct something, take something out, put something in, and make a new positive – so that you have a whole series of changes that are not documented. The whole notion that something is a work – one material manifestation of a certain point in time – is done away with completely. You could make changes to something on a weekly basis. So, in a way, historicity is done away with.

—PCU: But does this historicity remain visible? Or is the viewer led to believe – because no one is actually told about the subtleties involved in the process – that, for example, this is actually Dreyer's *Joan of Arc,* shown in a form which simulates the absence of a negative? Is this going to be perceived as a historical object, "the real thing"?

—ML: Most likely the real thing. Audiences cannot recognize the difference. The work is there. In a way, if you get rid of the historicity you weaken your own decisions. Analog reconstructions – utilizing physical material, selecting, deselecting, splicing shots – make your decisions manifest. Although you wouldn't destroy original elements, you're thinking in terms of destructive editing – every decision has physical consequences (as in life in general!). This is testimony to decisions made with the clear conscience that at one point in time you need to fix your decisions, even if they prove to be wrong in 20 years. It has a certain seal – an author's signature, if you want. On a digital level it's always possible to reconfigure, never to regard decisions as permanent, but as something reversible tomorrow. You lose authority. I mean, I'm not speaking about dogmatic views, which say this is cast in stone, but you weaken your own decisions, because you can always redo them or do away with them.

—PCU: Well, yes. But what I'm hinting at, and what I would like to hear your opinion on, is the possibility that one peculiarity of the digital technology applied to the preservation of cinema heritage is that digital has the intrinsic ability to conceal the historicity of the process. You may find out that it happened, but you do not necessarily know when. So does the digital technology applied to archival and museum work have the power to hide this historicity?

—ML: Yes, definitely. By its own logic it does. Historicity is a function of the material, something that comes from the material. Very generally speaking, the moment you turn something into pure information there are no more hierarchies. So, by the intrinsic logic of digital, yes, it does hide it. The question is, can we use it in our simulation to actively make transparent what it does to our object, what it does to our artefacts, to our heritage, and to make that process visible?

___PCU: Today, we can still say we are watching a 1956 print of *Joan of Arc*. We can say this is the 1956 restoration of *Joan of Arc,* with its own peculiarities, mutations, and the presence of a certain amount of silver in the emulsion of the print. This is not possible with digital technology. I know that by saying this I'm taking the risk of presenting ourselves as the ongoing sceptics regarding digital technology. But if digital technology tends to erase the historicity of the artefact, is this fundamentally a wrong tool for our job, which is the job of protecting and promoting historicity, insofar as history matters to a curator – which may or may not be the case in the future?

___ML: Then it most definitely is, but it depends on which level you employ digital technology. If you preserve *Joan of Arc* digitally, and it becomes your preservation master, there's something inherently wrong with that on a philosophical level. If you make a conscious decision, for instance, to publish a digital edition of the film, but the final result of your preservation is an analog master that is time-stamped, and is a material with a certain historicity, then I think the question moves away from a complete deadlock.

___PCU: When I consider this, I find it interesting that in the field of archiving relating to recorded sound, digital preservation is all we have. Preservationists of recorded sound now take it for granted that preservation is done digitally. There is no such thing as analog preservation; the best

you can aim at is that you can still listen to an original cylinder in very special circumstances. But otherwise, the fact that you can hear a recording made in 1901 using digital means is considered perfectly acceptable. And I suspect that this uncontroversial attitude towards digital preservation may soon touch our shores, if it hasn't already.

___ML: The thing archives which are as sceptical as we are can do is to keep hiding behind the technical limitations of digital technology, and say, "This might be a solution for sound recordings, since current equipment is capable of a sample rate that far surpasses the frequency range of analog recordings, etc." With film you can still say, "Well, you can't properly represent colour, grayscale, grain, etc." But, in a way, this is the last line of defence. After this is breached, all that remains are philosophical arguments. And then sound preservationists who are pro-digitization can say, "Nobody cares for analog sound anymore, and we've solved the technological problems. So where's your problem?" I don't know any answer to this.

___DF: May I join the conversation?

___PCU: We were talking about Dreyer, the digital presentation of *Joan of Arc* without analog intermediate. Remember the FIAF Congress in São Paulo, back in 2006? We were told, "You are about to see the film as if it didn't have to go through the negative intermediate process." Which effectively means we were seeing something that the original audience never saw.

___ML: We arrived at the conclusion that in the current digital culture, all the historicity in the analog production process is like an obstacle to the actual appreciation of the work, and that digital culture puts forward the idea of an ideal film, of representing as if it were real something that is entirely virtual to the analog production process. As if we could emulate the situation where the image of an actress was directly transmitted onto our retina.

___DF: The worry I have with going directly from the negative is that the positive is what was seen by the public, and that positive was graded in a certain manner for presentation at that time. If you do phase reversal, you don't have the ability to make the positive image match a particularly graded and presented copy. So, effectively, what you're doing is you're allowing the digital engineer even more flexibility to change the nature of the original experience. Now we all know that you can't recreate the experience, but by going to the negative you're making it even more difficult to approximate the positive as seen originally. And there are so many problems anyway associated with digital preservation, because, unless your digital engineer is also your curator, they're going to produce the best results according to their terms of reference, not according to the historicity of the object, where they have no experience.

___PCU: In this sense, finding a film exclusively in the form of an original camera negative may not be the best option.

___DF: No, this is what I'm saying: I don't think it is the best option, unless you had present a positive copy from that negative, which the digital engineer would be able to access for reference purposes during the making of the digital master.

___PCU: Now you are aware – and I'm doing a very violent jump-cut here – that we are talking about something that the vast majority of the archives around the world would consider as an unrealistic, abstract discussion, which has very little bearing on the reality of collections that are decaying and in need of protection. In other words, we are talking about a luxury which most archives cannot afford. And as our conversation is technically about so-called "platforms", I would like to bring the focus to the crude reality of the vast majority of archives, for which the sudden presence of the digital opportunity is perceived rightly or wrongly as a chance to do what otherwise would have been impossible to achieve with photochemical means. My view is that yes, this approach provides these archives with new tools, but it also presents them with a different kind of challenge. Until the advent of the digital era, to put the question into blunt terms, the alternative that an archive in distress would have had, would be to say, "I have half a million dollars. With this I could probably properly preserve ten feature films, or I could put my entire collection on videotape. What do I prefer to do?" So, let's translate this into the digital world, and you have an archive curator saying, "With the money I have at my disposal, I can digitize my entire collection in a highly compressed way to make it available, or I can pay for uncompressed preservation of a more limited portion of my collection." So the same problem will present itself, but in a different way. If you were the curator of the National Film Archive of Indonesia, with a very large collection of works in rapid decay, and the years are passing, and along comes this new tool, what would be your approach?

___ML: If I only had those two choices?

___PCU: Well, if there's a third one, please tell us!

___ML: The third one would be to traditionally preserve a selected number of films that are representative of different aspects of the collection, and produce access masters in digital form to further promote my archive and disseminate knowledge about it. What is the purpose of digitizing something in a highly compressed format? The only advantage it gives you is that you make your collections more visible, either to researchers or for commercial use, or to funding agencies.

___DF: I agree to a certain extent. I think that generally the potential saving that you gain by digitizing to a lower level is not significant in terms of storage. So you might as well digitize your archive, but how you chose to release the material or make it available is a different matter. But at least if you digitize to a reasonably high level, you've got a choice in making it available in several ways according to need. My problem with your question is that it had no time frame. Are you talking about what I would do if I were trying to do something for 100 years, or are you talking about what I would try and do if I were doing it for a 5-year plan? Because I would have a totally different answer. If you say 100 years, I would have to say first of all I've probably got to put away $50,000 of that to invest it, so that when I need to refresh my master and make new digital access copies I have something to do it with. Otherwise everything I'm doing now is for a short period of time, and that is not the concept behind an archive.

___PCU: Let me rephrase my hypothetical scenario. I operate in an archive in a tropical country. I have a collection of, let's say, 50,000 feature films, where I cannot even ensure proper climate control in my vault. In the foreseeable future, unless there is some predictable change in the government, I can expect to have a pre-

servation budget of $100,000, if I am lucky. So there is a clear disproportion between the magnitude of the collection and my ability to take proper care of it. Let's say that I operate in an environment where I still have analog options.

___DF: Well, I think what I would do is to make a very strong case for as little a compression as possible, because that would give me the option if things got better of making a physical film copy back from the compressed material. If it so happened that Indonesian cinema became important in the world, and someone else was interested in making it accessible… So if I went down the digital route, and I understand a lot of the reasons for doing so, I would do it to the highest level of compression, because I wouldn't have lost the option of film.

The other factor is, of course, it sort of assumes that in a country like Indonesia there is an ability to go from a 35mm copy to a digital environment. I think the chances are that they are going to have to go out to at least Hong Kong, or somewhere nearby, in order to do anything like that. It's not a simple issue.

___ML: It depends. It would only make sense if it has been agreed upon that digitizing is (a) considerably cheaper than a traditional analog preservation, and (b) the staff or infrastructure in your county allows for the same level of care in digital preservation as with analog preservation. If those two pre-conditions are fulfilled, then it might be a route. But, on the other hand, you can be faced with something which you could preserve with analog means 20 times, and with digital means 28 times. But your staff do not know enough, or do not have enough choices in the methods of digitizing, to really evaluate whether this is going to be a usable representation, even in 10 years' time. Are we choosing the right format? Do we have the proper means for storing the digital data?

__PCU: I assume that the risk faced by an archive in this situation – even if the archive was given the means to massively digitize its collection because of a special grant, or because of a governing body which supports the digitization of a collection – would be the possibility that if the archive is not able to refresh their data on a periodic basis, the solution would actually lead to a catastrophe.

__DF: Yes, I agree. But if you've gone down the route of high digitization, when it comes to refreshing data you still have two options in front of you. You have the option to refresh, and you have the option to make a film copy. To me, if I'm recommending to someone in this field, in this immediate stage, at the moment I would say, "Fine, go for the digital approach, but don't sacrifice by digitizing to a lower level than necessary, because that would take away options for the future."

__PCU: So does this mean – and I'm talking to you, Michael, as a representative of a specific generation of archivists – that the choice between analog and digital is a false distinction?

__ML: My instinct tells me that it is a false distinction, in the sense that it is presented as if there were no other possibilities. I always get nervous when something is positioned by the industry or by agenda-makers as something where there is only one possibility. This is something which very much goes against all my instincts.

__DF: But you see, I think Paolo's original question came from the perspective of developing countries reading our work, and if they're reading our work we don't want them to say, "This is totally irrelevant to us." And yet we want them to understand the issues. But in the end I think they will only take our work seriously if we address their situation. Now, we're going to have to put a lot of the technical considerations to one side, because it's not that digitization is necessarily any easier in that environment than making a film copy. If you have the opportunity of digitization and a reasonable level of quality, I think I would come out and say to you, "Yes, this is a reasonable expenditure of the money you have available, providing you realize that before you do your digitization you must clean and repair the original film, so that you get from that film the best copy, because that then becomes the master for any future material that is going to be created." If I had to give a positive answer, that would be my answer.

__PCU: Yes, you're absolutely right. Especially in relation to someone who reads this book, and thinks, "I work in India, and I cannot reasonably expect my government to listen to my plea to allow me to invest in the preservation of the cinematic heritage in 35mm. So, reasonably, my only option is to ride the tiger of digital preservation in a way that does not betray my curatorial principles." We need to be able to say something on this matter.

__ML: Go for the best quality available. The most dangerous thing would be to compromise between quality and accessibility. I think a wrong answer would be to produce 2,000 mediocre, heavily compressed access copies, because this is also a route so many private collections have taken. For instance, in Austria you had the film archive of the Workers' Movement, who transferred all their original 16mm films from the 1930s onto half-inch tape in the 1980s, because video technology then was something that was easily available. And of course they destroyed the film prints.

___DF: I think that's a very good point. We should look back at what happened when video came in, and see what everyone was saying at that time. It must have been a very similar conversation.

But going back to what we were saying before, something that might be worth doing is to talk to developing archives about differentiating the material they have in their collections. If they have a VHS cassette they might as well copy that on a production-line technique, and not spend too much money on it, because VHS has already lost so much of the resolution of the original that you would be wasting money trying to record it to a higher level than the information it contains. For instance, at the Library of Congress, what we were doing was, anything that we got on VHS was put through a 24-hour machine, which copies it into the digital environment at a reasonable level, which potentially can be used to make that accessible. And which in numerical terms appears to be making a lot of your collection accessible. Then you concentrate your skills on doing the things which are more important, and where there is justification in going for higher quality.

Now I would like to say to other countries that you need to look at your collections, because if, for instance, you've got a 16mm negative of a film shot in your country, that's likely to be the only such material available, it has to be treated differently. Even if it is a 16mm, it may be the only one that exists. But if you have television, videos, etc., on VHS cassettes, you might as well do something with that on a fairly

production-line technique. But the 16mm print in, let's say, Africa, is going to be the same as the 35mm original print in Europe, in terms of the heritage of that particular country. And in some ways it may be more valuable, because there may be fewer copies of it. The chances of finding another copy in another tropical environment, in a part of the world where distribution wasn't very great, means that you may be dealing with literally the only copy. It's not just another copy of *The Red Shoes* or *The Birth of a Nation;* it may be the only copy. And I wouldn't want for that to necessarily follow the same route I'd want for something else. So I think what I want to talk about, in answer to the question, is breaking collections down into different types of material, and dealing with them in different ways, and allocating your money according to the opportunities you have and the material you have.

___PCU: Let me raise a question about those cultures where the difference between platforms is seen as fundamentally irrelevant. I'm thinking of the case of ethnic minorities, such as Aboriginal cultures in Australia, where the importance of preservation of the visual heritage is completely separate from the notion of platforms. There would perhaps be an active dislike of any obstacle to the preservation of a culture based on a platform. People say, "Don't give us that nonsense about platforms! We just want to re-appropriate our own culture."

___ML: This is about visibility. It was one scenario that I won't propose now for our discussion, because platforms also involve a certain hierarchy of what is visible and what is not. To go back to the last example: If you had the choice, with a certain budget, to do two digital restorations and preservation, but with the same money you could, from a certain corpus of work in your collection, produce access masters for active use in education or in providing visibility, what would you do? Say you've got a collection of material on aboriginal cultures which has been traditionally preserved, and you can now choose whether to produce access masters, be they QuickTime movies or DVDs or maybe a Web platform, with hundreds of hours already catalogued and preserved for society's use and the sake of visibility. Or would you use it to save a few more works? As a curator this presents you with an ethical dilemma.

__PCU: The solution that has been found by Indigenous cultures has been a collaboration between a national institution and the Indigenous communities. The Indigenous communities would allow the national institution to pursue the preservation of the collection according to the highest possible (Western) standards, while at the same time guaranteeing that the maintenance of these standards would not be an impediment to the immediate accessibility of the material. So the archive is a caretaker of a kind of integrity which the community does not necessarily care about, but it matters to the national institution. It's a way of saying, "Do things the way you want to, but don't use this as an excuse to prevent us from re-acquiring what we consider our cultural ownership."

__ML: And in this case, a digital environment makes complete sense as a platform for distribution and simulation, or even to gain more support within communities. You've just outlined that this is a contract between the communities and the archive as a caretaker with its own criteria.

__DF: We have the same issues with the Native American communities in the USA. They take it one step further, and say, "We want you to claim us so that we can do the transfer, because we're the only people who have the sensitivity to understand the material. So it's not a question of just making the material available to us in any form. If you're going to put it in the national collection in a high-quality form, we have to be there doing that. And until we are in that position we're happy with low-quality material for access purposes. We don't want the institution to handle this without us present." Now, obviously, to a certain extent this is an activist role in the community, of saying, "Look, we are a county within a country. This is our heritage, and we want to be able to decide on its future and how it is handled." Wherever there are indigenous communities, more and more they're using the case of preservation in all fields as an activist approach.

__ML: This is a fascinating case for archives as museums. But, on the other hand, imagine the same thing in a traditional arts and crafts museum. Indigenous communities have for decades fought a case for getting back artefacts held in, for instance, museums of anthropology. Objects which they see as essential to their identity. Museums don't want to restitute those objects because they say, "You can't look after them." In the case of film, those communities are perfectly content with a copy, even with something we perceive as down-graded. Sometimes museums and archives won't provide this, because they say, "What is essential is the artefact and the original elements, and we don't produce lower-level facsimiles of what we do." This is a really fascinating case.

_PCU: In my view, it's important to take things even a step further, and accept the fact that certain communities may advocate the right to treat collections in a way which openly contradicts our own values. For example, our notion of the artefact as something fundamentally untouchable for the sake of our own idea of integrity is something that certain communities just don't agree with, as they claim the right to alter, make inaccessible, or even destroy the works which belong to their tradition. I find this a healthy reminder of the historicity and specific connotation of curatorship as a cultural concept.

~

_PCU: Speaking of which, Michael, may I throw in an impromptu thought on a totally different matter, in relation to a (yet to be written) history of film curatorship? It just occurred to me that when we started working on this project, YouTube was a good idea on the rising path. Now it's a *fait accompli*. Other similar initiatives, such as Rick Prelinger's Internet Archive, are quickly gaining ground. The YouTube model is questioning the very *raison d'être* of film archives and museums in their current form: every user becomes the curator of his or her own visual preferences in a growing collection put together by everyone with a computer. The days of film archives and museums "as we know them" may be numbered, don't you think?

_ML: I couldn't agree more, and it's telling that YouTube became a global phenomenon in the relatively short time between our first conversation and the last one. And the archival community just can't understand its impact – everybody's panicking about "pirate copies" of their precious holdings showing up on one of the portals, but no one seems to notice that this exactly figures as a "mindmap" of the global, contemporary media- and mind-scape: the ephemeral and the masterpiece, the childhood "guilty pleasure" and the nasty, become equal. The curatorial principle is individual, idiosyncratic, and collective at the same time; it's as if the idea of the "moving image archive" had taken a huge leap to where historical sciences have taken us during the last decades: from artefacts-as-documents, the archive as a repository of historical records, to a *lieu de mémoire* – a site of memory.

I can hardly contain my excitement, talking about this – as it leaves me in a state of perpetual amazement, and a feeling of uncertainty as to what this means for our profession.

But I'm rambling... You said that the days of archives are numbered? In a way I share the feeling of a tidal wave rolling along, but I don't know whether they're "numbered". Don't you believe in some kind of "split reality", where both concepts share a place in the public arena? Or will the new regime prove the old to be obsolete?
_PCU: Let me stress what I put between quotation marks. For how long do we think film archives and museums will be allowed to operate in what you call a "split reality"? This may be possible for the short term, but sooner or later they may face an unsustainable dilemma: either embrace the YouTube model, or become irrelevant. Look what happened to recorded sound archives. How visible are they? How many people make use of them? I'm an avid listener of rare music, but I never had to contact a phonotheque in order to find what I want. This phenomenon may in fact deepen the gap between film museums and film archives, thus

radicalizing the very same distinction David finds so objectionable.

Let's put it this way: on one hand there's a MoMA or a *Filmmuseum,* somehow managing to exhibit (in one form or another) and convey a certain sense of (film) history, necessarily limited to a shrinking élite; on the other there's the YouTube-type archive, an ocean of moving images in which users can swim at their own discretion. In a way, I welcome this short circuit as an opportunity to achieve a much-needed shake-up of our notions of visual culture, and – perhaps more importantly – to accelerate the collision between copyright and the real world. One may argue that it's perfectly fine to be able to look at a Dziga Vertov film on YouTube; according to this viewpoint, a bad photocopy is better than nothing, and someone may eventually want to see the actual thing (whatever that may be). Vertov himself may have probably endorsed such *modus operandi.* But I feel there's something flawed in this line of reasoning.

—ML: Well, it's flawed in the sense that we – archives, museums, curators – believe ourselves to have authority over the ways in which moving pictures can be encountered, interpreted. In a way we try to advocate a consciousness of historicity – works shall be preserved and made available for future generations not only as content but as a "functioning system". This runs counter to the idea of consumption, where moving images become a commodity that is disseminated in the most convenient and economical wrapper, for instant, individual use. You said that the YouTube model allows users to swim at their own discretion? It does; and its promise – for the user on the receiving end as well as the broadcaster/video jockey/curator –

is that collective memory, heritage, can be easily incorporated into one's own "home cinema". The idea I heavily dislike about this "privatization" of collective memory is that it turns cultural artefacts into souvenirs, something that can be gathered effortlessly, consumed casually, and disposed of easily. Cinema was never like that – you never "own" a film, but you partake in a social activity, in a communal experience. I wonder how we – as curators – can reinforce this aspect: that collective memory is something that belongs to mankind without the concept of "property" fragmenting its totality into bits and bytes; that appropriation doesn't mean "stealing"?

—PCU: I had always thought that "stealing", together with "cheating" and "lying", is part of the creative process, in the sense that the artist (and the curator, to the extent that the curator is an artist) appropriates the ideas of other people, other forms of expression, other frameworks of knowledge, to create something new. What I'm hinting at is that the YouTube way of thinking may be the first evidence of another form of curatorship we're still not aware of. The problem with YouTube is the problem of the Internet as a medium, that is, its overwhelming power to dissolve originality into anonymity: a case in point is the story of a writer who had a sexual fantasy, found it so beautiful that she decided to share it in a chat room, and suddenly felt that her fantasy was not beautiful any longer, it had become something banal.

Having said this, one may argue that we are dealing with curatorship of "film" and not of YouTube nor of sexual fantasies, so the question becomes, how do we make film curatorship meaningful in a YouTube visual culture? The obvious answer from an outsider's viewpoint will be "Why should I care?", and it won't be enough to say "Yes, you should". We must be able to come up with persuasive, if not compelling, arguments to this effect, without questioning the right to "steal", "cheat", and "lie" with film in the name of genuine invention. Because if we, members of the last generation born in a "film" world, can't formulate these arguments, who will?

~

From: PCU
To: AH; DF; ML
Date: 2 April 2007
Dear all,
Please check out Kristin Thompson's recent blog entry on digital access. I think we should include her argument in our book; her text seems a natural to me in this context. Do you agree?

THE CELESTIAL MULTIPLEX
Kristin Thompson

The Internet is mind-bogglingly huge, and a lot of people seem to think that most of the texts and images and sound-recordings ever created are now available on it – or will be soon. In relation to music downloading, the idea got termed "The Celestial Jukebox," and a lot of people believe in it. University libraries are noticeably emptier than they were in my graduate-school days, since students assume they can find all the research materials they need by Googling comfortably in their own rooms.

A lot depends on what you're working on. For *The Frodo Franchise,* studying the ongoing *Lord of the Rings* phenomenon would have been impossible without the Internet. A big portion of its endnotes are citations to URLs. On the other hand, my previous book, *Herr Lubitsch Goes to Hollywood,* a monograph on the stylistic and technical aspects of Ernst Lubitsch's silent features, has not a single Internet reference. Lubitsch can only be investigated in archives and libraries, where one finds the films and the old books and periodicals vital to such a project.

Vast though it is, the Internet is tiny in comparison with the real world. Only a minuscule fraction of all the books, paintings, music, photographs, etc., is online. Belief in a Celestial Jukebox usually works only because people tend to think about the types of texts and images and sounds that they know about and want access to. Yes, more is being put into digital form at a great rate, but more new stuff is being made and old stuff being discovered. There will never come a time when everything is available.

Even so, every now and then someone proclaims that in the not-too-distant future all the movies ever made will be downloadable for a small fee, a sort of Celestial Multiplex. A. O. Scott declared this in "The Shape of

Cinema, Transformed at the Click of a Mouse" (*New York Times,* March 18, 2007): "It is now possible to imagine – to expect – that before too long the entire surviving history of movies will be open for browsing and sampling at the click of a mouse for a few PayPal dollars." Not only that, but Scott goes on, "This aspect of the online viewing experience is not, in itself, especially revolutionary." He's more interested in the idea that online distribution will allow filmmakers to sell their creations directly to viewers. That would be significant, no doubt, but as a film historian, I'm still gaping at that line about "the entire surviving history of movies." Such availability would not only be "revolutionary," it would be downright miraculous. It's impossible. It just isn't going to happen.

I will give Scott credit for specifying "surviving" films. Other pundits tend to say "all films," ignoring the sad fact that great swathes of our cinematic heritage, especially in hot, humid climates like that of India, have deteriorated and are irretrievably lost.

Dave Kehr has already briefly pointed out some of the problems with Scott's claims, mainly the overwhelming financial support that would be needed: "Tony Scott's optimism struck me as, well, a little optimistic." On the line about "the entire surviving history of movies," Kehr suggests, "That's reckoning without the cost of preparing a film for digital distribution – the same mistake made by the author of the recent vogue book '*The Long Tail'* [Chris Anderson, 2006] – which, depending on how much restoration is necessary, can run up to $50,000 a title. None of the studios is likely to pay that much money to put anything other than the most popular titles in their libraries online." As Kehr says, the numbers of films awaiting restoration and scanning isn't in the hundreds, as Scott casually says. No, it's in the tens of thousands, even if we just count features. It's more like hundreds of thousands or more likely millions, if we count all the surviving shorts,

instructional films, ads, porn, everything made in every country of the world. To see how elaborate the preservation of even one short medical teaching film can be, go to www.jhu.edu/~gazette/2003/21jul03/21film.html.

Putting aside the need for restoration, newer films present a daunting prospect. To help put the situation in perspective, let's glance over the total number of feature films produced worldwide during some representative years from recent decades (culled from *Screen Digest*'s "World Film Production/Distribution" reports, which it publishes each June): 1970, 3,512; 1980, 3,710; 1990, 4,645; 2000, 3,782; and 2005, 4,603. For me the numbers conjure up the last shot of *Raiders of the Lost Ark,* only with just stack upon stack, row upon row of film cans.

Scott isn't the first commentator to prophesy that all films will eventually be on the Internet. It's an idea that crops up now and then, and it would be useful to look more closely at why it's a wild exaggeration. It's not just the money or the huge volume of film involved, though either of those factors would be prohibitive in itself. There are all sorts of other reasons why the advent of practical digital downloading of films will never come close to providing us with the entire history of cinema.

Coincidentally, two experts on this subject, Michael Pogorzelski, Director of the Film Archive of the Academy of Motion Picture Arts and Sciences, and Schawn Belston, Vice President, Film Preservation and Asset Management for Twentieth Century Fox, visited Madison this past week. Mike got his MA here in the Dept. of Communication Arts and now returns about once a year to show off the latest restored print that he has worked on. Schawn isn't an alum, but he has also visited often enough that most students probably think he is. The two brought us the superb new print of *Leave Her to Heaven* that Fox and the Academy have recently collaborated on.

I figured it would be very enlightening to sit down

with these two and talk about why the Internet is never going to allow us to watch just anything our hearts desire. They kindly agreed, and with my trusty recorder in tow we went for burgers – and fried cheese curds, a commodity not available in Los Angeles – at the Plaza Tavern. I'm grateful for the fascinating insights they provided into some of the less obvious obstacles to putting films on the Internet *en masse*.

No Coordinating Body

Before we launch in, though, one point needs to be made: there is no single leader or group or entity out there organizing some giant program to systematically put all surviving movies on the Internet. There isn't a set of guidelines or principles. There's no list of all surviving films. How would we even know if the goal of putting them all up had been achieved? When the last archivist to leave turned out the light, locked the door, and went looking for a new line of work?

Most of the physical prints that would be the basis for such transfers are sitting in the libraries of the studios that own them or in the collections of public and private archives (including many individuals). The studios would make films available online for profit. The archives might be non-profit organizations, but they still would need to fund their online projects in some fashion, either by government support, from private grants, or by charging a fee for downloads. Most archives are more concerned about getting the money to conserve or restore aging, unique prints than about making them widely available. Preservation is an urgent matter, and making the resulting copies universally available for public entertainment or education is decidedly a secondary consideration.

Mike works for a non-profit archive, Schawn for a studio, so together they provide a good overview of some key problems facing the creation of an ideal, comprehensive collection of movies for download.

Money

People who claim that all surviving films could simply be put on the Internet don't go into the technology and expenses of how that could be done.

Of course, Schawn says, studios want to "digitize the library." That phrase is highly imprecise, however. He specifies, "For the purposes of this idea of media being online, available, downloadable, streamable, whatever, that's something that we're dealing with now using existing video masters. So there isn't an extra cost to quote, unquote digitize. But there is a cost to make the compression master, what we're calling at Fox a 'mezzanine file,' which is basically a 50 megabit file. That's the highest-quality 'low' quality version of the content from which you can derive all of the different flavors of compression for the various websites that have downloadable media.

"There's a huge problem with this, in that Amazon, iTunes, and Google all have a slightly different technical specification of how they need the files delivered to them. If you don't have this kind of mezzanine file, you have to make a different compressed version for each one of these, which costs something, certainly. It's not incredibly expensive, but it's not free.

"So why? What's the motivation to us to compress at Fox the entire library? I don't know. Are we going to sell enough copies of *Lucky Nick Cain* [a 1951 George Raft film] compressed on iTunes to cover the costs of making the compression? I don't think so."

Compatibility and the Onrush of Technology

Schawn's mention of the variety of files needed by the big download services raises the problem of compatibility. It's not just a matter of supplying the files and then forgetting about the whole thing, assuming that the film is available to anybody forever. What about new standards and formats?

Shawn: "Just as with consumer video, the standard

changes, so what used to be acceptable yesterday isn't acceptable now in terms of technical quality." As time passes, plug-ins make access faster and cheaper, and eventually the original files don't look good enough. He points out that currently iTunes can't download HD. If it becomes possible later, "If you want to get *24* in HD, what Fox will have to do is go and re-deliver all the files in HD." And presumably re-deliver again when the next big format revolution occurs.

Mike explains further, "Using the mezzanine file, you would just have to continue to reformat it to whatever the players demand. The lowest of the low quality will keep going up as people have broadband and can handle larger chunks of data faster."

What about the film you've already downloaded? You acquire films using plug-ins, which change. Think how often you're told that an update is now available. If you go ahead and keep updating, the changes accumulate. Eventually you may not be able to play the download you paid for. QuickTime will have moved way beyond what the technology was when you made your purchase.

Schawn and Mike both point out that at this stage in the history of downloading, the level of quality is still pretty bad in comparison with prints of films in theaters or on DVDs. It would be nice to think that the virtual film archive could provide sounds and images worthy of the movies themselves, but that will take a long, long time – not the "before too long" that Scott envisions.

Copyright

I raised another matter: "But what about copyright? Every time I hear something about restoration or bringing something out on DVD, it's, 'Well, there are rights problems.' And some of those rights problems don't get resolved. I assume that quite a few films that they blithely believe can be slapped up for downloading can't be slapped up."

Schawn: "Sure, and there are often not any kinds of provisions in the contract about Internet distribution – obviously! So you're right, how do you deal with that?" He pointed to *Viva Zapata!* as a film that Fox has restored but can't make available due to rights issues. The potential sales are not thought to warrant paying to resolve those issues. "I'm sure there are lots of titles in everybody's libraries that you can't just pop up on the Internet and start selling."

The copyright barrier is worse for archives, which seldom own the exhibition or distribution rights to the films they protect. Usually – though not invariably – the studios do not object to archives owning and preserving prints. Making money through showing them or selling copies would be quite another matter.

Mike described the online presence of archival prints. "On a much smaller scale, this is being attempted in the archive world already, like on Rick Prelinger's site [Prelinger Archives] or on the Library of Congress's site, where they've put up dozens of moving-image files. True, it's not independent cinema and it's mostly commercials and the paper prints that have recently been restored. On Prelinger's site it's all the industrial films that he's collected over the years. That has seen a good amount of traffic, but it hasn't created new audiences for these films, I would argue. At least, not on a huge scale."

Prelinger's site contains only public-domain items, including the ever-popular *Duck and Cover,* allowing him to avoid the problem of copyright. Similarly, the Library of Congress gives access primarily to films in the pre-1915 era.

Suppose an archive and a film studio both have good-quality prints of a minor American film made in the 1940s. The archive does not have the legal right to put it online, and if the studio decides that it does not have the financial incentive to do so, that film will not be made available for downloading. A private collector might possibly create a file and make it available, but he or she would risk being threatened by the copyright-holder.

Piracy

We briefly discussed the methods used to prevent pirated copies being made from downloaded films. Like DVDs, downloads can be pirated, with people sending copies to their friends or even offering downloads for a fee in competition with the copyright-holder. Copy-protection codes might make it necessary for a purchaser to keep a downloaded copy only on a hard-drive without being able to burn it onto a DVD. Another type of code could erase the file once the film had been viewed once or twice. That's not exactly conducive to the ideal archive of world cinema, where we would hope to be able to study a film in detail if we so choose.

One might think that piracy protection mainly applies to studios, with their need to make money. Mike points out, though, that the need for such protection "even applies to the archival model, too. For films that you mention that have gone out of copyright, there's still the same costs associated with putting out a silent film that no one owns – digitizing it, creating the compressed master that goes on the Web – and they aren't the kinds of subjects that people are going to get rich on at all, so there isn't a lot of piracy. You don't hear many archivists complaining, 'Hey, you took my 1911 Lubin film, damn you! You can't put that on your Web-site. That belongs on the archive's Website.' But that scenario becomes more of a likelihood for more popular titles. The obscure 1911 Lubin film is on one extreme, but *Birth of a Nation,* a well-known silent film a lot more people would like to see, is on the other. Let's say the highest-quality copy is on the Museum of Modern Art's Website and can be easily lifted and posted on your own site. And even if you just say, 'Oh, I'll charge 99 cents or I'll charge 50 cents to stream it,' it's still going to be someone taking over something that the archive put all of the high-end effort and money into doing. Frankly, I think unless it's an archive with a national mandate and a little bit higher budget to digitize and to put the contents of their archives online, there's not going to be any motivation to make that high-end investment up front."

Thus an archive may simply not bother to put a film on the Internet because it can't guarantee recouping the costs that would be generated.

Language and Cultural Barriers

Scott's notion of easy access to all of surviving world cinema implicitly depends on an idea that all these films are either English-language or already subtitled or dubbed for English-speaking users.

That's not true for a start, so there would remain a great deal of work to translate films that have never been released in English-language markets. That's another huge, expensive task.

Then there's the opposite side of that coin. For truly complete access, everyone in the world, whatever language they speak, would be able to download and appreciate every film. Of course, there are billions of people without computers or Internet access, and it looks unlikely that being able to go online will become universal anytime soon. (For figures on numbers of people with Internet access, check https://www.cia.gov/library/publications/the-world-factbook. Percentages can be calculated by clicking on each country and finding the total population. In Tajikistan, for example, .07% of the population was online in 2005. One has to assume that a lot of connections in some of those countries are dial-up, so downloading films would be virtually impossible.)

So let's just say that for the foreseeable future downloadable films would "only" need to be subtitled in the languages of countries or regions where significant numbers of people subscribe to PayPal.

In our conversation, Schawn pointed out that digital compression files mean that there can be huge numbers of versions, with different soundtracks dubbed in or different subtitles added. Technically it's possible to do all that translation. Still, "It's very complicated. So for worldwide distribution of anything, like you're talking about your silent film. If you're in Pakistan, do you get the American version of the movie, or do you get the version of the movie with the intertitles appropriate to wherever it is that you're showing it? If so, that quickly compounds the amount of stuff that's digitized."

I responded, "Yeah, or a 1930s Japanese film put on the Internet for downloading, subtitled in every language where there are people that can pay for it. The more you think about it, the more absurd it becomes."

Scott must be implying as well that there is some single "original" version of a film and that that version would be the one available in this ideal collection in cyberspace. Yet any archivist or film historian knows that multiple versions of a given film are typically made, depending partly on the censorship laws of the different countries where it is originally shown. In making

downloadable files available, does a studio or archive use only the original version of a film made for its country of origin, and thus risk having it include material offensive to viewers in some places where it might be downloaded? Or does a whole slew of different versions, one acceptable in, say, Iran, another inoffensive to the Danes, and still another compatible with Senegalese social mores, get put online? How could one even gather all such versions and digitize them? National film archives tend to have government mandates to concentrate primarily on preserving their own countries' films. Not every version of every film gets saved.

The Bottom Line

For all the reasons noted here and others as well, film availability for download will follow pretty much the same economic principles that have governed film sales in other media. Mike's opinion is, "Whether they're from an archive or a studio, I think things'll start going online in the same pace that they came onto DVD, in an 8 to 10-year cycle. And there still will be large gaps." Schawn interjects, "Just as there are on DVD." Mike concludes, "There's stuff that will never go online. Yeah, just as on DVD."

Chapter 9

Film Curatorship: The Making of a Definition

From: PCU. Subject: Definition of curatorship! Dear Alex, David, and Michael: What do you think of this? I don't believe we can publish a book on film curatorship without offering a definition. Your opinions and amendments would be welcome.

FILM CURATORSHIP: The art of interpreting and explaining the aesthetics, history, and technology of cinema through the collection, preservation, and public presentation of cinematic artefacts, experiences, and events. Paolo

From: DF. Subject: Re: Definition of curatorship! Dear Paolo, I think your definition is excellent.

I am just not sure that one can collect events.

I would like to re-order your definition: **"The art of building, preserving, documenting, and making accessible a collection of films, artefacts, and related materials, and using it to interpret and explain the aesthetics, history, and technology of cinema."**

What do you think? Best wishes, David

From: AH. Subject: AW: Definition of curatorship! Dear Paolo + David,

Many thanks for starting the definition process.

I agree with David that "events" can't be "collected".

On the other hand, I tend more towards Paolo's definition, because it stresses the interpretation/explanation aspect by putting it first.

[A side issue that's involved here: Do we also accept as FILM CURATORSHIP the work of somebody who is not an archivist, not part of an institution/collection, but who still – in staging a film exhibition/series by bringing together films from various sources – "interprets and explains the aesthetics, history and technology of cinema"? I am not sure. I DO believe it is important to highlight the continuum between collection-preservation-exhibition.]

My own version would probably read something like this:

The art of interpreting and explaining the aesthetics, history, and technology of cinema through the collection, preservation, and documentation of films and their exhibition as cinematic events. All best, Alex

From: PCU. Subject: Re: AW: Definition of curatorship! Dear Alex and David and Michael:
Indeed, one can't collect "events". However, I felt that including "events" in the definition was important in light of the discussions we had so far; hence my clumsy attempt to squeeze the word in.

This is to say that I like Alex's "intermediate" version. It has all the right ideas at the right place. To avoid the possible objection from archivists, "but isn't this what we are already doing?", may I add one word, "selective", as follows:

The art of interpreting and explaining the aesthetics, history, and technology of cinema through the [selective] collection, preservation, and documentation of films and their [selective] exhibition as cinematic events.

I have put the word "selective" in two different parts of the phrase, but we have to pick just one. I see advantages and disadvantages in both options, but I'd prefer to put it before "collection", to finally declare that archives and museums can't collect and preserve everything.

Or, do you think that "selective" is too strong and normative as a term? What do you think? Warmest regards, Paolo

From: AH. Subject: AW: AW: Definition of curatorship! I wholeheartedly agree – would put "selective" before collection.
What do you think, David+Michael? Alex

From: DF. Subject: Re: AW: Definition of curatorship! Dear Paolo et alia,
I am happy with Alex's version. I suppose because I have been a film archivist for a long time. I think that building a collection, documenting it, and preserving it comes before interpreting it and providing access to it. Curatorship is involved in both the building and the interpretation, but as we are more concerned with the interpretation at this stage in the history of film archives, I think Alex's proposal is the best. I do however agree with Paolo that we should include the word "selective". I like it before "collection". Regards, David

From: ML. Subject: Re: Re: Definition of curatorship! Dear all,
Recovering from a cold. I find this discussion very inspiring. As I do agree with all your input I'd be happy with the following:

The art of interpreting and explaining the aesthetics, history, and technology of cinema through the selective collection, preservation, and documentation of films and their exhibition as cinematic events.

I was wondering whether "their exhibition as cinematic events" is too narrow – don't we explicitly exclude curated presentations such as digital presentations

(DVD, Web, etc.) or installations? Of course our focus is on theatrical presentation, and this definition even allows for the before-mentioned exhibition formats, as long as the artefact (or its facsimile) is exhibited as a "cinematic event" – which includes different exhibition formats which nevertheless acknowledge and communicate the cinematic character of the original. Right?

Secondly, I wonder whether we should amend three short sentences which reinforce the idea that curatorship is connected to a collection, and that it is essential to an institution's overall policy. I've been reading a lot of 1920s/30s documentary film theory lately, as well as on the history of compilation film, and Grierson's (and Rotha's) dicta still do impress me. So what about something that reads:

Curatorship is the creative treatment of artefacts. Its aim is to interpret and to contextualize historical traditions for contemporary audiences. Thus the curator is responsible for the intellectual policy of the institution.

This might be redundant, though – please let me know. Best wishes, Michael

From: PCU. Subject: Re: Re: Definition of curatorship! Dear all:

I have now read and digested Michael's perceptive comments, with the following results.

Please correct me if I'm mistaken, but my understanding is that one of the goals of the definition is to highlight the importance of the cinematic event. While I don't think this excludes a priori the use of other media, it also stresses the value we attribute to the projection event in its original medium, whatever that is.

I should also stress that the definition I have been seeking is for "film curatorship", as I think this is the overall goal of our project.

The second definition offered by Michael raises some further questions:

⋆ I believe in the power of single sentences (if they are not too complex). What are your feelings on this?

⋆ "Creative treatment of artefacts": This could also be said of an assemblage of artworks for the creation of a new artwork, don't you think? We need to be more specific.

⋆ "for contemporary audiences": I think curatorship must also look at the future. We don't build or preserve collections (both are forms of contextualizations) only for contemporary audiences, right?

⋆ "the curator is responsible for the intellectual policy": In my view, one of the goals of our book is to demonstrate that virtually every position in a film archive or museum potentially plays a curatorial function. I fully agree that someone must be in charge of curatorial policies, but we don't want to give

the impression that these policies are simply dictated to the rest of the staff.
In any event, let me stress that it is absolutely crucial to ensure that all four of us
are 100% behind whatever definition we will present. This is the right time to iron
out the issues described by Michael, as well as any other question that may arise.
Warmest regards, Paolo

From: ML. Subject: Re: Definition of curatorship! Dear Paolo,

Thanks for the thorough comments. I'm trying to play devil's advocate here to
spot potential misunderstandings and criticism for the definition, and your reaction
actually makes the definition appear even stronger.

*Please correct me if I'm mistaken, but my understanding is that one of the goals of the
definition is to highlight the importance of the cinematic event.*
*While I don't think this excludes a priori the use of other media, it also stresses the value
we attribute to the projection event in its original medium, whatever that is. I should also
stress that the definition I have been seeking is for "film curatorship", as I think this is the
overall goal of our project.*
This is important: We should definitely call it "Film curatorship" then. This is a
strong emphasis that must be retained in the glossary and in the respective chapter.
★ *I believe in the power of single sentences (if they are not too complex).*
What are your feelings on this?
Single sentences are great. I feel the urge to "over-explain" definitions, which in a
way lessens their impact and makes them appear too "diplomatic". So yes – I think
it must be a one-sentence definition, but I wonder whether we should include our
e-mail exchange in the book as a documentation of our thought process?
★ *"Creative treatment of artefacts": This could also be said of an assemblage of artworks
for the creation of a new artwork, don't you think? We need to be more specific.*
While this is rather broad I think it is also true. Every process – the restoration of
a film, its interpretation, its projection, or the designing of a venue / event where it
is projected – is a creative act. This blurs the border between the curator and the
artist, which of course has dangerous implications and is a tendency heavily
criticized, e.g., in the art world. On the other hand it challenges the notion of
archives and museums as mere wardens of film history, as administrators of
pre-existing intellectual heritage. It emphasizes our proactive role.
★ *"for contemporary audiences": I think curatorship must also look at the future.*
*We don't build or preserve collections (both are forms of contextualizations) only for
contemporary audiences, right?*
Well, that's what I meant to say, but obviously "contemporary" does not imply
"future" by itself in English.

★ "the curator is responsible for the intellectual policy": In my view, one of the goals of our book is to demonstrate that virtually every position in a film archive or museum potentially plays a curatorial function. I fully agree that someone must be in charge of curatorial policies, but we don't want to give the impression that these policies are simply dictated to the rest of the staff.

Point taken. When writing my reply I was still thinking of an earlier model we have long overcome ("the curator vs. the archivist"). Our conversations clearly establish a far more radical idea of "curatorial conscience" on all levels of archive / museum work.

In any event, let me stress that it is absolutely crucial to ensure that all four of us are 100% behind whatever definition we will present. This is the right time to iron out the issues described by Michael, as well as any other question that may arise.

So now I hope this has helped in shaping the (short) definition! Reading it again, I think it is a pretty good one... Kind regards, Michael

From: PCU. Subject: Re: Definition of curatorship! Dear Michael:

Thank you for your prompt feedback. Here are my two comments on your points:

★ I am the first to concur about the fact that curatorship involves a creative act; however, we also want to make sure that those who will read the definition (I'm referring especially to archivists and curators) can relate to it and identify with our proposed formula. Using the term "creative act" for someone who – for instance – is building a collection may involve the risk of provoking unwanted answers, such as "hey, I'm not an artist". Maybe we are discussing this because your emphasis is on the "curator of film programmes", while I'm trying to address the Holy Trinity of the collection builder, of the "preservationist" (aka laboratory technician), and of the curator of a film exhibition. The way I have proposed to address the "creative" aspect of all forms of curatorship in a way that is intelligible to all the players in this game has been the adoption of the term "art" as the first word of the definition, as opposed to "science", or the more neutral word "discipline".

★ I am all for reproducing the correspondence in the book, if the others agree.

So let's see what David and Alex think before wrapping the definition. As I said before, it is important that we all feel comfortable with it, rather than signing off because we're tired of too many e-mail exchanges. Warmest wishes, Paolo

From: AH. Subject: AW: Definition of curatorship! Hi friends,

I like the discussion.

I agree with Paolo, and while I'm not sure if the complete e-mail discussion on this issue of definition makes sense in the book, I'd find it interesting to put a separate box under the definition which includes Michael's variant plus some of the (edited) responses – just so that the reader can see how it's possible to inflect these terms differently, and what the "cloud of connotations" might look like that always hovers around such a term/definition. Best, Alex

From: DF. Subject: Re: Definition of curatorship! Dear Paolo, Michael, Alex,

I think Michael's definition is more appropriate if we are not just talking about curatorship in film archives. Although I hope the book will be read by archival personnel in other fields, I feel our text should be specifically related to film archives; therefore I still support the definition that Alex offered. In the current climate it is important to stress interpretation over acquisition and preservation. The collections are largely built. We are falling behind on the contextualization front.

The only phrase I still worry about is "cinematic events". I hope our readership will be informed, but they are unlikely to have as much commitment to archival concepts as we have. If in doubt, I think we should move towards simplicity. With this in mind, I wonder whether we should just end the definition at "exhibition". Regards, David

From: PCU. Subject: Re: Definition of curatorship! Dear all:

I have consulted with Edith Kramer, and she also believes that it would be best to end the sentence with the word "exhibition", as follows:

The art of interpreting and explaining the aesthetics, history, and technology of cinema through the selective collection, preservation, and documentation of films and their exhibition.

Edith argues that while "cinematic events" is an important concept, definitions should be as clear and unequivocal as possible. She argues that it's best to have the concept of "cinematic event" being discussed throughout the book, as not everybody may be familiar with what we mean by that.

Please let me know if you would agree to go for the above definition. All the best, Paolo

From: AH. Subject: AW: Definition of curatorship! Dear all,

I certainly do not want to make this a never-ending story, but as much as I see Edith's and David's points, I feel that the word "exhibition" at the end (without further qualifications) leaves far too much room for all sorts of practices that we probably (?) do NOT want to subsume under FILM CURATORSHIP.

It is exactly because "we are falling behind on the contextualization front" (David)

that this aspect needs stronger focus – and the exhibition side of it IS the most contested aspect of any contextualization. Few people take issue with the process of interpreting, explaining, contextualizing cinema by way of building+ maintaining a collection or by way of writing academic (or non-academic) books and essays about it. What many people DO quarrel about are the thousands of ways in which this interpreting, explaining, contextualizing can be done and IS done by way of exhibition.

If we just say "exhibition", then we'd include in it all sorts of making films visible and accessible, either as a whole or in part, either in a contextual way (series/exhibitions/retrospectives) or just "for fun", "randomly", either as "cinematic events" or via all other media.

This is why I can't get rid of the feeling that a further qualification is needed (nevertheless honouring the aim of clarity and precision).

I know I'm going a few steps backwards here, but at this very moment I feel that adjectives are needed more on the exhibition than on the collection front. So, if I may, I'd put in one last version for your discussion. It certainly limits the range of what might be understood as "film curatorship", but that would be fine for me. It is shorter at the beginning, but "doubly cinematic":

The art of interpreting cinema through the collection, preservation, and documentation of films and their exhibition *as cinema*.

I feel that the "explaining" is somewhat covered by the "interpreting", and that "the aesthetics, history, technology" can be subsumed under the whole of cinema – at least for the purposes of a clean sharp definition. But if this seems too shortened, a longer version might read like this: **The art of interpreting the aesthetics, history, and technology of cinema through the selective collection, preservation, and documentation of films and their exhibition *as cinema*.**

Sorry for making everything complicated again... What do you think?
All best, Alex

From: PCU. Subject: Re: Definition of curatorship! Dear Alex:

Never be afraid of reopening the debate! This discussion is too important to leave room for uncertainties.

I was so pleased with the previous version that I would prefer to go to that one and see what we can put instead of "cinematic event" at the end of the sentence. I think we have better chances of coming up with something that addresses your concern.

I'd like to hear what the others think. My suggestion is to be careful not to propose a definition that is too normative (i.e., "it's true curatorship only if you curate the way we want to"), without losing sight of that fact that, indeed, we don't want to implicitly endorse "curatorship" as everything under the sky, "for fun", with internet clips, and so on. I really think that ending the sentence with "as cinema" gives it a very prescriptive tone.

As for deleting "explaining", don't you think that one could interpret just for oneself without telling anybody about it? Curatorship is an outward activity.

I don't feel I'm being curatorial if I juxtapose the viewing of different sequences on DVD in my private home.

Michael, David? I'm also copying Edith into this. Maybe she has a suggestion in relation to your (very legitimate) doubts. All the best, Paolo

P.S. As a reminder to all, this is what we had so far:

The art of interpreting the aesthetics, history, and technology of cinema through the selective collection, preservation, and documentation of films and their exhibition.

From: DF. Subject: Re: AW: FOREWORD, TAKE 2

The Definition. I understand Alex's point, but I am afraid the addition of "as cinema" still isn't unequivocably clear for me. We are trying to recreate the experience audiences would have had when a film was first released, so there is a logic in using the word "exhibition", but because this (once again) is an industry word it needs a qualifying adjective that will separate it from commercial exhibition. The only thing I can come up with is the obvious "archival exhibition". What other words are there? "Access" is now banned, "dissemination" is too vague. "Archival presentation(s)" might be a possibility. In the end the best I can do is "archival exhibition". I hope someone else can do better.

By the way I like Alex's longer version better. Best wishes, David

From: ML. Subject: AW: AW: FOREWORD, TAKE 2 Dear all,

I do share David's argument.

I'd propose the following: **The art of interpreting the aesthetics, history, and technology of cinema through the selective collection, preservation, and documentation of films and their exhibition in archival presentations.**

"Archival" here is a better term than "museal", since a "museum" presentation is "museal" by definition. What emphasizes the high standards and the scrupulous attention to the historical artefact (the "work") is "archival", which is a term well introduced by now ("archival copy", etc.).

Do you think that this sounds clumsy in English? Till later, Michael

"Archival presentations" has the advantage of addressing my argument about "interpreting and explaining". You may recall that "interpreting" didn't seem enough for me, as it excluded the interaction with the external world. Just to be on the safe side, are you all happy with deleting the word "explaining"?
If so, I think we're OK with the definition. Paolo

PS: have received the following input from Edith Kramer. There's useful stuff here:

Maybe a start is just to ask the question, do you want your DEFINITION to be an opening statement that leads to the detailed discussions or the ending and a summation of sorts? That might clarify what you have to include or not. Or it can be both at the beginning and the end, a place to start the argument and place to conclude the argument, but realizing that whatever is published will lead to more discussion, nothing is final and perhaps the purpose is to make people think about what they are doing and need to do.
Best practices at this moment with what we know and foresee. And then there is the very human intellectual curiosity, the need to examine, analyze, philosophize, justify. What you have all been doing is in one sense an intellectual exercise, and I mean this in the best way, building the mind's muscles to deal with problems and provide inspiration to go on, and not become victims of fads, mindlessness, pomposity, vanity, etc., etc.
It would be nice if our institutions could be as good as the best individual can be as a citizen! I would hope that the outcome of all this work is not to distinguish between museum and archive practice; those distinctions seem today and for the future no longer valid. And those that would see such distinctions are I suspect not really interested in the larger issues of curatorship, but only concerned with their daily duties in the narrowest sense. Even non-museum affiliated archives have parents, like governments that change policy with political change, and could hardly care about good curatorship since they are not likely to recognize it anyway.
Cynical of me, but look around at the world we live in, where and who are the visionaries, how long does any institution chart a good course and keep the course, or understand how to adjust to new challenges. It's a human dilemma as well.

Chapter 10

Film Curatorship: A Definition

The art of interpreting the aesthetics, history, and technology of cinema through the selective collection, preservation, and documentation of films and their exhibition in archival presentations.

Glossary of Terms

access Physical and/or intellectual exhibition or delivery of audiovisual materials and related documentation based on confirmed level of copyright protection.

access – open Archive collection material which has no restrictions, and which may be made readily available for general exhibition purposes through on- or off-site viewing.

access – restricted The term applies to archive collection material whose access requires special technical precautions and requirements, or which has secret, offensive, or sensitive content, and which is only available for audition, viewing, or reproduction after appropriate clearances have been received from copyright and/or traditional owners.

access – appropriate Access to audiovisual materials and related documentation based on confirmed level of copyright and – where applicable – on other forms of cultural ownership.

acquisition The formal process of collecting cultural works and artefacts for the purposes of inclusion in a collection, preservation, and long-term access to the work or artefact.

artefact (cultural) A human-made object which gives information about the culture of its creator and users.

Audiovisual (AV) Moving images and/or recorded sounds embodied in any medium now known or yet to be invented. "Audiovisual" includes – but is not limited to – the formats of film, video, and audio tape, video and audio discs, computer files, and machine-readable or encoded data embodying sound and/or moving images; the distinctive technologies by which these images and sounds are reproduced and made accessible; the context in which they are created and disseminated; and their experience by an individual or collective audience.

carrier Audiovisual media include images and sounds (the "work") recorded on film, discs, magnetic tape, or other materials ("carriers"). Because physical decay and/or format change mean that most carriers have a limited shelf life, preservation of the "work" eventually requires copying to another carrier. Whenever possible, this process must result in the creation and availability of the "work" in the same format and on the same media in which the original works were created. In some cases, the copying process may involve technical judgements, and the original media or carriers may have attributes that cannot be copied; curatorial judgments as to their appropriateness are therefore necessary. For access purposes, replaceable copies may be made in formats or media other than the original one (depending on demand), as long as permanent availability in the original media and format is guaranteed wherever possible.

classification 1. Application of index terms such as subjects, formats, class, and genre, to facilitate the retrieval of works. 2. Classification of level of restriction; or, classification of material as either "Restricted" or "Open".

conservation All the activities necessary to prevent or minimize the process of physical degradation of the artefact, whether such an artefact is newly produced by the archive or is an already existing object acquired by the archive. An underlying principle of the conservation process is that the activities described above should be carried out with minimal intervention or interference with the artefact.

deaccession The permanent removal of collection items from the collection with accompanying documented record.

deposit Collection material placed on "deposit" with the institution for safekeeping. Unlike material that is purchased or donated, the physical item on deposit remains the property of the source until such time as the source may transfer ownership to another person, community, or organization.

depositor The person, organization, or company that deposits audiovisual material with the institution for safekeeping. Unlike material that is purchased or donated, the physical item on deposit remains the property of the depositor until such time as the depositor may transfer ownership to another person, community, or organization.

disclaimer Introductory text or announcement inserted at the beginning of a film, video, sound recording, television or radio broadcast, and digital-born work, or given as accompanying text in the presentation of documentation items.

documentation The material produced before, during, or after the completion of a film or sound production, providing meaningful information on audiovisual works, their creation, exhibition, reception, and influence. It includes – but is not limited to – scripts, publicity materials, stills, business and private papers, and press clippings.

donation Collection material that is gifted without charge to the institution, so that the physical item becomes the property of the organization. The work(s) and other materials included in the item may still be subject to copyright, and/or may require the agreement or clearance of the traditional owners before access to and/or use of the work may occur.

donor A person, organization, or company that donates material to the collection by gift or legacy. Material that is donated becomes the physical property of the organization, although the work or parts of it may still be subject to copyright.

duplication The set of practices related to the creation of a replica of an audiovisual work, either as backup of existing original or preservation material, or as a means to provide access to the audiovisual works. While the duplication process is performed with the goal of obtaining a copy as close as possible to the source, such a process is a necessary but not sufficient requirement of the preservation and restoration processes. A duplicate may be restored, but not subject to enhancement.

education programmes Programmes and activities that foster inquiry about, and understanding of, the cultural life and environment of a country through its audiovisual heritage.

enhancement A separate and distinct process of rearranging or adding content, altering, or adding qualities such as colour, reverberation, or effects which were not part of the original production, but which may increase contemporary appeal. A new enhanced work is a recreation, not a restoration, and should not take place to the detriment of the availability of the original audiovisual work and its experience.

heritage (cultural) Physical features, both natural and artificial, associated with human cultural activity. These include sites, structures, and objects possessing significance – either individually or as a grouping – in history, architecture, archaeology, or human cultural development. Cultural resources are unique and non-renewable. Cultural heritage is also defined as "our legacy from the past, what we live with today, and what we pass on to future generations" (UNESCO World Heritage).

interpretation The act of explaining items in the collection, making clear their context, experience, meaning, and cultural significance.

item A discrete physical copy (including the original) of a work or part of a work (for instance, a sound negative) on one or more carriers.

licensee A person, organization, or company that is granted a licence to use items from the collection in a public manner (usually by way of display, screening, broadcast, etc.).

migration Transferring data *en masse* onto a new system capable of carrying the same data, in a similar but not necessarily identical form.

moral rights The right to be named as creator, and the right for the work to keep its integrity.

National Collection (The) The group of objects acquired by an institution as defined by its [mandate and its] Collection Policy. The National Collection consists of various formats, including – but not limited to – film, television, and (where applicable) recorded sound. In addition, the National Collection includes associated documentation (that is, material produced before, during, or after completion of a moving image or sound production, including scripts, publicity materials, stills, and other artefacts). There is no conclusive definition of what is or is not "National". The institution regards material produced in, by, or about the nation, or experienced by national audiences, as "national heritage". Ongoing curatorial judgements are needed to monitor the application of the concept.

outreach The provision of programs off-site, aimed at achieving access, educational, and awareness-raising objectives.

presentation A live event designed to deliver information about the collection. A presentation may include seminars, interactive discussions, guided tours, and the experience of items from the collection.

preservation The overall complex of procedures, principles, techniques, and practices necessary for maintaining the integrity and organizing the intellectual experience of a moving image or a recorded sound on a permanent basis. The purpose of preservation work is threefold: ensuring that the surviving collection artefact is no further damaged or altered in its format and content; bringing it back to a condition as close as possible to its original state; providing access to it, in a manner consistent with the way in which the artefact was meant to be exhibited and perceived. Taken individually, other activities, such as duplication, restoration, conservation, reconstruction (where appropriate), access, and exhibition in proper conditions, are possible or necessary but not sufficient actions aimed at achieving preservation. Enhancement is not part of the preservation process. The purpose of preservation is to enable access to the sound and image heritage in the long as well as short term. As such, short-term access should not be achieved at the expense of preservation that enables access in the long-term future.

preservation (active) See also "Preservation". Physical treatment of carriers or artefacts in their original format (for instance, cleaning or consolidation), a condition for restoration and transfer of the works (duplication, printing).

preservation (passive) See "Conservation". The storage, packaging, and all the other non-interventionist means of prolonging the life of a carrier or artefact in its original form. It includes – but is not limited to – cyclical maintenance (such as monitoring condition or respooling).

preservation and **access** Material may be acquired either with the intention of preservation (and subsequent access), or solely for access purposes. In the latter case, preservation is assessed against the likelihood that the work is or will be adequately preserved by another organization in the country of the archive, or abroad, so that the archive does not need to duplicate that task.

preservation component The original or earliest generation held by the archive; the best technical quality element; the most complete, and/or the most stable or robust. A preservation copy is the result of a complete, unedited, and unaltered transfer of the work from an unstable original component.

product Objects created for sale, using material from the collection, including (but not limited to) videos, compact discs, and paper-based items.

provenance The history of ownership of a collection or item, which may include ownership of the physical item, the creative and production history, and the intellectual property rights.

public domain The legal status of material in which no copyright currently exists.

public programmes Suite of public activities designed to foster and increase awareness of the audiovisual heritage, and to interpret it for the benefit of diverse audiences, nationally and abroad.

purchase Collection material that is financially and legally acquired by the institution, so that the physical item becomes the property of the organization. The work(s) and other materials contained in the item may still be subject to copyright, and/or may require the agreement/clearance of the traditional owners before access to and/or use of the work may occur.

repatriation The return of materials to relevant organizations and communities as either copies or originals. Repatriation may also sometimes imply that the physical location of the item remains unchanged, but the recognized status of ownership changes (for instance, ownership may transfer from an organization or collector to a community, while the item itself remains in the same location, such as a designated collecting institution, for safekeeping and archival storage).

research Private, educational, or commercial investigation into archival holdings to identify material and subject matter which may subsequently be requested for further access, reference, or incorporation into publication, production, or private archives.

restoration The set of technical, editorial, and intellectual procedures aimed at compensating for the loss or degradation of the audiovisual artefact, thus bringing it back to a state as close as possible to its original condition when created and/or released. The restoration process is not complete if it does not jointly address the content, the technological context, and the distinctive experience linked to its accessibility. In the absence of one or more of these components, the process may be called "simulation", "recreation", or, in limited cases, "duplication".

use Active incorporation of collection material held by the institution into an event, production, publication, or presentation. Use is always subject to the confirmation of prior clearance from identified rights-holders, when applicable.

work A distinct, identifiable cultural or intellectual creation that may have one or more parts.

About the Authors

Paolo Cherchi Usai, *1957, is co-founder of the L. Jeffrey Selznick School at George Eastman House and of the Pordenone Silent Film Festival. He directed *Passio* (2007), a film adaptation of *The Death of Cinema* (BFI Publishing, 2001). His latest book is *David Wark Griffith* (Editrice Il Castoro, 2008). He is currently Director of the National Film and Sound Archive of Australia.

David Francis OBE, *1935, was for 16 years Curator of the British National Film Archive, where he established the J. Paul Getty Jnr. Conservation Centre (Berkhamsted), and from 1991 until 2001 was Chief of the Motion Picture, Broadcasting, and Recorded Sound Division of the Library of Congress, where he was responsible for the planning and design of the Library of Congress National Audio-Visual Conservation Center's state-of-the-art Packard Campus in Culpeper, Virginia. His many publications include the ground-breaking study *Chaplin: Genesis of a Clown* (Quartet, 1977), written with Raoul Sobel.

Alexander Horwath, *1964 in Vienna, has worked as a film critic, writer, and curator since 1985. Director of the Viennale – Vienna International Film Festival (1992–97); Director of the Austrian Film Museum since 2002. Author and (co-)editor of publications on the American Cinema of the 1960s and 70s, Austrian avant-garde film, and film-makers such as Josef von Sternberg, Michael Haneke, and Peter Tscherkassky.

Michael Loebenstein, *1974 in Vienna, studies in film history and film theory at Vienna University. Has worked as a freelance writer and critic, film programmer, and DVD author, and since 2004 works as a curator and researcher at the Austrian Film Museum.

FilmmuseumSynemaPublikationen

Vol 1
CLAIRE DENIS. TROUBLE EVERY DAY
Edited by Michael Omasta,
Isabella Reicher

"There is no other filmmaker like Claire Denis, and what a beautifuil gift to us all!" (Jim Jarmusch) During the 1990s, with films such as *Chocolat, Nénette et Boni* or *Beau travail,* French director Claire Denis has become one of the major figures of contemporary cinema. This book deals with her personality, her radical aesthetic and her cultural influences. Contributors include Peter Baxter, Jean-Luc Nancy, Christine N. Brinckmann, Ralph Eue, Martine Beugnet, Ekkehard Knörer, Vrääth Öhner, Michael Omasta, Isabella Reicher and Jim Jarmusch (preface). The volume is concluded by an extensive interview section and the first detailed filmography of her work.
Vienna 2005. 160 pages, with numerous illustrations and an annotated filmography. In German. ISBN 3-901644-15-6

Vol 2
PETER TSCHERKASSKY
Edited by Alexander Horwath,
Michael Loebenstein

The films of Peter Tscherkassky have played a central role in the international reawakening of interest in avant-garde film. At the turn from a photographic to a digital culture of moving images, his work has run an exciting course – from the anarchic gesture of Super-8 filmmaking through an engagement with psychoanalysis and semiotics towards a newfound pleasure with the physicality of the medium and its potential to overwhelm the audience in more ways than one. This first book on the artist engages with his work both visually and in writing. Essays about – and by – Tscherkassky are complemented by a rich variety of stills and frame enlargements published here for the first time.
Vienna 2005. 254 pages, with 260 illustrations in colour and b/w, an annotated filmography and bibliography. In English and German throughout. ISBN 3-901644-16-4

Vol 3
JOHN COOK. VIENNESE BY CHOICE,
FILMEMACHER VON BERUF
Edited by Michael Omasta,
Olaf Möller

Canadian-born filmmaker and photographer John Cook (1935–2001) was one the key figures in the "Austrian New Wave" of the 1970s. A maverick artist still to be discovered among international cinephiles, Cook almost single-handedly introduced a type of freewheeling auteur cinema in Austria, reminiscent of both Italian neorealism and the French New Wave. This volume offers two books within one – a section of essays and interviews is followed by Cook's previously unpublished autobiography: *The Life* deals with Cook's Toronto childhood, his life as a photographer in 1960s Paris and his struggle as an independent filmmaker in 1970s Vienna. This literary account is accompanied by previously unpublished photographs from the artist's estate.
Vienna 2006. 252 pages, with numerous illustrations and an annotated filmography. In German (part 1) and English (part 2) ISBN 3-901644-17-2

Vol 4
DZIGA VERTOV.
THE VERTOV COLLECTION AT
THE AUSTRIAN FILM MUSEUM
Edited by the Austrian Film Museum,
Thomas Tode, Barbara Wurm

For the Russian filmmaker and film theorist Dziga Vertov (1896–1954) KINO was both a bold aesthetic experiment and a document of contemporary life. This book presents the Austrian Film Museum's comprehensive Vertov Collection for the first time: films, photographs, posters, letters as well as a large number of previously unpublished sketches, drawings and writings by Vertov, including his extensive autobiographical "Calling Card" from 1947. Additional essays and commentaries by the editors and international contributors intend to stimulate further academic and artistic projects and to "activate" Vertov's legacy for the here and now.
Vienna 2006. 288 pages, with 220 illustrations in color and b/w. In English and German throughout ISBN 3-901644-19-9

FilmmuseumSynemaPublikationen

Vol 5
JOSEF VON STERNBERG
THE CASE OF LENA SMITH
Edited by Alexander Horwath,
Michael Omasta

In his 1929 Hollywood production *The Case of Lena Smith*, director Josef von Sternberg vividly brought to life his youthful memories of Vienna at the turn of the last century. Critic Dwight Macdonald called it "the most completely satisfying American film I have seen". But only a short fragment survives – *Lena Smith* is one of the legendary lost masterpieces of the American cinema.
Assembling 150 original stills and set designs, numerous script and production documents as well as essays by eminent film historians, the book reconstructs Sternberg's dramatic film about a young woman fighting the oppressive class system of Imperial Vienna.
With contributions by Janet Bergstrom, Hiroshi Komatsu, Gero Gandert, Franz Grafl, Alexander Horwath, and Michael Omasta.
Vienna 2007. 304 pages, with hundreds of illustrations.
In English and German throughout
ISBN 978-3-901644-22-1

Vol 6
JAMES BENNING
Edited by Barbara Pichler,
Claudia Slanar

James Benning's films are among the most fascinating work in American cinema. He explores the relationship between image, text and sound while paying expansive attention to the "vernacular landscapes" of American life. This volume traces Benning's artistic career as well as his biographical journey through the United States, from Wisconsin to the East Coast to Southern California.
With contributions by James Benning, Sharon Lockhart, Allan Sekula, Dick Hebdige, Scott MacDonald, Volker Pantenburg, Nils Plath, Michael Pisaro, Amanda Yates, Sadie Benning, Julie Ault, Claudia Slanar and Barbara Pichler.
Vienna 2007. 264 pages, numerous illustrations in color and b/w. In English
ISBN 978-3-901644-23-8

Vol 7
JEAN EPSTEIN. BONJOUR CINÉMA UND
ANDERE SCHRIFTEN ZUM KINO
Edited by Nicole Brenez and
Ralph Eue, translated from
the French by Ralph Eue

Jean Epstein, the great unknown amongst the geniuses of film, was an essential figure in the invention of modern cinema – both as a theorist and as an artist. For the first time, a selection of Epstein's writings on film are published in German in this volume.
Vienna 2008. 160 pages, numerous illustrations. In German
ISBN 978-3-901644-25-2

Vol 8
LACHENDE KÖRPER. KOMIKERINNEN
IM KINO DER 1910ER JAHRE
Claudia Preschl

Claudia Preschl's study focusses on short comedies and comedy serials between 1910 and 1918 and is a contribution to the rediscovery of the early „other" cinema in which comediennes such "Rosalie", "Léa" or Asta Nielsen played a decisive part. *Lachende Körper* describes the variety of preposterous body-language and shows how anarchistic body-politics and rebellious strategies of Gender in Early Cinema can be decoded for today.
Vienna 2008. 208 pages, numerous illustrations. In German
ISBN 978-3-901644-27-6